About Island Press

Island Press is the only nonprofit organization in the United States whose principal purpose is the publication of books on environmental issues and natural resource management. We provide solutions-oriented information to professionals, public officials, business and community leaders, and concerned citizens who are shaping responses to environmental problems.

In 1994, Island Press celebrated its tenth anniversary as the leading provider of timely and practical books that take a multidisciplinary approach to critical environmental concerns. Our growing list of titles reflects our commitment to bringing the best of an expanding body of literature to the environmental community throughout North America and the world.

Support for Island Press is provided by Apple Computer, Inc., The Bullitt Foundation, The Geraldine R. Dodge Foundation, The Energy Foundation, The Ford Foundation, The W. Alton Jones Foundation, The Lyndhurst Foundation, The John D. and Catherine T. MacArthur Foundation, The Andrew W. Mellon Foundation, The Joyce Mertz-Gilmore Foundation, The National Fish and Wildlife Foundation, The Pew Charitable Trusts, The Pew Global Stewardship Initiative, The Rockefeller Philanthropic Collaborative, Inc., and individual donors.

About The Growth Management Institute

The Growth Management Institute is a nonprofit organization established in 1992 by a group of distinguished practitioners and scholars recognized nationally as experts in the field of growth management. Under the guidance of Douglas R. Porter, the Institute encourages effective and equitable management of growth in human habitats and provides a forum for the constructive exchange of ideas and information about growth management. The Institute promotes strategies and practices to achieve sustainable urban development and redevelopment while preserving environmental quality. The Institute is based in Chevy Chase, Maryland.

MANAGING GROWTH IN AMERICA'S COMMUNITIES

DOUGLAS R. PORTER

In cooperation with members of
The Growth Management Institute

ISLAND PRESS

Washington, D.C. • Covelo, California

Cover photos: (*Top*) Farmland in Calvert County, Maryland. (*Bottom*) The same parcel of land after housing development.

Library of Congress Cataloging-in-Publication Data

Porter, Douglas R.
    Managing growth in America's communities/Douglas R. Porter; in cooperation with members of the Growth Management Institute.
      p.   cm.
Includes bibliographical references and index.
ISBN 1-55963-442-1 (pbk.)
1. Cities and towns—United States—Growth. 2. City planning—United States. 3. Regional planning—United States. 4. Community development—United States.   I. Growth Management Institute.
II. Title.
HT384.U5P67   1997
307.1'416'0973—dc21   97-14941
                                                 CIP

Printed on recycled, acid-free paper ♺

Manufactured in the United States of America

10 9 8 7 6 5 4 3 2 1

Contents

ни H tеарийtеl

Preface

Communities of all shapes and sizes across the nation are practicing growth management, adopting and implementing policies and regulations to guide the location, quality, and timing of development. Programs and techniques that have been evolving over decades are being employed in company with federal, state, and regional policies and programs that also influence community development. Through these efforts, public decision makers and their constituents attempt to improve the quality of life in the places where we live, work, and relax. In the process, professional and citizen planners are broadening their understanding of the vital linkages among development, the environment, and social and economic conditions of everyday life.

The primary purpose of this publication is to draw on these community experiences to describe proven strategies, policies, programs, and techniques for managing growth in American communities. This book traces the emergence of a new paradigm for guiding community development, one that builds bridges across traditional divisions among physical, economic, social, and governmental regimes, and brings cohesion to typically segmented professional, academic, and citizen perspectives on community growth and change.

The term "growth management" encompasses public efforts to resolve issues and problems stemming from the changing character of communities, whether they are rapidly growing small towns and suburbs or mature and even declining communities. All must cope with change to retain valued qualities of community life. All must establish public policies to guide new development. As we grow increasingly concerned about the sustainability of development on this planet, we understand the importance of developing our communities in ways that respect the natural ecosystems they occupy. Managing community growth and change, therefore, is part and parcel of managing sustainability. In this spirit, the book identifies and explores a variety of growth management approaches and mechanisms to help clarify the public discussion of what to do and how to do it.

My work on this book was aided in many ways by many people. Over the years of my planning and development practice, and especially during my long experience at the Urban Land Institute, I learned much from professional planners working in communities and regions all across the nation. Their dedication to their work and willingness to share experiences never ceased to amaze me. Time and time again, planners "on the ground" tolerated my attempts to burrow beneath surface policies to determine fundamental responses to plans and regulations. Others also contributed to my knowledge.

The comments and perspectives of developers and builders, civic activists, elected officials, and other professionals helped shape my understanding of community experiences. Their contributions were invaluable in enriching the content of this book. I would like to thank the many board members of The Growth Management Institute who contributed to this publication, including John DeGrove, Lindell Marsh, Erik Meyers, Larry Orman, Arthur Nelson, James Nicholas, Ingrid Reed, Paul Tischler, Richard Tustian, and David Winstead.

I also want to thank David Salvesen, Libby Howland, and Paul O'Mara, old friends from ULI days, for digging out material from hard-to-get places. And, of course, Heather Boyer, my editor at Island Press, whose comments on drafts and prompting about schedules kept me on course. Most of all, I would like to acknowledge the patience and support of my wife, Cecelia Porter, and my grown-up children, Rebecca, Elizabeth, Bart, and Lawrence, all of whom had to listen too much to my trials and tribulations in getting this book to a finished state.

1

Introduction to Growth Management

Forty years ago, in the mid-1950s, the citizens of Fort Collins, Colorado recognized that they had a problem, or probably several. Founded in 1864 as a military outpost, Fort Collins developed into a small college town and a trade and shipping center for the surrounding livestock and sugar beet industries in the area. A century after its founding, the town still boasted fewer than 15,000 residents. In the 1950s, however, the college began expanding and new industries arrived; suddenly growth was everywhere. From 1950 to 1960 the town's population rose by two-thirds. Propelled by continuing college and industrial expansions, the number of residents kept rising, by 7 percent a year during the 1960s and 5 percent annually during the 1970s. From 1950 to 1980 the town frantically annexed land to accommodate development, virtually doubling the incorporated area each decade.

When this growth spurt started, town officials could notice development taking place on a daily basis. Traffic clogged roads, schools became overcrowded, water and sewer systems needed expansion, and parks were scarce. The town's rudimentary zoning ordinance appeared inadequate to deal with these problems. A task force, formed to consider solutions, recommended short-term public investments in new facilities but hardly touched on the larger ramifications of continuing growth. Years later, a member of that task force viewed its principal accomplishment as building a cadre of community leaders concerned with the town's future development.

Soon after the infrastructure crisis was resolved, at least temporarily, many of the participants in that effort determined that the town should embark on a more ambitious planning project. A "Plan for Progress" was formulated in 1967 that laid out future land uses, street patterns, and utility services. Although the plan had little effect on development, it prepared the ground for citizens' continuing interest in planning. From 1975 to 1977, city officials, the business community, and citizens' groups worked together to produce a statement of goals and objectives for city development. Unfortunately, a follow-on effort to formulate a traditional land use plan based on those goals and objectives failed to reach consensus.

Further efforts involving another task force, extensive public hearings, and a failed ballot initiative to limit growth finally led to the city council's adoption in 1979 of a four-part comprehensive plan: a land use policies plan, a land use guidance system (adding flexible development standards to existing zoning), an agreement with the county that defined an urban growth area, and a cost of development study. These plans and programs, some of them innovative and all refined considerably over the years, continue to provide the principal framework for guiding development in Fort Collins to this day.

The experience in Fort Collins over four decades mirrors the principal features of growth management programs in many communities throughout the nation:

- Sudden unplanned development caused major problems in the community, provoking citizens' concerns for managing growth.

- Consensus on workable ways to address those problems evolved over many years, during which community leadership coalesced and a variety of solutions was tried.

- City officials gradually learned that a single solution—meeting infrastructure needs—fell short of satisfying wider community concerns.

- The continuous involvement of many organizations, interests, and individuals built strong support for public guidance of the development process.

- The city's program today is an amalgam of both conventional and innovative planning and growth management components, closely tailored to its particular attitudes and needs.

In short, Fort Collins' citizens found that managing growth is a time-consuming, messy, and constantly evolving process, at times exhilarating and at other times deeply frustrating. Efforts to manage growth and change seldom produce quick solutions. Long-term investments of time, interest, innovation, and follow-up are absolute necessities.

These difficulties are rooted in the ways our communities develop. As Fort Collins' story demonstrates, growth brings changes: in habits of daily life, in needs for larger and more complicated systems of public fa-cilities, in impacts on environmental qualities and open space once taken for granted, even in how local governments must learn to deal with competing interests and other jurisdictions, including state and federal agencies. In Fort Collins, additions of one or two houses at a time gave way to development of 100-lot subdivisions. Instead of a new store open-ing on Main Street, a new shopping center with 20 stores sprang up on an open field out on the highway. Residents of Fort Collins found that growth brings opportunities but also generates needs and issues. They learned that growth fosters needs for better public management of the development process.

Citizens, public officials, and city planners in many communities are becoming accustomed to a comprehensive view of the challenges of com-munity growth and change. They are eager to anticipate and deal with potential problems before those problems overwhelm community re-sources. Especially, they understand the need to incorporate a broader sense of shared values and concerns in the community development process. Many citizens are involved in public decisions about commu-nity development. In addition, public officials have made great strides in recognizing important environmental, transportation, social, and other goals in decisions about development.

These initiatives fall under the heading of growth management, an in-clusive approach to thinking about, and acting upon, community devel-opment strategies. In the following pages, the term growth management and its principal purposes are further explored to set a solid foundation for the remainder of the book.

Growth and Change in America's Communities

Communities throughout the United States continue to grow and change. In the early days, waves of immigrants poured through the ports into the hinterland. People staked out farms and towns, villages grew into towns and cities. When the industrial age arrived, people moved from the land to towns that quickly grew into new urban centers. Over the centuries, towns expanded into cities, and cities into metropolitan areas.

America's population keeps growing. The Census Bureau projects that the 266 million people now resident in the United States will increase to 394 million by 2050. Although fertility rates are not expected to rebound to earlier levels, average life expectancy probably will increase and im-migration will continue.

Most of the increased population will flock to towns and cities clus-tered in metropolitan areas. Almost 90 percent of the nation's increase in population since 1980 has occurred in cities, towns, and urban counties. About four out of five Americans live in metropolitan areas today, and those areas are growing at almost twice the rate of rural areas, according to the 1990 census. That tremendous expansion of urban and suburban population, the U.S. Census Bureau predicts, will continue well into the twenty-first century.

Many members of the "baby boom" generation of Americans are retiring to once-rural areas and telecommuters are moving farther away from cities. Most, however, cluster in and around existing settlements, sometimes reviving declining rural towns and often creating satellite communities just as suburban in character as the suburbs of large cities.

Meanwhile these population trends, coupled with economic shifts, propel interregional population movements and structural economic shifts across America. Some regions grow at the expense of others. Sunbelt states continue to attract residents and employees from the "Rustbelt" states of the Northeast and Midwest. About 85 percent of the nation's population growth during the 1980s occurred in the west and south, bringing unprecedented growth to California, Florida, Texas, and other western and southern states. The Los Angeles/Long Beach metropolitan area, for example, gained almost 1.3 million people in the 10 years before 1990. Some suburban counties around Los Angeles grew by as much as 45 percent in a decade.

Further migrations are taking place in the 1990s, most visibly into the Rocky Mountain states. Much of the urban growth occurring in places such as Boise, Idaho; Denver and the Front Range communities in Colorado; and Albuquerque, New Mexico draws from rural areas in those states, although fueled to some extent by an exodus of jobs and retirees from California and movement from other parts of the nation. And Texas, Florida, and California have emerged from their late-1980s economic doldrums to lure in-migrants once again.

At the same time, many older cities continue to lose population. St. Louis' population dropped by 41 percent since 1970 and by 7 percent since 1990. Pittsburgh's population declined by 31 percent and Cleveland's by 34 percent since 1970. Among large eastern and midwestern cities, New York stood out by gaining 7 percent since 1990 as a result of in-migration.

Even metropolitan areas losing population experience change. People move from inner-city neighborhoods and older suburbs to newly forming urban areas. While metropolitan Detroit's population dropped almost 2 percent from 1980 to 1990, for instance, the suburb of Troy increased its residents by more than 8 percent. Reflecting this phenomenon, all of the population increases in midwestern and northeastern regions during the 1980s occurred in suburbs rather than central cities. And in the cities, needs change as the demographics change.

Community growth and change, therefore, happen everywhere, not just to a few cities or regions. Some municipalities and counties in virtually all parts of the nation must cope with the phenomenon of urban development.

Many communities expect and even welcome development. Historically, Americans have sought the good life by moving outward, establishing new communities and leaving old ones behind. Growth has meant expansion, pushing into the countryside, building on new ground. Much of that expansion has been necessary to accommodate rapid population increases and a growing economy. But moving outward also generates problems and issues that defy simple solutions.

Fort Collins' experience is not unique. For almost a century its small-town ways made few demands on public facilities and its citizens saw no need to guide growth. Increments of development were small and easily assimilated into the town and its infrastructure systems. Town administrators were accustomed to dealing with relatively straightforward development issues. Rapid growth changed all that.

Growing communities often experience radical and disorienting alterations. Open farmland turns into subdivisions full of new houses practically overnight. Rural crossroads are transformed by new shopping centers. Green fields become industrial parks and golf courses. Office buildings replace old country stores.

With these highly visible changes come shifts in social and economic aspects of daily life. Different kinds of people arrive, some with different ideas about lifestyles. Some are wealthy and make higher bids for housing while others are poor and require special services. Demands for public facilities and services change as well. Roads and utility lines and schools must be expanded to serve additional people, and in addition a larger population desires a higher quality of services and more varieties of facilities. Gravel roads must be paved, paved roads widened, and new roads built. New schools, libraries, fire stations, and other facilities are required, each designed according to the latest standards. In turn, local governments scramble to secure funding and administer the construction and operation of ever-larger systems of public services and facilities.

Some communities fear that these changes will alter the comfortable character of their living environment. Growth can threaten the way of life of residents of small towns and rural communities. Instead of a relaxing shopping trip to the corner store, residents encounter a nerve-racking drive on congested highways to a busy shopping mall. Once-verdant views of rolling farmlands and wooded hills may be blocked by new buildings.

Patterns of growth also threaten essential environmental qualities and features, and thus the sustainability of life. Over the past few decades, development in metropolitan fringe areas has been increasingly consumptive of land. Densities of development have been declining as

homeowners elect to settle on larger and larger lots. Land that could remain in a natural condition or used for farming and forestry is cut up
into lots and covered with houses and pavement. Hundreds and thousands of individual wells and septic tanks alter the aquifers and groundwater. Wetlands, drainage areas, and wildlife habitats are invaded. Residents must use automobiles for long-distance commuting and shopping
trips, sending fumes into the air.

But growth is not the only agent of change. Declining cities and towns
are constantly evolving and adapting to new economic and social realities. When growth bypasses inner cities, neighborhoods decline and employment opportunities wane, leaving them mired in hopelessness. Communities compete for growth by maintaining desirable living areas,
increasing job opportunities, and undertaking the redevelopment of underused areas. In many cities that have seen residents departing for the
suburbs, new downtown office buildings, sports arenas, and civic buildings are revitalizing central-city economies, and middle- and upper-in-
come inner-city neighborhoods are flourishing.

Community change can be beneficial. New development can be a positive force for improving the lives of many residents. More and better employment opportunities may become available, not just in construction
but in businesses and industries expanding or moving to the area. New
stores and businesses may offer goods and services previously difficult to
find. Residential development may provide wider choices of housing
styles and prices to fit the preferences of a more varied population. New
development may produce a sounder long-term fiscal base for the community and diversify possibilities for social and cultural activities. Development can be designed to be compatible with environmental features rather than destroying them.

The Hazards of Unmanaged Development

Community growth and change challenge both citizens and governments
to prepare for new circumstances. Citizens must find ways to adapt personal living styles, and structures of government must meet new needs.
Governments of developing jurisdictions often find the pace, quality, and
amount of advancing growth difficult to deal with. Fort Collins' sudden
attraction for development caught town officials by surprise. No one had
anticipated the college's rapid expansion nor the industries that arrived
seemingly overnight. Although the prospect of growth was welcomed by
business and property owners and by families that saw possibilities for
new and better jobs, its implications for the town's way of life went un-
examined. Public officials worried about the tax rate and were excited
about additions to the tax base, but they were unaccustomed to looking

beyond these current events to evaluate the potential longer-term effects of growth.

Like public officials in Fort Collins, elected officials in growing rural areas and small towns often are overwhelmed by expanding needs associated with growth. They are unprepared to envision new governmental responsibilities and often unwilling to take decisive steps to meet them. Even professional administrators in local governments are often unready to take on the managerial and operational complexities of planning, financing, and operating larger systems of public services and facilities.

The combination of residents' negative reactions and government officials' fumbling response to growth and change spells trouble of several kinds. When local governments are slow to recognize emerging needs, they neglect to insist on appropriate standards of development and fail to program and deliver facilities required to support new development. Postponing planning and facility funding can quickly affect citizens' quality of life; citizens view inadequate roads, schools, water systems, and other basic services as inconveniences in their daily lives and potential threats to property values.

Unfortunately, for decades throughout the United States, all levels of government have underinvested in community infrastructure. Roads, water supply, sewerage, and other critical support systems in many older communities have not been maintained. Those in newer communities often lack capacity to expand without major investments. Simply catching up with existing system deficiencies will take substantial funds in many communities. Meanwhile, growth continues to erode capacities and qualities of vital services.

As the gap between needs and expenditures has expanded, consumers want more and better services, spelling higher costs for new infrastructure. Furthermore, as public officials approve higher standards of facilities for new developments, residents of older neighborhoods expect equal treatment, thus adding to fiscal burdens.

Unplanned growth also may endanger important natural and cultural assets of the community and region. Haphazard development consumes valuable open spaces and prime farmlands, disturbs wildlife habitats and wetlands, and destroys historic and cultural features that link the community to its heritage.

Communities that pay insufficient attention to potential growth and change are caught short when it occurs. When public officials simply let growth happen, they miss opportunities for creating value in the community, for maintaining important community characteristics, for establishing stability in the development process, and for providing efficient systems of infrastructure for all residents. Unfortunately, their reactions often are too little and too late, putting the entire community behind the curve of dealing effectively with development.

Local voters tend to react angrily to these outcomes of unplanned growth. As development swamps valued community qualities, citizens often demand public actions to slow down or even stop development. Sometimes public officials respond by taking punitive actions to limit development. Unfortunately, most such actions cannot cure the problems and often prevent reasonable solutions. Over the long term, stop-gap solutions and crisis-reactive management perpetuate political turmoil and community conflict.

Managing Development Means Planning Ahead

Growth and change may be blamed for many community ills, but failure to plan for growth is the fundamental problem. Public officials turn opportunities into problems by neglecting to anticipate and cope with community expansion. Their dereliction not only harms their own communities but usually affects nearby communities as well. By contrast, communities that plan ahead to foresee and meet the needs associated with urban development can capitalize on the benefits of growth.

Such a positive approach to future growth is supported by a great many people. Several studies have shown that support for growth management is not confined to a few elitist or environmental groups. The studies tested the hypothesis that growth restrictions and regulations are pursued by certain organizations or exclusive communities that wish to restrict access to their communities and increase their property values. As summarized by Elizabeth Deakin, these studies found that "characteristics such as education, income, home ownership, and political attitudes [are not closely related to] attitudes toward growth."[1] There are some differences among attitudes: More educated and less fiscally conservative people tend to worry more about environmental issues, and less educated and more fiscally conservative people tend to be more concerned with economic issues. But Deakin points out that many kinds of communities adopt growth controls, usually because they are undergoing rapid rates of growth, loss of farmland, traffic congestion, and fiscal distress.

Growth management, therefore, is supported by a variety of people and groups in many types of communities as a useful means of coping with growth.

The Concept of Growth Management

The idea of managing growth in urban and rural communities was hatched in the late 1960s and nurtured by Americans' increasing inter-

est in environmental protection then sweeping the nation. The confluence of concern for growth management with the environmental movement probably accounts for the emphasis of many early growth management programs on controlling growth to preserve environmental
resources. With time, however, and after considerable practical and academic exploration of the concept, growth management came to be seen
as a planning and administrative approach that focused on supporting
and coordinating the development process—a much wider perspective
than placing limits on development. Through years of practical experience with growth management approaches and techniques, the concept
became a positive force for guiding community development rather than
a means for restricting growth.

The concept of managing development is well understood in the business world. Corporate managers know that management of private enterprises requires the formulation of a thoughtful strategy to guide future
actions. In turn, this calls for a rational sequence of actions: estimating
trends in basic conditions, defining goals and objectives, determining
workable approaches to achieve those goals, and programming investments necessary to implement those approaches. Moreover, managers
understand that they need to constantly review and revise their strategies, goals, and approaches to keep their enterprises viable.

Management of community development follows a similar path, with
essential differences: community management programs demand a public–private partnership and consensus among a large variety of stakeholders. Public programs and regulations generally are adopted by local
governments to guide development that is carried out by private developers, builders, and landowners who operate within the economic marketplace. At the same time, public growth management must respond to
the interests of many "shareholders" in the public enterprise. Within
communities, residents of established neighborhoods, property owners,
and business leaders voice differing perspectives on development issues.
For that reason, growth management programs must acknowledge and
reconcile tensions between economic development, needs for social jus-
tice, and protection of essential environmental qualities—the concept of
sustainable development. A public management approach to community
development provides a useful process for responding to all those concerns.

Most growth management programs of local governments today aim
to accommodate development while maintaining community qualities
of life and livelihood and preserving environmental qualities. So, too,
with regional growth management efforts and with the wave of state
growth management laws that now influence the actions of local governments in at least 10 states. State and regional growth management programs, in fact, are chiefly concerned with making certain that local gov-

ernments manage the development process to achieve an equitable blend of public and private interests.

Defining Growth Management

Established definitions of growth management usually describe an all-inclusive concept that provides ample room for further definition while suggesting a masterly approach to guiding community development. The authors of *Constitutional Issues of Growth Management,* an early publication that influenced an entire generation of growth managers, define growth management as "a conscious government program intended to influence the rate, amount, type, location, and/or quality of future development within a local jurisdiction." The authors go on to note that practitioners intend growth management "to influence certain characteristics of growth and [to use] a variety of governmental policies, plans, regulations, and management techniques. . . ."[2]

The encyclopedic series of volumes called *Management and Control of Growth,* published by the Urban Land Institute, stated that managed growth

> means the utilization by government of a variety of traditional and evolving techniques, tools, plans, and activities to purposefully guide local patterns of land use, including the manner, location, rate, and nature of development.[3]

These broad definitions suggest that growth management programs can provide policy and action frameworks for a wide variety of development activities.

A more incisive and yet comprehensive definition recently was framed by Benjamin Chinitz:

> Growth management is active and dynamic . . . ; it seeks to maintain an ongoing equilibrium between development and conservation, between various forms of development and concurrent provisions of infrastructure, between the demands for public services generated by growth and the supply of revenues to finance those demands, and between progress and equity.[4]

Condensing that statement provides a practical definition of growth management as "a dynamic process in which governments anticipate and seek to accommodate community development in ways that balance competing land use goals and coordinate local with regional interests."

This definition reflects the outlook and content of this publication. Several key aspects of this definition deserve further explanation.

- Growth management is a *public, governmental activity* designed to direct and guide the private development process. Growth management puts public officials in a proactive position regarding development. The concept of growth management requires them to pay attention to development issues early and often. It also suggests that community development is too important to be left to developers alone.

- Growth management is a *dynamic process,* more than formulation of a plan and a follow-up action program. Growth management foresees an evolving and ever-changing program of activities, a continuous process of evaluating current trends and management results and updating both objectives and methods.

- Growth management *anticipates and accommodates development needs.* The principal purpose of growth management is to foresee and shape the scope and character of future development, identify existing and emerging needs for public infrastructure, and fashion governmental actions to assure that those needs will be met. With few exceptions, growth management programs generally are formulated to accommodate rather than limit expected development.

- Growth management programs provide a forum and process for determining an *appropriate balance* between competing development goals. Public interests must be weighed against private property rights. Furthermore, individual public objectives are meaningless unless their value is weighed against the importance of other goals of growth management. Growth management programs must make the difficult choices of emphasis, priorities, and coordination that translate general intentions into workable plans for future action.

- Local objectives in growth management must *relate local and regional concerns.* Ideally, growth management encourages communities to reach beyond their individual interests in future development to reflect region-wide needs and goals as well. Local governments' management of growth must recognize that communities function within a context of metropolitan economic and social activities, goals, and needs.

Growth management is both a political and technical tool for guiding community development. In addition, it incorporates and builds on traditional planning tools, and extends to encompass economic and social concerns as well as interests in physical development.

Growth management is one of the processes our political institutions use to solve problems. In seeking community consensus on the composition, quality, and location of future urban development and determining specific actions to implement that consensus, public officials are practicing growth management. Growth management programs offer ways and means to shape a strategy and policy framework to guide the many political decisions that otherwise would be made incrementally, without coordination. Growth management involves adoption of official public plans, enacted regulations, and budgeted programs—all determined by elected officials acting in their capacity as legislators and executives.

Growth management also involves technical processes requiring technical knowledge. Skilled professional staff must identify future development trends; define options for desirable forms of development; and specify policies, programs, incentives, and regulations that can be employed to achieve those forms of development. These tasks require an understanding of complex relationships among geography, resources, social and economic institutions, and other factors that contribute to each community's special character. Knowledge of programmatic and regulatory approaches is also necessary. Growth management requires and benefits from technical competence and continuous administrative coordination among various agencies responsible for guiding development.

Growth management also encompasses and builds on traditional planning tools. Comprehensive planning and zoning were practiced long before the concept of growth management came on the scene. When the term *growth management* was invented in the late 1960s, it was intended to embrace and extend the ideas of comprehensive planning, zoning, subdivision regulations, and capital improvement programs that are commonly used by local governments. Some planners think of growth management as a more proactive form of urban planning—that is, growth management incorporates action programs that go beyond mere plans and common regulations. However, Eric Kelly in his book *Managing Community Growth* says "growth management is a tool to implement planning."[5] His comment reflects the widespread use of the term in western states to mean special types of regulatory techniques used to control, often limit, growth.

In practical terms, however, growth management should be viewed as a community's collection of plans, programs, and regulations that will accomplish the community's development objectives. To the extent that community objectives are achievable through the use of basic planning techniques, those tools can constitute a satisfactory growth management program. If public officials desire a more hands-on approach for guiding the development process, or if innovative or experimental techniques are considered necessary, then the growth management program will extend standard planning and zoning to incorporate a larger package of techniques.

The hallmark of *effective* growth management, however, is that these individual techniques are interlinked and coordinated in a synergistic manner rather than applied incrementally and independently. In addition, growth management programs recognize that successful approaches to growth management depend as much on administrative and consensus-building leadership as on specific policy or regulatory techniques and provisions.

Growth management approaches and techniques also are applicable to all types of communities in all types of development circumstances. Early growth management programs typically were adopted by suburban communities undergoing rapid development. Many people still think of growth management as primarily a suburban concern, although many rural towns, larger cities, urban counties, and even regional agencies also manage development by using growth management approaches and techniques. The term can be as inclusive as necessary to treat problems associated with community development. Growth management programs, for example, increasingly include affordable housing elements and can also incorporate programs dealing with employment opportunities, housing assistance, child care, and other social and economic problems.

Central cities practice growth management in undertaking redevelopment activities, infrastructure renovations, neighborhood upgrading, and other public actions. These programs require coordination, which can be accomplished through development management programs using some if not all the techniques employed in suburban growth management.

In summary, growth management is a public response to the potential effects of growth and change in community livability. Communities of all kinds—large and small, urban and rural—use growth management approaches and techniques to resolve development problems before they become crises and to keep the public and private sides of the development process synchronized and in balance. Chapter 2 explores the ways in which conventional planning techniques and more recent growth management techniques contribute to growth management programs.

2

Growth Management
Approaches and Techniques

The United States traditionally has relied to an extraordinary extent on spontaneous economic forces (the "free market system" or "free enterprise") to develop the places in which we live and work. The right of private individuals to own and determine how they will use real estate is a cherished and constitutionally protected tradition. But the public sector always has been a strong force in establishing the rules of the development game and even in participating in the development process. Governments provide the legal framework for land ownership and contractual understandings. They support development by planning and securing funding for underlying infrastructure and major capital facilities that stimulate development, an activity described in detail in Chapter 6. Governments also prescribe standards for development and regulate the character and location of development. At times, governments participate in joint ventures to obtain development that meets public objectives.

The roles of the public sector as regulator of private development and participant in selected projects are constantly evolving. At one time, governments played relatively passive roles in land development. More recently, some local governments have imposed limits on development in response to voters' wishes to slow or even stop growth. Environmentalists and other interest groups have pressed for more rigorous standards and complex requirements to protect specific areas, natural features, and buildings. Neighborhood residents have succeeded in obtaining special zoning protection against new developments in their vicinity.

15

Many local governments, constrained by limitations on powers of taxation and changing attitudes toward development, have shifted much of the burden of financing development-related infrastructure to the private sector.

Today, the development process functions within a complex array of public policies, regulations, restrictions, and incentives, all of which are continually evolving in response to changing public goals and responsibilities. This chapter examines the roles of government in managing community development and describes the chief approaches and techniques currently in use in community growth management programs.

The Public Sector as Regulator of Community Development

In ancient times, governments founded cities and towns—historically in colonies recently subjugated—and took responsibility for their layout and construction of major public buildings, often populating them with new residents. In Colonial America, great landowners such as William Penn and James Oglethorpe borrowed many of the ancient ideas of town building—a gridiron street pattern, systems of open spaces, highly visible civic buildings—in designing their new towns. The difference was their status as landowners and as developers and speculators. From that time onward, communities in the United States were developed as private ventures. The Revolution helped the process by abolishing many of the feudal public claims on land ownership; soon thereafter, the Ordinance of 1785 established the rectangular survey system that allowed speculators to identify and trade in land they never saw.[1]

Governments' roles in community development consisted mostly of municipalities assisting the private development process: establishing and maintaining land records to protect ownership; building and managing basic facilities such as roads, prisons, schools, water and sewer systems; donating land to lure new industries for economic development. The City Beautiful movement initiated by the Columbian Exposition of 1893 helped inspire cities to build imposing civic edifices and parks and to create wide boulevards that increased values of adjoining private lands.

The first two decades of the 1900s saw the first stirrings of greater municipal involvement in guiding community development. Stimulated by concepts of the "City Beautiful" and motivated by concerns over teeming slums in the major cities, civic reformers called for establishing housing and building standards and for more attention to the quality of civic spaces, such as roads and parks. Committees of leading citizens com-

missioned well-known civic designers to provide plans for future development of their up-and-coming cities. In 1916, New York City adopted
the first comprehensive zoning law to regulate land use as well as building characteristics. Municipal zoning quickly spread across the nation,
opening the door to increasing public regulation of development.

The Regulators

Local governments in the United States possess the most direct powers
to regulate development. Although most of the 19,000 municipalities and
3100 counties existing throughout the nation are too small or lack authority to enact development regulations, many local jurisdictions actively guide development through adoption of official policies and regulations. Certainly, most cities over 25,000 population and many
suburban jurisdictions and small towns with smaller populations guide
community development. Townships in some states and counties in
other states also regulate development. (Many other states deliberately
limit county governmental powers to certain rurally oriented duties such
as highway maintenance and social services.) And in some states, several
cities and counties have combined to jointly regulate development.

Thus, thousands of local governments are engaged in governing the
development process. In a typical metropolitan area, development patterns and characteristics may be regulated by dozens of municipalities
and some counties. Regional agencies have been formed in metropolitan
areas to coordinate local efforts, but rarely do they posess enough power
to truly affect the course of development.

State and federal agencies also regulate development, although not in
the same manner as local governments. State laws and regulations may
require special permits for drilling wells or installing septic tanks in rural
areas, or for opening access from a property to a state highway, or for developing certain types of facilities, such as airports and hazardous waste
dumps. States often adopt building codes as guides for codes of local jurisdictions. Both state and federal environmental laws require permits
for development that affects wetlands, habitat of endangered or threatened species, and water quality. Development that directly affects state
or federal lands and facilities may require special evaluations and/or permits. As described in Chapter 8, nine states have adopted state growth
management acts with additional requirements for local governments
and property owners to abide by.

Thus regulation of development is a multilayered and complex process
that can create substantial obstacles to development. Regulation of the
development process encompasses a host of laws and ordinances en-

acted at federal, state, and local levels of government. For almost 80 years these laws and ordinances have been tested in the courts, creating a large body of case law that continues to evolve.

The Legal Foundation for Public Regulations

State and local governments' regulation of land development is based on the police power—the right and obligation granted to states by the Tenth Amendment to the Constitution—to protect the health, safety, and general welfare of citizens. Oddly, the police power is not a constitutional power of the federal government except in cases of interstate commerce, land in federal ownership, and private land subject to major federal public works, such as dams and irrigation systems. Rather, the police power is reserved for the states, which usually elect to delegate that authority to local governments for purposes of guiding land development.

Most states enacted enabling legislation in the 1920s and 1930s that gave local governments the authority to regulate real estate development through use of the police power. Since then, local officials have become accustomed to thinking of these regulatory powers as theirs by right. They believe that regulations affecting the growth and character of their communities should be determined and administered by local governments that are closest to the people and the land most affected. Increasingly, however, states are moving to reassert a role in managing the development process through state growth management acts. A reminder of state prerogatives in land use control occurred in Fairfax County, Virginia in 1990, when the state legislature threatened to rescind the county's downzoning of industrially zoned land.

Courts recognize the right of local governments to exercise the police power, but they also are concerned with safeguarding private property rights. The history of land use law in the United States describes the working out of an uneasy—and continuously evolving—balance between the rights of local governments to protect the public's health, safety, and general welfare and the rights of individuals to unfettered enjoyment of private property. That balance has shifted as the courts have expanded their interpretations of "health, safety, and general welfare" to include aesthetic and other concerns.

The courts also allow local governments wide latitude in adopting legislation under the police power. Under the doctrine of "legislative presumption of validity," the courts give great deference to regulations that are properly enacted by local governments, generally holding them valid unless clearly proven otherwise. Local governments' use of the police power therefore has grown considerably in scope and application.

Two early court cases, *Welch* v. *Swasey* in 1909 and *Hadacheck* v. *Sebastian* in 1915, established the right of local governments to regulate development. A major judicial step supporting regulation of the police power occurred in 1926, when the U.S. Supreme Court, in *Euclid* v. *Ambler Realty*, upheld zoning as a valid form of regulation. Through countless court decisions since then, the courts consistently upheld the right of local governments to regulate land use and development so long as they established a legitimate public interest for the action and followed due process in adopting and administering it.

Under the police power, governments may severely limit private property owners' rights to use of their property. In appropriate circumstances, governments may legally curtail or prohibit development to preserve such natural features as floodplains, wetlands, sand dunes, and habitats of endangered species, and may restrict the amount or height of development to protect erodible hillsides, mountain views, access to beaches, solar access, and other public interests.

Courts, however, have established legal constraints on rights to use the police power. The extent to which regulations can restrict the use of land remains an open and controversial legal question. If regulations are too restrictive, they can be defined as a "taking" of private property, which governments cannot do without compensating the property owners.

Four famous U.S. Supreme Court decisions sounded warning notes about overly expansive use of the police power. In a 1987 court case, *Nollan* v. *California Coastal Commission*, the Court ruled that the Commission had not established an appropriate connection between a regulation and the public interest when it required property-owner Patrick Nollan to allow public access along his beach frontage, citing as a reason the goal of providing public views of the ocean. The Court indicated that, in cases of this type, it would more closely scrutinize governmental actions to ensure that regulations were properly related to public purposes. In the same year in *First English Evangelical Lutheran Church of Glendale* v. *County of Los Angeles*, the Court ruled that if regulations are found to take property, the public authority may be required to compensate the owner. (In this case a state court later determined that the regulations, which prevented rebuilding of structures destroyed by a flood in a floodplain, were not a taking.)

In 1992, in *Lucas* v. *South Carolina Coastal Council*, the U.S. Supreme Court held that a taking had occurred and damages were due because the Council's regulations against beachfront development deprived Lucas of all use of his two lots on the ocean. These decisions suggest that governments' regulation of development must follow strict

Some Important Land Use Cases

Douglas R. Porter

Welch v. Swasey, 214 U.S. 91 (1909). The U.S. Supreme Court upheld Boston's height restrictions within districts.

Hadacheck v. Sebastian, 239 U.S. 394 (1915). The U.S. Supreme Court upheld a city ordinance prohibiting the continuance of brick manufacturing within designated areas as a nuisance to nearby residents as a proper exercise of the police power.

Village of Euclid, Ohio v. Ambler Realty Co., 272 U.S. 365 (1926). This was the first U.S. Supreme Court case to uphold zoning as a valid form of regulation of the police power.

Golden v. The Planning Board of the Town of Ramapo, 285 N.W. 2d 291 (N.Y. 1972). This case is one of the first and most important cases upholding regulations for timing, phasing, and quotas in development generally and in Ramapo specifically, making development permits contingent on the availability of adequate public facilities.

Southern Burlington County NAACP v. Mt. Laurel Township, 336 A. 2d 713 (N.J. 1975) and 456 A. 2d 390 (N.J. 1983). In these two cases, the state court ruled that Mt. Laurel Township and other New Jersey municipalities must provide for development of a fair share of lower-cost housing and impose court oversight of the process.

Avco Community Builders, Inc. v. South Coastal Regional Commission, 132 Cal. Rptr. 386, 553 P. 2d 546 (1976). The California Supreme Court held that Avco did not have vested rights to develop despite having secured local approvals and made expenditures of over $2 million. The decision led directly to the state development agreements act.

Penn Central Transportation Co. v. New York City, 438 U.S. 104 (1978). The U.S. Supreme Court upheld New York City's imposition of landmark sta-

rules, with due caution for rights of private property owners. The Court's 1994 decision in *Dolan v. City of Tigard* determined that the government has the burden of justifying requirements for dedication of property for which the owner is not compensated.

The other, more widely applied, brake on governments' use of the police power is public opinion, expressed through political means. Many U.S. citizens own property and place great store on their rights to use it. It is not surprising, therefore, that local public officials, when deciding to regulate land use and development, usually attempt to allow property owners a reasonable economic use of their property. In writing and administering zoning regulations, for example, city councils and public ad-

tus on Grand Central Station, thus preventing construction of an office building over the station, as a justifiable regulation that required no compensation.

Kaiser Aetna v. United States, 444 U.S. 164 (1979). The U.S. Supreme Court upheld the owners of a private lagoon in their claim that a taking had occurred when they were forced to allow public use of the lagoon.

Agins v. City of Tiburon, 447 U.S. 255 (1980). This case was one of a series in which the U.S. Supreme Court held that the cases were not "ripe" for a decision, usually meaning that the plaintiffs had not exhausted the administrative procedures that might have resolved their complaint before going to court.

Nollan v. California Coastal Commission, 483 U.S. 825 (1987). The U.S. Supreme Court ruled that the California Coastal Commission had not established an appropriate connection between a requirement for an exaction and the cited public objective for the exaction.

First English Evangelical Lutheran Church of Glendale v. The County of Los Angeles, 482 U.S. 304 (1987). This decision was the first by the U.S. Supreme Court that a regulatory taking of property can require compensation to the owner, even if the regulation has only a temporary effect.

Lucas v. South Carolina Coast Council, 112 S. Ct. 2886 (1992). The U.S. Supreme Court ruled that damages are due in the relatively rare situations in which a governmental entity deprives a landowner of "all economically beneficial uses" of the land.

Dolan v. City of Tigard, 114 S. Ct. 2309 (1994). The U.S. Supreme Court ruled that the government has the burden of justifying permit conditions that require dedication of property without compensating the owner.

ministrators take care to allow property owners fair use of their property and provide for special treatment of hardships. Attitudes of public officials on this question vary considerably from state to state, affected to some extent by past and present pressures for development, fiscal discipline, and environmental protection. Regulatory restrictions considered reasonable for Californians might be anathema for Virginians.

Thus, local governments have a great deal of latitude in determining how to regulate development. State enabling legislation provides a starting point and court decisions erect a legal framework, but final decisions often depend on the attitudes and political positions of the public officials making them.

The Property Rights Issue

Erik Meyers

Few topics ignite such deeply held and poorly informed views as the current conflict between property rights and development regulation, especially regulation for environmental protection. Many development interests and some landowners denounce environmental and land use regulation as an unwarranted, illegal, or unconstitutional intrusion of their "property rights." They assert the right to use private land unfettered by concerns of society and seek compensation for even temporary restrictions. A similarly extreme view at the opposite end of the spectrum is raised by some public officials and environmental and civic activists, who claim that protection of a community's right to a clean environment should always trump a private interest in land.

Perhaps at no time has the pace of change in the United States been as dramatic as it has since World War II. Individual liberties and civil rights have experienced near-revolutionary change. Protection of the environment has moved from being a fringe, counter-culture issue to becoming a core American value. Laws by the score were enacted and billions of dollars expended to protect environmental features and qualities. Based on the immensity of those shifts, the current clash between property-rights advocates and environmental protection proponents could have been predicted.

Often unacknowledged and thus unappreciated in the current debates is that the legal doctrines that determine the balance between private and public prerogatives and rights in land have been evolving for centuries. Since the earliest days of the American colonies our law has recognized the shared interests in land between sovereign and individual owner. Private ownership was never unfettered: One of the most enduring concepts in common law is the obligation to use property in a manner that does not adversely affect one's neighbor. American law has long recognized the necessity of fairly allocating the burdens and benefits of property ownership.

The Fifth Amendment to the Constitution contains a provision (extended to the states by the Fourteenth Amendment) that states in part: ". . . nor shall private property be taken for public use, without just compensation." Since the 1920s, the courts have acknowledged that the exercise of validly enacted regulations could affect a "taking" of private property if application to a particu-

The Local Framework for Regulating Development

Cities, counties, and other local governments undertake planning, zoning, and additional forms of development regulation according to state enabling statutes and, in some cases, through home rule charters

lar parcel resulted in leaving the owner without a viable use of the property. This established doctrine, however, only starts the process of determining whether a law or regulation so severely impacts a property that compensation is due the owner.

Law students encounter the concept of property as a "bundle of sticks" that includes the right to occupy and use property for an economically productive purpose, to exclude others, to convey title or ownership interests, and to convey by will the property to others. Each stick is limited by laws and limitation or loss of one stick does not automatically mean abrogation of one's property rights in a constitutional sense. In many modern cases, the extent of a regulation's economic impact on property is often a critical question. Regulations that protect water resources or scenic vistas can negatively affect the market value of a specific property, however, while enhancing market values on others. Established law requires an owner's expectations of value to be reasonable and backed by some investment. Recent U.S. Supreme Court decisions have placed greater emphasis on public authorities defining specific ways in which regulations may legitimately affect property values.

The rate of doctrinal change has been evolutionary, not revolutionary. Property rights advocates, seeking more rapid and far-reaching change, have solicited support from federal and state legislatures for their views. In particular, they have pressed for economic impact assessments of new regulations and set a lower threshold of regulatory impact that would trigger compensation. Although these pursuits have netted a few state laws, they have encountered resistance based on Americans' high valuation of environmental protection. The recent report of the President's Commission on Sustainable Development, endorsed by business, environmental, and other leaders, expresses those values in calling for maintaining an equitable share of the nation's natural wealth for future generations. Although no end to the debate is in sight, the genius of American law is its ability to avoid abrupt shifts, respecting precedent but continually adapting to accommodate society's changing needs and expectations.

granted by states. The four cornerstones of local governments' regulatory programs are comprehensive plans, zoning ordinances, subdivision regulations, and capital improvement programs. Almost all local governments regulate development using these tools. Many communities also adopt additional measures to manage growth and development.

1. Comprehensive Plans

The basic, guiding document of the public regulatory process is the comprehensive plan, sometimes known as the general plan or master plan. A comprehensive plan describes the ways in which a community should develop over a 10- to 20-year time frame. Usually a plan consists of written development goals and policies, supplemented with maps. The plan provides guidelines for local officials in decisions about the quality, location, and amount of development.

Comprehensive plans are distinctive for their long-range outlook and broad scope of development concerns. Thus, plan statements of overall development objectives and policies may be quite general. However, the plan may also incorporate or be supported by more detailed plans for specific elements of development, such as housing and infrastructure systems, or for particular areas of importance, such as central business districts.

Depending on specific state statutes and court decisions, comprehensive plans may be optional or mandatory for local governments. They may be merely advisory in nature or legally binding on public decisions. From state to state, and often locality to locality, therefore, comprehensive plans differ greatly in content and significance. Although many jurisdictions now formulate and regularly consult their comprehensive plans as serious policy documents to guide decision making of local officials, some local governments continue to treat them as strictly advisory and highly flexible guides to community development. For that reason, plans often become outdated, are written to be overly general, and ineffectively influence decision making on development issues.

2. Zoning Ordinances

Zoning is the most widely used form of land use regulation. Most homeowners understand zoning; most neighborhood associations routinely track rezoning issues; council members' positions on specific zoning cases can spell defeat or victory for their reelections. Zoning was invented in the early years of this century and zoning regulations quickly spread across the land. Many local governments adopted zoning before any other type of development regulations.

Zoning ordinances include written requirements and standards that define the permitted uses of land and buildings, the height and size of buildings, the size of lots and yards around buildings, the supply of parking spaces, size and type of signs and fences, and other characteristics of development. These provisions are spelled out for a variety of zoning districts, which are delineated on maps. When a local government adopts a zoning ordinance, every property within its jurisdiction is designated within a specific district and its use is regulated by the ordinance provisions for that district. The ordinances also establish procedures for changing zoning.

The fundamental purpose of zoning is to separate incompatible uses of land. Housing is separated from smoky or noisy industries; shopping centers that generate traffic are separated from residential neighborhoods; tall buildings are separated from low ones. Through years of practical experience and litigation, single-family homes have emerged as the primary beneficiary of zoning. In most communities, zoning is largely a device for protecting old and new residential neighborhoods from other uses viewed as incompatible.

Because traditional zoning is rather inflexible, however, a host of alternative zoning approaches have been formulated, as summarized in the box on page 26. According to planning theory, zoning is supposed to be based on the comprehensive plan. In a sense, zoning is a detailed application, in written and map form, of the more general policies spelled out in a plan. In states not requiring consistency between plans and zoning, however, zoning may vary from the plan, causing a great deal of unpredictability in the community development process. Furthermore, some local governments persist in treating both comprehensive plans and zoning regulations as transitory documents subject to constant amendment and revision to meet short-term pressures for development.

Subdivision Regulations   3.

Subdivision regulations provide public control over subdivisions of land into lots for sale and development. The regulations require all subdivision developers to obtain approval of detailed plans before they can record and sell lots. The plans must satisfy requirements and standards pertaining to the size and shape of lots, design and construction of streets, water and sewer lines, other public facilities, and other concerns such as protecting environmental features. Thus subdivision regulations act as a principal point for public regulators to impose special requirements for facility improvements and other conditions.

Capital Improvement Programs   4.

These programs are adopted by local governments to provide a construction schedule for planned infrastructure improvements, including expected sources of funds to pay for them. Usually the program is adopted each year for a six-year period. It furnishes a guide to when and where public improvements will be made, and therefore where development is encouraged.

Until recently, capital improvement programs in many jurisdictions were subject to year-to-year political wheeling and dealing, so that they

Selected Zoning Innovations

Douglas R. Porter

Conventional zoning, especially as practiced up to the 1950s, has been supplemented by many special types of zoning to address needs for greater flexibility in regulating development. Some of the most significant variations are summarized below.

Planned unit development (PUD): An optional procedure for project design, usually applied to a fairly large site. It allows more flexible site design than ordinary zoning would allow by permitting options or relaxing some requirements. A PUD frequently permits a variety of housing types and sometimes other uses as well. Usually a PUD includes an overall general plan that is implemented through specific subdivision plans.

Cluster zoning: Allows groups of dwellings on small lots on one part of the site to preserve open space and/or natural features on the remainder of the site. Minimum lot and yard sizes for the clustered development are reduced. Like PUDs, site designs are subjected to more detailed reviews.

Overlay zoning: A zoning district, applied over one or more other districts, that contains additional provisions for special features or conditions, such as historic buildings, wetlands, steep slopes, and downtown residential uses.

Floating zones: Zoning districts and provisions for which locations are not identified until enacted for a specific project. Such zones are used to anticipate certain uses, such as regional shopping centers, for which locations will not be designated on the zoning map until developers apply for zoning. They usually require special review procedures.

Incentive zoning: Zoning provisions that encourage but do not require developers to provide certain amenities or qualities in their projects in return for identified benefits, such as increased density or rapid processing of applications. Incentives are often used in downtown areas to gain open space, special building features, or public art in connection with approved developments.

Flexible zoning: Zoning regulations that establish performance standards and other criteria for determining appropriate uses and site design requirements rather than prescribe specific uses and building standards. Performance provisions are rarely applied to all zoning districts but are often used for selective locations or types of uses (e.g., PUDs).

were not effective predictors of actual future improvements. With more private involvement in funding improvements and greater fiscal concerns of local governments, capital improvement programs have become more significant as a regulatory tool.

These four basic regulatory tools function as the principal framework for growth management programs in most jurisdictions. With skillful use, they alone can act as an effective growth management program. As described later in this chapter, however, most local governments have added other regulatory techniques to manage development more effectively.

Regulatory Procedures

The regulations adopted by local governments establish procedures that require property owners and developers to obtain zoning, building, and occupancy permits. Depending on site conditions and circumstances, other permits—for wells and septic tanks, use of environmentally sensitive lands, and special uses—may be required as well. Applications must be submitted for these permits, usually with supporting documentation. If the type of development is allowed "by right" according to zoning for the property, an administrative official can approve the proposal without further action. If the proposed development is allowed only under certain conditions or requires a change in zoning, special hearings and other procedures are necessary, some of which can be quite lengthy.

As development regulations become more complicated and convoluted, applicants are faced with many decisions about making their way through the permitting process. For a specific project it may be necessary to request changes in adopted plans or zoning or to use special procedures that allow alternative uses or more flexible design treatment. A request for changes or special procedures usually exposes a project to closer scrutiny by public officials and the general public and often creates opportunities for public officials to require additional amenities or private contributions to infrastructure.

Use of these special "discretionary" procedures has grown in recent years. In part this occurred because public officials discovered that they can control the size and quality of development more directly through case-by-case reviews rather than through written regulations. In part developers opt for discretionary procedures to avoid overly restrictive regulations and to achieve greater flexibility in site design and development. But special interest groups and citizens' groups also discovered that such procedures open opportunities for intervening in decisions The result is that negotiations over conditions of development approval can be quite lengthy, require additional special studies, and involve a number of interests.

A time may come when the local regulatory process clearly needs to be rethought and reorganized. Communities frequently form task groups, comprising both public and private interests, to review existing regulations and procedures and recommend ways to streamline them. As described in Chapter 7, complex or overlapping requirements and lengthy, bureaucratic procedures can be simplified to reduce wear and tear on both the public and private sectors in the permitting process. At the same time, design and construction standards can be brought in line with community objectives, particularly if reducing housing costs is a concern.

Public Participation in Development

An important governmental activity often overlooked in growth management programs is public participation in specific developments, either in determining sites for major community facilities such as stadiums and convention centers or in public/private project partnerships. Although public and private sectors most often perform independent functions in the development process, in actuality public development activities can have significant effects on community development.

Public Facility Siting

Decisions about the location and nature of major public facilities can play an important role in stimulating or steering private development. Communities often determine to fund construction and operation of convention centers, for example, to improve the economic climate; they choose locations for convention centers to interact effectively with existing and planned hotels, restaurants, and other convention-related private businesses. Similar decision making is applied to stadiums, sports arenas, performing arts centers, and other facilities that can stimulate community development. At the other end of the spectrum, public officials must weigh the development *disincentives* of locating such facilities as landfills and halfway houses.

Public/Private Ventures

The usefulness of public participation in private development projects as a particularly proactive means of managing community development has been proven over and over. There are many examples of public assistance given to stimulate private development in the interest of promoting local economic and business opportunities, as well as obtaining community amenities not otherwise attainable. For decades, federally assisted programs such as urban renewal, new communities, housing subsidies, model cities, and urban development action grants provided funds and processes for engaging in public/private development efforts. With cutbacks in federal aid, local governments sponsored similar joint projects to develop or revitalize town centers, industrial areas, residential neighborhoods, transit station areas, and even recreation areas. Many such projects, like Baltimore's Inner Harbor redevelopment, aimed at revitalizing deteriorated sections of older cities and towns. Other projects, however, such as a regional shopping center promoted as the town center for Fairfield, California and a mixed-use project on county-owned land at a Miami rail-transit station, are in developing suburban areas. Through these types of projects, an impressive body of experience has been gained by local officials in ways to design and implement public/private projects.

Thus, beginning early in the century and continuing through the immediate postwar period, local governments sought to guide development using basic techniques for planning, zoning, subdivision regulation, and programming capital facilities. While those tools proved useful, the public role in community development is ever-changing, requiring local governments to respond to emerging conditions and needs. Types of policies, regulations, and programs that local governments can employ for guiding development have steadily widened as communities experimented and refined approaches and techniques. In many communities, these efforts evolved into comprehensive, far-reaching growth management programs, using approaches and techniques described in the next section.

The Emergence of Growth Management

The concept of growth management arose in reaction to the surge of urban growth that swept across the nation soon after World War II. Pent-up demands for development suppressed by the lean Depression years of the 1930s, followed by the restrictions imposed by the war during the first half of the 1940s, generated a burst of development unlike any that had gone before. The Federal Housing Administration and Veteran's Administration underwrote housing mortgages for the common man. Automobiles, which had just begun to be the travel mode of choice prior to the war, poured onto the highways, taking their passengers to find homes in the countryside. Developers ushered in the era of big projects—huge subdivisions of new houses on sites scraped clean of vegetation, the spread of innovative shopping centers and industrial parks. Development quickly spread beyond city boundaries into areas soon incorporated into separate suburbs.

During this time, growth was considered a plus for any community. Local progress was equated with the number of new houses built, new jobs created, increases in local spending, and the like. Growth expanded small communities into large ones that were a source of pride to the business community and most residents. Growth was expected to expand the local tax base, bring a broader range of goods and services, raise income levels and create job opportunities, provide a wider choice of housing, and lead to more and better community facilities to be enjoyed by all.

However, although developers were simply catering to the mass market—and then to its creators, the baby-boom generation—the picture generally was not a pretty one. The media—newspapers and magazines in those days—printed photo after photo of the new developments, usually using aerial angles guaranteed to show the immensity and bleakness of suburban development. Standards of development were not high; the usual procedure was to bulldoze the site into shape without worrying too much about stands of trees and stream valleys. Environmental sensibilities were virtually unknown. Many of the first developments took place on small lots platted in the 1920s, planting houses a few feet apart on a deadly dull gridiron street pattern. Post-development landscaping took years to gain a foothold.

Then, as Randall Scott observes in his introduction to the *Management and Control of Growth* volumes published by the Urban Land Institute in the 1970s, "the backlog of demand for more adequate and improved facilities could no longer be ignored: the 'catch-up' costs tended to be high, setting the stage for taxpayer reactions against increased costs, poor land use management, and further development."[2]

Adding to the strength of that reaction, Rachel Carson's *Silent Spring*, published in 1962, opened many eyes to the degradation of the environment taking place on a national and global scale.[3] The resulting environmental movement led to the passage of the National Environmental Policy Act in January 1970.

The environmental concerns that drove desires for managing development were reflected in the work of a national Task Force on Land Use and Urban Growth, which in 1973 published *The Use of Land: A Citizen's Policy Guide to Urban Growth*, a highly influential publication for the next generation of environmental advocates. Said the task force:

> There is a new mood in America that questions traditional assumptions about urban growth and has higher expectations of both government and new urban development. . . . It is time to change the view that land is little more than a commodity to be exploited and traded.[4]

Later in the report, the authors described the consequences of 600,000 new residents settling in Nassau County on Long Island from 1950 to 1960, doubling its population:

> . . . an unrelieved pattern of low-density, single-family homes, shopping center sprawl, and haphazardly sited business, industry, and entertainment. Once-blue bays are polluted; once-com-

mon shellfish have disappeared, wetlands are bulkheaded and beaches are eroded; in many areas open space is virtually gone.[5]

These kinds of conditions, repeated in region after region across the nation, energized civic activists to demand better regulation of the development process. Even as the National Environmental Policy Act was being signed into law, local governments in widely scattered areas were formulating and adopting the first growth management acts.

The Pathbreakers

Several early experiments with new forms of development regulations gave wide publicity to some of the basic techniques of growth management. In fact, three led to court cases that established fundamental legal justifications for growth management. The communities of Ramapo, New York; Petaluma, California; Boulder, Colorado; and Boca Raton, Florida borrowed approaches to growth management from a variety of ideas then circulating in the planning world. Their early innovations, however, put them on the map as pathbreakers for the growth management movement.

One of the best-known early growth management programs was adopted by the town of Ramapo, New York in 1969. Ramapo was a semi-rural community within commuting distance of New York City. Following growth pressures created by completion of two major highways, the town adopted a comprehensive plan that called for low- to moderate-density development. Then it amended the zoning ordinance to require that residential development could take place only as public facilities were available to support it. An 18-year capital facilities budget accompanied the amendment. Each proposed project was rated according to a point system that awarded points based on availability of sewers, drainage, public parks, recreation facilities, major road facilities, and fire houses. Projects not receiving 15 points would be postponed until facilities were available or the developer constructed them.

After adoption of this ordinance, Ramapo's housing construction dropped by two-thirds. Builders sued but the development control system was upheld by New York's highest court in 1972, in *Golden v. The Planning Board of the Town of Ramapo*. Although the system was criticized because the town itself controlled provision of only parks, sewage collection, drainage, and some roads, its innovative requirements, positive judicial support, and widespread publicity made it a decisive influence in the spread of growth management.

The small community of Petaluma, California, with 15,000 residents in 1960, stood in the path of suburban growth pushing north from San Francisco. Between 1968 and 1972, 2000 new residents a year moved to the city. Although the town had planned for residential development and provided a full complement of services, by the early 1970s its sewer and water systems were operating almost at full capacity and elementary schools in newer parts of the city were on double sessions. In 1971 a moratorium was put in place to give time to rethink the general plan. In 1972 the city adopted a "residential development control system" that limited development to 500 new housing units a year, applicable to any development of more than four units. (This limit was substantially lower than recent rates of development.) In addition, the system set quotas for various housing types and their distribution throughout the city; the city also established an annual competitive evaluation of proposed projects according to criteria that included consistency with the plan, availability of services, urban design features, and provisions of needed public facilities.

The city was sued by homebuilders in 1973 over the annual limit on new dwelling units. After lengthy court battles, including a decision by the Federal District Court against Petaluma's system, the U.S. Supreme Court settled the issue in 1976 by letting the residential development control system stand. Interestingly, Petaluma's pace of development after 1976 never again approached the 500-unit limit. The system has been modified considerably over the years, especially focusing on design issues; a growth limit has been maintained.

Boulder, Colorado, another city undergoing rapid growth during the 1960s and 1970s, adopted a growth limit in 1976. The move came in response to an initiative by the Boulder chapter of Zero Population Growth to halt development at the level of 40,000 housing units. The city's counter initiative, which won, called for the city to keep growth "substantially below" the 1960s' growth rates. Following the work of a blue-ribbon commission, the city drafted an ordinance patterned after Petaluma's, called the "Danish Plan" after its primary author and sponsor. It limited annual housing development to an increase of 1.5 percent, or an average of 450 units per year. Various exceptions to the limit allowed a growth rate of about 2 percent. As with Petaluma, subsequent growth rates generally fell below that limit. However, Boulder has continued to innovate with many growth management techniques that are described in several later chapters.

Boulder's success at controlling residential development was not paralleled by its regulation of nonresidential development. A lengthy boom in commercial and business growth prompted Boulder to adopt controversial limits on that type of development in 1995.

Another example of early attempts to impose growth limits occurred in Boca Raton, Florida. Citizens appalled at the rate of development in that resort community during the 1960s pressed for and got city action in 1972 to limit development to a maximum of 40,000 housing units, or a population of about 105,000. This was implemented by adopting a moratorium on all but single-family and duplex residential development and rezoning to reduce permitted densities. In 1979 a Florida court, in *City of Boca Raton* v. *Boca Villas Corporation,* 371 So. 2d 154 (Fla. App. 1979), struck down the limit because it was not based on sound studies and deliberations. However, the court let the rezonings stand.

The regulatory innovations, subsequent experience, and court decisions resulting from these communities' growth management efforts gave public officials and planners across the nation license to proactively guide their community's development process, even to the point of limiting the amount, pace, and location of future growth.

The Growth Management Paradigm

The swirl of publicity and activity concerned with growth management that built on these early examples lent the term a certain mystique in the land use and development field in the early 1970s. Academicians, researchers, and attorneys soon fashioned a theoretical construct that postulated an awesome combination of content and process for growth management. Growth management in some circles meant a broadly comprehensive but meticulously detailed program enacted by public entities to control all aspects of development—the classic "management" scenario.

In other circles, growth management offered an opportunity to slow or stop growth. Population control advocates, active then as now, exerted a great deal of effort (as illustrated by Boulder's experience) in proposing limits on the amount of growth in specific communities. Today, proponents of population control remain opposed to the positive aspects of growth management, because a successful growth management program accommodates growth—and hence a larger population.

Elsewhere, in the places where growth management programs actually were adopted and functioned, growth management became a more mundane, practical concept. Selected techniques for carefully managing growth were simply added to existing planning and zoning programs. Over time they were tinkered with, revised, and extended to respond to specific community concerns. It turned out that growth management programs were helpful approaches to public guidance of the development process but a far cry from total control. The experience of Montgomery County, Maryland demonstrates many of the approaches—and some of the perils—of growth management as practiced in many communities.

The Case of Montgomery County, Maryland

Montgomery County, an affluent suburban jurisdiction in the Washington, D.C. region, has managed growth through a comprehensive, multifaceted program for almost 70 years. The county earned a nationwide reputation for imaginative and aggressive planning and growth management, using a variety of increasingly complex techniques. Montgomery County's program of managing growth incorporates many of the techniques used by other communities throughout the nation.

Populated by almost 800,000 residents in 1995, Montgomery County adjoins the northwestern boundary of the District of Columbia. Until the 1950s, its pastoral landscape was dotted with rural settlements; near the District border, a few subdivisions sprang up catering primarily to higher-income families seeking a country-club or rural setting. During two postwar decades, from 1950 to 1970, however, the county experienced rapid growth as development spilled over the District boundaries, attracted not only by the county's suburban lifestyle but also by the construction of Interstate 270 and the I-495 Beltway.

During the 1970s the pace of growth continued, abetted by the completion of Metrorail connections. But the nature of growth changed: The county began accruing the commercial and industrial features of an urban center. High-tech and bio-tech industries were attracted by the presence of the National Institutes of Health and the Bureau of Standards, among several federal agencies. Today, with 474,000 employees, almost two-thirds of county residents work within the county, and commuting into the county exceeds commuting out of it. Bethesda, Rockville, and Silver Spring, once small-town market centers, evolved into major business, shopping, and governmental centers focused on Metrorail stations. In the process, the county became the fifth highest local jurisdiction in the nation in terms of income-per-capita and the fourth highest in percentage of adults with 16 or more years of schooling. The county became a large, diverse, affluent urban center.

Strategic and Detailed Planning. The county's planning process began in 1927, when the Maryland General Assembly established the Maryland–National Capital Park and Planning Commission as the planning, zoning, and park acquisition body for Montgomery and neighboring Prince George's counties. Montgomery County adopted a home-rule charter in 1948 instituting a county planning board as part of the Park and Planning Commission, and in 1968 the charter was revised to establish a county executive and a county council that, unusually, was given authority for planning. Today, the planning board prepares and administers plans and ordinances; the county council appoints most board members and all hearing examiners and officially adopts plans and ordinances; and the county executive appoints some board members, programs facilities in the capital improvement program, prepares water, sewer, and solid waste plans, reviews and comments on other plans, and may veto planning board appointments and budget items, subject to council overrides.

In 1957 the Commission adopted the first master plan for the entire two-county area. The plan was revised in 1969 as the major development policy document for the counties. Entitled "On Wedges and Corridors" the plan proposed to contain urban sprawl by focusing development within two major transportation corridors, the I-270 corridor and the State Highway 29 corridor, and by preserving large areas of low-density development and open space between them. Although revised and detailed since then, the major concepts in that plan remain the cornerstones of the county's planning efforts.

The plan was augmented by "community" and "sector" plans prepared and adopted to apply more detailed land use guidance to specific areas, including plans for business districts and transit station areas. In recent years, the plan has been supplemented by issuance of annual growth policy reports that assess conditions and recommend course corrections. Zoning and subdivision ordinances have expanded in scope and detail to respond to a wide variety of concerns. A capital improvements program is adopted annually to provide facilities in concert with development.

Montgomery County's planning program is highly participatory, so a number of task forces and special working groups have reviewed the policies of the general plan over the years. In general, the groups have continued to support the basic elements of the plan, reaffirming the concentration of development around existing settlements and the preservation of farmland and open space in the northern part of the county.

Plan Implementation. The county implements the plan through the usual regulatory and programmatic devices such as zoning, but four initiatives deserve special mention and discussion: (1) the use of adequate public facilities measured as a core concept for year-to-year management of development; (2) the agricultural land preservation program; (3) the county's inclusionary housing program; and (4) its encouragement of development around Metrorail stations. All are keys to effective growth management that have attracted nationwide attention.

An adequate facilities ordinance was adopted in 1973 to require a review of facility capacities available to serve prospective development as a condition of project approval. With this ordinance, the county's programming of capital facility improvements (water, sewer, roads, transit, schools, police and fire protection, and health clinics) became a life-or-death matter for developers. A sewage moratorium in effect from 1970 to 1978 introduced both public and private interests to the intricacies of rationing available capacities. Subsequently, the planning board employed computer-assisted models to estimate traffic and fiscal impacts of proposed developments.

Since 1986, the county has prepared an annual "growth policy report" that defines the available capacities of facilities for new housing and employment in 18 policy areas throughout the county. The test of adequacy is based primarily on the adequacy of roads, which are the most vulnerable part of the infrastructure system at present (although in some cases school capacities are also considered). The annual report identifies the areas in which development can continue and those where development must await improvements or where transportation-demand measures must be adopted.

The measurement of "adequate" facilities, however, has been complicated by the unpredictable delivery of improvements promised in the capital improvements plan (CIP), affected by the usual annual politically inspired decisions, by the difficulty of matching incremental demand increases to the timing of major facility construction, by continuous changes in consumer demands and expectations for facilities, and by reductions in state and federal funding for capital facilities. The slump in development from the late 1980s to mid-1990s meant that many projects were postponed indefinitely.

The planning board responded to these problems by introducing ever more complex methods for projecting and calculating demands and for meeting projected demands. The annual growth policy report incorporates the results of policy-area transportation studies, but each proposed project is also subject to a local-area transportation review. With the slowdown in public funding of facilities in the 1970s and 1980s, developers were forced to resort to higher levels of "contributions" to counter the lack of planned or available capacity, especially for roads. Another tack encouraged by the county calls for developers to commit to traffic reduction measures such as carpools, van pools, and transit subsidies. About 100 trip-mitigation programs have been approved by the planning board, which has created a full-time staff position for monitoring the results.

Over time, however, the county discovered that the adequate facility requirements were prohibiting further development in the areas planned for higher-density growth, especially around Metrorail stations. The level of private improvements required by the system also was forcing developers to forego development of affordable housing. Accordingly, the county revised adequate facility requirements in 1994 to permit continued development and affordable housing near the Metrorail.

Another important policy involves preservation of agricultural land, a major part of the planned "wedge" between and around the transportation corridors. In 1980, after several years of studies, the county council adopted a "plan for preservation of agriculture and rural open space" (see Figure 2.1) that established a 25-acre minimum lot size for the northern one-third of the county—91,000 acres—and proposed the use of transferable development rights (TDRs) to partially compensate affected property owners. Later, "receiving areas" were identified in the master plan to which development rights could be transferred, resulting in somewhat higher permitted densities.

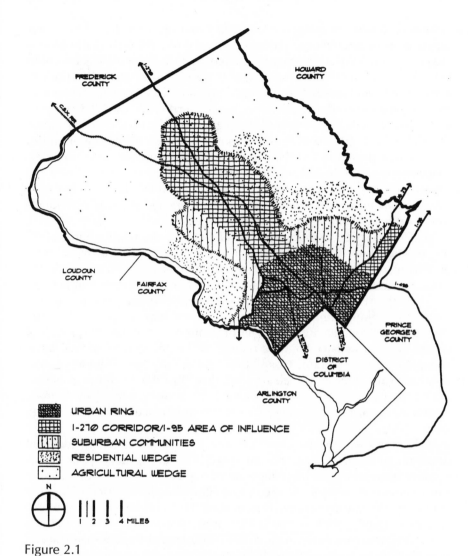

FREDERICK
COUNTY

HOWARD
COUNTY

LOUDOUN
COUNTY

FAIRFAX
COUNTY

PRINCE
GEORGE'S
COUNTY

DISTRICT
OF
COLUMBIA

ARLINGTON
COUNTY

▓ URBAN RING
▦ I-270 CORRIDOR/I-95 AREA OF INFLUENCE
▨ SUBURBAN COMMUNITIES
▨ RESIDENTIAL WEDGE
⠂ AGRICULTURAL WEDGE

N

| | | | |
1 2 3 4 MILES

Figure 2.1

Montgomery County plan/agland preservation area. The wedges and corridors that demarcate urbanized and agricultural areas in Montgomery County's General Plan are shown in this map included in the most recent revision of the plan. (From *General Plan Refinement, Goals and Objectives*, prepared by the Montgomery County Planning Department, 1993, p. 11.)

This program was quite successful in lowering the political heat that might be expected from up-county property owners (especially after a judge, in upholding the program, noted that the county legally could have downzoned without resorting to TDRs). The program did run into considerable controversy in the neighborhoods selected to be "upzoned" by receiving added development rights. Nevertheless, by 1993 the program had set aside 30,000 acres for agriculture, protected from future development. A 1988 report of the county council's Commission on the Future strongly supported the continuation of the agricultural and open space reserve, calling it Montgomery County's "Central Park." The 1993 report incorporating revisions to the general plan commented that "the 'Wedge' is as important today as it was 30 years ago. . . . It is very much the green lung of Montgomery County." (p. 7)

In 1973, faced with mounting housing prices, the county adopted an inclusionary housing program requiring developers of 50 or more units of housing to set aside 15 percent of the units for low- and moderate-income housing. In return, developers could obtain an increase in permitted density. Although builders and developers grumbled about the program, the county amassed 9183 units of moderately priced housing through the program. Recently the program was modified to provide a sliding scale of density bonuses related to the percentage of total units allocated to the program. In addition, the county has augmented production of moderately priced housing through other county-sponsored affordable housing programs. Its accessory housing zoning provisions, for example, authorized creation of 800 in-home accessory apartments since 1984.

Reflecting a central theme of the general plan that called for focusing development along transportation corridors, Montgomery County has pursued aggressively the development of higher densities around Metrorail stations. Of particular value in this effort was the creation of floating zones that permit higher densities in some business areas subject to design review and contributions of amenities. The zoning provisions have been applied particularly in rail/bus station areas to encourage transit-friendly development and a high order of design and appearance. Figure 2.2 shows design parameters for buildings and spaces.

The zoning incentives helped to focus a substantial amount of development around stations in Friendship Heights, Bethesda, Silver Spring, White Flint, and other business centers in the county, transforming rather drab business areas into a series of major suburban employment and shopping centers. In Bethesda, millions of square feet of office space and hundreds of residential units were developed within three or four blocks of the Metrorail station during the 1980s. Within that area, zoning density options were subject to an overall development limit set by the sector plan and by traffic capacity measures, with the consequence that a "beauty contest" erupted to gain higher-density develop-

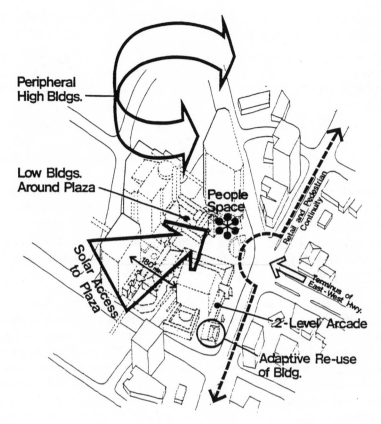

Figure 2.2

Bethesda urban design. In preparation for a development competition for a transit-station area in Bethesda, the Montgomery County urban design staff identified key design characteristics for proposed buildings and spaces. The design concept was followed in the final development. (From *Bethesda Metro Center Urban Design Study,* prepared by the Maryland–National Capital Park and Planning Commission, 1980.)

ment rights. Developers contributed a wide variety of public art, fountains, landscaping, and other amenities to obtain project approvals, in the process gaining substantial density increases. (Developers, of course, prefer the latter without the former; many county residents have clamored for the former without the latter.)

Consistency and Longevity. Over seven decades, Montgomery County steadily evolved an approach to growth management that has generally prevailed over attempts to change its direction and import. Richard Tustian, the county's planning director during the 1970s and 1980s, attributes this to four principal factors:

- The endowment of status as a chartered county, coupled with attitudes of state courts that generously applied the "fairly debatable" rule, both of which gave the county considerable latitude to develop its own planning approach

- The outlook and standards of early residents, many of whom came to Washington, D.C. as new dealers and who respected professionalism in government, and residents' high degree of affluence and education that allowed them to meet their high standards

- The early personalities who entered county government, who had the vision and political savvy to establish the bi-county planning commission and water and sewer agency

- The long-term strength of the Washington, D.C. metropolitan economy that has provided a fairly predictable stream of public and private investment capital to support community development

The confluence of these factors has tended to shelter the planning function from extremes of political and economic cycles, allowing it to evolve incrementally over time. Indeed, it might be said that the county's growth management system is continuing to build on the fundamental concepts laid down by the general plan 25 years ago. For many years, the planning board has been refining and improving both the high-level policy area and the nuts-and-bolts technical end of the system.

The county represents a populous, rapidly growing jurisdiction that has tried most of the bells and whistles that planners have contrived to expand ordinary planning and zoning into full-fledged growth management. In general, the county has attempted to keep pace with development rather than limit it, although its attempts have fallen short from time to time.

These innovations in planning, zoning, and implementation programs have not escaped controversy. Neighborhood groups, community coalitions, and even political parties were formed to resist or boost almost every new approach to development management. Particular issues in recent years focused on traffic congestion, school overcrowding, open space preservation, and rapid changes in the Silver Spring, Bethesda, and Rockville business districts. A vocal movement in 1986 to establish limits on development resulted in a council vote to cap growth, subsequently vetoed by the county executive. The next county election revolved around the growth issue, and a major business redevelopment plan for Silver Spring was subject to a referendum. Although the pro-development candidate won and the referendum lost, citizens' groups continue to apply pressures to reduce the pace of development.

These pressures have been tempered in the mid-1990s by a new appreciation of the value of economic development; however, the planning process appears to be spinning its wheels. Robert Marriott, the county's planning director from 1991 to 1995, believes that the complex structure of development decision making in the county virtually prohibits revisions to the basic approach. Under present conditions, he says, citizens fearful of runaway development will allow only tinkering with the planning and regulatory process.

Montgomery County's role in the broader regional development scene is also problematic. It is widely believed by Washington real estate watchers that the county's rigorous development reviews, restrictive agricultural zoning, and developer exactions have driven small developers, in particular, to other less demanding jurisdictions and, by limiting supplies of developable land, have escalated land and housing prices. Certainly Frederick and Howard counties, on Montgomery County's northern border, are undergoing real estate booms. Richard Tustian counters this argument by observing that the county has been simply "doing its growth management job." (It is not the county's fault, in other words, if developers elect to move their activities to jurisdictions with lower standards.)

A 1988 assessment of the general plan placed the blame for housing price increases on an unexpected spurt of economic growth in the 1980s that unbalanced the jobs-to-housing ratio. The resulting housing shortage, said the report, will be rectified by the market as long as there remains plenty of developable land for new housing. However, housing prices in the 1990s continue to be substantially higher than those in bordering counties. As an expanding economic center viewed as a highly desirable residential area, however, the county's housing prices are likely to remain high.

Like many other growing areas, the county has had its share of traffic woes, which are the leading cause of citizen outcries to dampen development and are responsible for moratoriums on development prompted by adequate facilities requirements in several parts of the county. Part of the blame for traffic congestion can be laid to a multiyear decline in road construction during the housing recession in the mid-to-late 1970s. The subsequent housing boom and accompanying rapid increase in commercial space could not be matched by increases in road capacity. At the same time, as in most metropolitan areas, home-to-work travel patterns were focusing more on intracounty travel and the number of cars per family was increasing.

The county responded to rising needs for road capacity with heroic measures, including encouragement of "road clubs" of developers to help fund improvements, adoption of impact fees in hard-hit areas, heavy emphasis on encouraging alternative transportation means, and, in some instances, the county's assumption of responsibility for funding state road construction. In the late 1980s, the state undertook major improvements to I-270 and several other critical highway arteries.

Still, traffic congestion continues to be a problem, requiring postponements of development in a dozen areas of the county. The recent downturn in development sharply cut developer initiatives to improve roadways. In addition, citizen demands for traffic improvements are matched by citizen resistance to road improvements in their neighborhoods.

A more basic issue is the extent to which the county planning board has been absorbed by its computer models, threshold standards, and number-counting to the exclusion of longer-range strategic development concerns. One planning consultant and citizen activist, Goldie Rivkin, commented that the planning board "had lost sight of long-term directions and goals." She observed that the general plan is over 25 years old and has been updated "by the grinding of models and numbers" without rethinking basic premises.

Robert Marriott points out that many of the county's planning woes are products of regional development forces beyond control of the county. Traffic problems, for example, are due more to through traffic pouring in from the growing counties to the north than to local travel. In that circumstance, he says, putting the brakes on development in one area of the county to meet adequate facilities standards is the equivalent of "shooting yourself in the foot." Only a more rational, workable regional planning process, highly unlikely in the Washington, D.C. area, would begin to overcome this problem.

Conclusions. In short, Montgomery County's growth management program emphasizes an approach that is comprehensive both vertically and horizontally. The program's long-term emphasis on ensuring development quality, focusing development along transportation corridors while preserving agricultural and open space lands, and requiring adequate facilities may be viewed as imposing extraordinary restrictions on the operation of the real estate market; but the program is strongly supported by county residents. Although the county may be faulted for failing to keep up with some aspects of growth (e.g., traffic and affordable housing), the program's policies and implementation practices have attempted to address future development needs in a highly professional and technically sophisticated manner, stressing the public interest but sensitive to meeting development demands. Many of the county's current problems with its planning structure flow from the lack of a strong regional framework that could deal with the effects of growth external to the county.

Growth Management Approaches and Techniques

The way Montgomery County has blended a variety of growth management provides a real-world introduction to the array of techniques available to many communities. The adoption of specific techniques, of course, depends on individual state legislative and judicial constraints on development regulation, as well as local attitudes and objectives. The most commonly used techniques are briefly identified and described below as an introduction to more complete descriptions of their characteristics and applications provided in subsequent chapters. The techniques build on the basic planning techniques of comprehensive planning, zoning, subdivision regulations, and capital improvement programs.

Thousands of communities have adopted some aspect of growth management; innovation and experimentation with new techniques is widespread. Some researchers have defined as many as 57 separate techniques that may be used in growth management programs, including special types of regulations, programs, tax policies, administrative approaches, review procedures, and more. Other experts have clustered techniques in a few categories. Some classifications have been based on the aspects of growth that are intended to be controlled, such as controls over population, types of development, and infrastructure. Other classifications have focused on the location of development, related infrastructure provision, and mitigating impacts of development.

This listing of growth management techniques reflects the primary concerns of each of the subsequent chapters, from Chapter 3 through Chapter 8. These chapters focus on the major goals or purposes of growth management.

- Techniques for managing the location and character of community expansion

- Techniques to preserve natural resources and environmental qualities and features

- Techniques to ensure efficient provision of community infrastructure

- Techniques to maintain or create a desirable quality of community life

- Techniques to improve economic opportunities and social equity

- Techniques for regional and state guidance of community development

The brief descriptions here are amplified substantially in the following chapters. However, because the science and art of growth management has blossomed so recently and is evolving rapidly even now, many growth management techniques do not fit neatly into categories and classes. The techniques are listed in the category that appears most germane to the issues addressed by this book, and their possible alternative uses are noted.

Techniques for Managing Location and Character of Community Expansion: "Where to Grow" *ref chap. 3*

The location and character of development is managed first and foremost by comprehensive plans, zoning, and subdivision regulations that specify where, how much, and what kind of development can take place. However, these traditional techniques can be supplemented by others that apply firmer policies about community expansion.

Urban Growth Boundaries. Urban growth boundaries restrict urban growth to a specific area around a community and prevent the spread of development into the surrounding countryside. Similar in concept to *urban service limits* and *designated growth areas,* boundaries typically incorporate enough land for about 20 years of projected development, adjusted periodically in response to development trends. Boundaries are intended to promote more efficient use and extension of infrastructure systems, encourage more compact development, and preserve open space and natural resources in rural areas. For all these purposes, the establishment of official boundaries to urban growth posts a reminder to public officials that urban growth should happen in some areas and not others. That objective can be achieved through zoning based on a plan, of course, but boundaries appear more long-lasting than zoning, which can be changed relatively easily.

Development Policy Areas. A variation on urban growth boundaries, development policy areas permit more options for steering development. The "standard" version delineates an *urban* area of established neighborhoods and centers, *urbanizing* areas where most new development will take place, and an *urban reserve* area where open space is preserved until some future date. Planning and zoning provisions are based on these broad policy delineations.

Promotion of Infill and Redevelopment. One way to curb urban sprawl is to direct more development toward existing developed areas, where vacant or underused sites can be redeveloped. Declining neighborhoods and commercial and industrial areas may be revitalized through programs that provide financial and other incentives to stimulate new development in those areas. Incentives may involve subsidized land costs, tax exemptions or reductions, infrastructure improvements, assistance from business development groups, and the leadership of community development organizations. Cities and suburbs can take advantage of federal and state programs to improve housing and stimulate economic development.

Extra-Jurisdictional Controls. Development that occurs outside a city or town limit may not be guided by adequate development controls or coordinated with existing development within the city or town. For those reasons, municipalities frequently attempt to control developing areas outside their jurisdiction through annexation policies, "extra-territorial" development controls, or interjurisdictional agreements. Annexation of newly developing areas can be relatively easy or difficult, depending on state laws regarding annexation. Some states instead allow municipalities to control planning and/or zoning for a certain distance outside their boundaries, although this control may be advisory rather than regulatory in nature. Lacking either of these possibilities, municipalities can formulate agreements with adjoining municipalities, townships, or counties about the amount and character of growth that should occur outside the municipality—for example, requiring that municipal standards be observed in such development.

Limits on Growth. Following the lead of early growth management programs, some communities continue to manage urban development by limiting the amount of growth that can take place. Typically, an ordinance limits the number of building permits issued each year, although some communities limit development through a schedule of infrastructure improvements. The most extreme version of growth limits is the moratorium, which halts all or most development to allow time for a policy or service crisis to be resolved.

Techniques to Protect Natural Resources and Environmental Qualities and Features: "Where Not to Grow"

In addition to programs and regulations to steer growth in certain directions, many techniques have evolved to prevent development on lands deemed important for natural resource or environmental purposes. The federal government and many states require protection of water quality, wetlands, floodplains, and habitats of endangered or threatened species. At the local level, however, a great variety of techniques is in use today, chiefly focused on the approaches listed below.

Land Acquisition. When open land is to be protected from development, acquisition is the most certain approach. Land may be acquired either totally (in fee) or by purchase of development rights or easements. Acquisition can be accomplished by local governments, regional or state agencies, land trusts, conservancies, and other nongovernmental organizations. Land may be donated or paid for through taxes, fees, grants, or incentives. Land or development rights so acquired can be used to conserve open space, protect environmentally sensitive lands such as wetlands and wildlife habitat, preserve agricultural or forested lands, and protect significant natural features important to the community such as ridgelines and dunes.

Conservation Planning/Zoning. Comprehensive plans and zoning maps are used to identify conservation areas in which communities propose to limit development. Conservation areas may include stream valleys, floodplains, ridges and hillsides, known wetlands and wildlife habitats, and other natural features. In many cases, such conservation goals are implemented through subdivision regulations that require developers to set aside identified conservation areas, sometimes in return for the ability to transfer development rights from those areas to adjoining or even remote developable areas. In other cases, zoning in conservation areas requires large lot sizes (e.g., 5 to 10 acres) that will presumably conserve substantial amounts of the resource. Such regulations, however, run the risk of triggering claims that they take property without compensation.

Water Quality/Erosion Control Regulations. Ordinances or subdivision provisions can require low-density development or no development on steep slopes, erosion control measures during and after construction, and preservation of stream valleys to reduce erosion that can degrade water quality. Particularly in areas that depend on groundwater for potable water supply, communities can protect groundwater quality from inappropriate development above the aquifer and around wellheads. In most cases, the amount of development is limited and/or types of development that might pollute the aquifer (such as some industries) are prohibited.

Delineation of Critical Areas. Through the federal coastal zone management program, many states have established the practice of designating critical areas in which special attention is paid to environmental preservation efforts. Some cities and counties also use this method of defining important areas for detailed planning and special management considerations. Most commonly, sensitive coastal environments are designated as critical areas in which development should be permitted only under special circumstances.

Mitigation of Development Impacts. Protection is not necessarily an all-or-nothing approach. Many regulations allow some development in natural resource or environmentally sensitive areas if the threatened resource can be largely preserved. Requirements to *cluster development* in and around rural settlements, for example, reduce the amount of land taken from agricultural use and intrusions in farming activities. *Set-asides or reservations* to retain significant natural features or highly valuable sensitive lands within development sites can allow some development. It is also possible to *define in advance of potential development* conservation areas that should be preserved. Use of *mitigation banks* to permit off-site replacement of environmentally sensitive lands under highly controlled circumstances is a growing practice.

Agricultural Land Protection. A variety of techniques are used to protect agricultural land from conversion to urban uses. *Agricultural districts* can be formed by farmers who wish to continue farming. The districts prevent sale of land for other purposes and retain tax assessments at levels suitable for agriculture. *Right-to-farm laws* protect farmers from nuisance suits and other problems raised by suburban residents living near farms who complain about noise, odors, and other accompaniments of agricultural activities. *Agricultural zoning* retains agriculture and associated uses as the primary permitted uses.

Watershed Planning and Management. River basin planning and management activities take place in many areas. Public agencies charged with watershed management attempt to guide land use to protect water quality, reduce flooding damage, and support water-related economic and recreational activities. The agencies accomplish these ends primarily through planning and educational efforts.

Environmental Threshold Standards. Some communities have established "threshold" standards for environmental qualities that determine when and where development may take place. Such standards are similar to a "carrying capacity" approach, in which the capabilities of the land, air, and water to absorb urban development are critical determinants of planned growth. Reasonable standards are established on a communitywide basis for air and water quality, energy consumption, preservation of important natural features, and other aspects of the environment. Proposed developments are not permitted to impact environmental qualities beyond the threshold standards.

Techniques for Efficient Provision of Community Infrastructure

One of the keys to growth management is managing the provision of public facilities and services that support community development. Comprehensive plans and zoning ordinances lay out a framework of development that presumably is responsive to the availability and efficiency of expanding infrastructure systems, including streets, water and sewer lines, schools, libraries, parks, and other common facilities. Subdivision regulations require developers to provide most or all of the facilities needed to support their projects. Capital improvement programs establish a schedule and funding basis for extending and improving facility systems. If well linked, coordinated, and constantly updated, these ways of managing infrastructure can be effective. Yet many communities find that they must rely on other means to ensure that infrastructure development corresponds to other aspects of community development, especially in meeting funding requirements. Many communities use some or all of the following techniques for these purposes.

Functional Plans. Many comprehensive plans incorporate or are supplemented by functional plans for the various community infrastructure systems. The plans spell out in detail the community's current inventory and standards for schools, roads, parks, and other facilities; project future needs for expanding and improving them; and indicate priorities of location and timing for their provision. In many cases, these plans are key guides to the location and sequencing of future community development.

Adequate Public Facility Requirements. These regulations require that public facilities are adequate to support proposed projects before building or subdivision permits are issued. First suggested as early as 1955, adequate facilities provisions are emerging as one of the most common forms of growth management. The provisions require that project developers show evidence that streets, schools, sewer and water lines, and other facilities in or near the project have capacity to serve the amount of development proposed. If not, development cannot proceed unless the developer is willing to build or fund capacity additions. The community's schedule of capital improvements thus governs the rate of development that can take place.

Exactions, Impact Fees, and Special Districts. In the past decade or two, many communities have taken steps to obtain more funding of infrastructure related to new development from developers and facility users rather than from the general public. They have increased the kinds and amounts of facilities to be contributed by developers as a condition of development. These "exactions" have been broadened from just basic on-site facilities to a larger array of on-site and off-site facilities related to the project. Many communities also impose impact and other fees and charges to provide funding for facilities and services. In addition, the use of special taxing districts has been expanded as a means of financing public facilities in developing areas. All of these funding methods tend to shift infrastructure costs from the community at large to specific benefi- ciaries of improvements.

Transportation Demand Management and Congestion Management Programs. Many communities have adopted techniques to improve air quality and reduce traffic on local streets and highways by reducing travel demands from new development. Typically these programs either mandate or provide incentives for using alternatives to single-person automobile travel, including high-occupancy vehicle lanes on major highways, carpool programs, financial subsidies for bus and rail fares, reductions in parking capacities, staggered peak hours, and so on. Such programs often require private involvement to reach public objectives.

Project Point or Rating Systems. Some communities have adopted project review systems to rate the acceptability of projects according to a list of criteria and standards. Projects that "earn" a certain threshold of points are approved. Point systems usually incorporate availability of adequate facilities and services as a major component; they may also include other factors such as neighborhood compatibility, environmental impacts, and locational criteria. Although such systems are essentially an evaluation procedure, they act as significant guides to the character and location of development.

Techniques to Maintain or Create a Desirable Quality of Community Life

Ultimately, all growth management techniques are employed to assure that communities can offer a desirable quality of life for their residents and workers. A number of techniques, however, are oriented most directly to maintaining existing qualities of development or guiding the quality of new development, as compared to the quantity or location of development.

Design Reviews. Local governments can establish special guidelines and procedures to review the design of proposed projects and buildings in parts of the community where specific qualities of design are particularly desirable. Design review criteria and procedures are established to provide more detailed guidance of design decisions than can be written into prescriptive regulations such as zoning. Design review procedures are frequently applied in downtown areas and historic districts, but also may be employed for complex mixed-use projects, industrial and commercial projects, or unusual housing developments such as clustered housing. Design reviews may be especially useful in guiding development in infill and redevelopment areas where compatibility with surrounding development is important, and in siting development within or adjoining environmentally sensitive lands.

Flexible Planning and Design. Many communities have adopted special regulations that permit more flexible treatment of site and building development than allowed by the rigidities of conventional zoning and subdivision regulations. The most common form of flexible planning is *planned unit development* (PUD), which offers options to developers for determining uses, densities, building placement, and other planning and design factors applied to their sites. PUD provisions establish overall parameters for development, such as average densities and open space requirements, but allow variable treatment of these factors within a given site. PUDs almost always require special review procedures (including design reviews) to approve these variations from normal requirements. In addition, *zoning overlay districts* can be adopted to provide for special treatment of certain areas such as historic districts, transit station areas, and downtown areas. Usually such districts add requirements for development but may also allow greater flexibility in meeting certain standards.

Incentive and Performance Zoning. Traditional zoning provides little flexibility to mix uses, employ innovative design techniques, or secure useful public amenities. Incentive zoning encourages developers to meet specified public objectives in development by offering advantages in the form of density bonuses, more flexible design treatment, and more expeditious processing of approvals. Performance-based zoning employs standards and criteria—rather than prescribed lists of uses and requirements—that allow more choices among potential land uses and design treatments. Standards and criteria set limits to the impacts of land uses to assure compatibility among adjacent uses and encourage development in preferred locations.

Historic and Architectural Preservation. Preservation of historic and architecturally significant buildings and districts can retain a community's unique heritage while offering opportunities for reuse and revitalization of older urban areas. Many communities have adopted legislation to encourage preservation of landmark buildings and significant districts, usually by requiring detailed reviews of building proposals and sometimes by offering incentives for preservation. Like infill and redevelopment policies, preservation measures help to retain the livability of existing urban areas and to reduce pressures for new development in fringe areas.

Neighborhood Conservation and Revitalization of Declining Areas.
Using a variety of protective devices (i.e., restrictive zoning, traffic-calming) and specific actions (i.e., rehabilitation programs, infrastructure improvements), many communities attempt to maintain desirable neighborhoods. Communities also may undertake efforts to revitalize areas of special importance to the community. Downtowns, arts districts, and older strip commercial centers are examples of especially significant areas often targeted for public support of development and redevelopment actions. These efforts, which require special planning, careful design, and realistic implementation programs, can provide critical support for market forces in maintaining and improving community quality of life.

Landscape Ordinances. Various types of ordinances and provisions have been adopted by local governments that establish standards for landscaping in new developments. Some provide for verdant scenery along major streets and at important community entrances. Other provisions are directed to mitigating impacts of development on adjoining development; usually these take the form of landscaped buffers or planted areas in surface parking lots.

Tree or Plant Conservation Requirements. Some communities adopted provisions in subdivision regulations to conserve existing trees or plants in proposed developments. The provisions specify the amount, size, and/or types of vegetation to be preserved, or require restoration of a percentage of formerly vegetated areas.

Techniques to Improve Economic Opportunities and Social Equity

All communities should be concerned with widening economic and social opportunities, either within the community or as part of a wider regional economy and society. Viewed as part of an overall strategy of managing community development, programs to enhance social and economic opportunities can help to strengthen existing neighborhoods and businesses and to reduce needs for spreading new development farther into the countryside.

Economic Development Incentives. Economic development incentives can include marketing programs to attract new jobs, various types of subsidies and tax relief policies to encourage business activities, and actions to revitalize declining business areas. Federally sponsored enterprise zones and empowerment areas incorporate these ideas. Most communities maintain such programs but few coordinate them with other aspects of their growth management program, such as infrastructure improvements.

Economic Opportunity Programs. Community-backed employment and vocational training and assistance programs and affirmative action programs provide ways for local residents to take advantage of employment opportunities offered both within and outside the community.

Affordable Housing Programs. Many communities have adopted incentives or requirements to encourage development of affordable housing, especially in areas where rising housing prices are excluding some elements of the population. Affordable housing programs can offer public subsidies for land and development costs or provide low-cost financing and other incentives to encourage development of affordable housing. Regulations can provide incentives such as density allowances to stimulate production of lower-cost housing. Affordable housing also can be mandated by inclusionary or linkage requirements. *Inclusionary housing* programs require developers to incorporate affordable housing in their developments, usually in return for densities. *Linkage requirements* usually pertain to developers of commercial space, who are required to contribute to affordable housing funds or build housing as a condition of development approval.

Techniques for Regional and State Guidance of Community Development

Many regional and state agencies guide community development, including planning for transportation systems, directing economic development activities, providing standards for schools and water and sewer systems, and other activities. State and regional growth management programs are described in some detail in Chapter 8. They influence the patterns and character of community growth most directly, however, by use of the following two types of mechanisms.

Coordination of Local Planning. Most regional planning agencies and some state planning agencies engage in coordination of local governments' plans. Sometimes this is accomplished through preparation of regional plans that provide guidance for local planning, especially regarding development issues that transcend purely local concerns. In addition, some states require local governments to prepare and adopt plans consistent with state goals established by state law.

Reviews of Developments of Regional Impact. Some regional and state agencies have been given powers to review large-scale project proposals that might affect several local jurisdictions. The agencies usually are concerned with reducing the potential negative effects of such projects on surrounding areas.

Conclusion

Clearly, communities may employ a great variety of techniques in practicing growth management. The subsequent chapters illustrate in detail how these techniques have been and are being applied in specific circumstances. In addition, the final chapter describes how the techniques can be mixed and matched to structure a balanced program that meets community objectives. The use of visioning approaches, collaborative planning, and benchmarking help communities reach that balance.

Growth management has come of age. The concept is now seen as a fundamental means of organizing community efforts to anticipate future development and provide ways to guide that development toward goals that meet communitywide objectives. As the following chapters make clear, the practice of growth management can be complicated, both politically and technically. Techniques and approaches must be carefully tailored to specific community needs and attitudes, and constantly adapted to changing circumstances. The evolution of the growth management approaches and techniques described in this chapter will continue to open up new possibilities for managing community development.

3

Managing Community Expansion: "Where to Grow"

One of the principal objectives of growth management is to determine the most desirable locations and character of future development. To accomplish this goal, communities large and small crafted comprehensive plans and zoning ordinances that spell out public policies to guide development, show how infrastructure systems will be extended to serve planned development, and define in regulations and on maps the details of the types and locations of anticipated development.

Over decades of experience, however, public officials and civic activists discovered that comprehensive plans and zoning ordinances frequently lacked the strategic force required to adequately control the development process. The myriad policies and provisions contained in the bulky documents often confused rather than clarified public decision making about development. Requirements became increasingly outdated as market and political interests changed. In many communities, the result was a continuous stream of plan amendments and rezoning actions that eroded the principal aims of local planning.

In reaction to this fragmentation of control over the development process, public officials sought to ensure long-term certainty about ways to achieve major public goals concerned with growth. The concept of growth management gave them the tools they needed to impose larger, more strategic purposes on guidance of the development process. In particular, the techniques of setting specific limits on where and how much growth could take place, directing some growth inward rather than outward, and controlling development outside the local jurisdiction provide firmer direction over long-term guidance of community development.

County commissioners in Sarasota County, Florida had these goals in mind when they established that jurisdiction's first growth boundary in 1975. The county was just beginning to assume responsibility for development outside the three principal towns along the coast, and the commissioners wanted to make a firm statement about the extent of that responsibility, in spatial terms at least. They chose the centerline of Interstate 75, a north–south highway then in the planning stage, as a convenient cutoff line for urban development. The areas east of the highway were to remain as open space, chiefly agricultural and wetlands. The comprehensive plan concentrated its development policies on land west of the highway. As of 1996, more than 20 years later, the line has held fairly firm, although it is beginning to crumble under the outward pressure of development. The county government has taken advantage of those two decades to organize and implement the infrastructure systems and services necessary to support urban development.

Forces of Change

The need for greater public guidance over development arose from the evolutionary forces stimulating urban development in the United States and elsewhere over the past century and a half. During the long evolution of human settlement, people clustered in cities and towns within walking distance or a brief horse-ride of each other. Their mutual proximity made it possible to trade goods and services, manufacture products, participate in religious rites, attend schools, enjoy entertainment and simple social contact, and protect themselves from marauding invaders. Physically, therefore, people lived and worked close together and urban centers were quite dense to afford maximum accessibility among all these activities.

The railroad and its urban counterpart, the trolley, began to open up opportunities to live and work in different places. From the 1850s onward, horse and then electric trolleys began transporting people throughout expanding urban centers, and commuter rail lines snaked into the countryside to bring in people from towns miles away to their work. Beginning in the early 1900s, the automobile gave individuals freedom to travel long distances in their daily lives. The dense urban center then became a problem for mobility rather than an opportunity for accessibility, and the countryside beckoned one and all. The automobile loosened the forces that had once pulled people together.

The result was an unprecedented sprawl of urban development into the countryside, especially after World War II when cars were plentiful, federally backed home mortgages were available, and the economy was on the move. By the 1980s and 1990s, suburbia was a way of life for many Americans and rural living was on the increase.

These changes in metropolitan development patterns have been studied by urban planners and urban geographers concerned with defining "optimum" urban form—the relative benefits of various patterns of city and regional development. These interests surface in evaluations of potential models of metropolitan development such as those postulated in regional transportation studies. These models are used as shorthand ways to describe changing patterns of city growth. The suburban "edge cities" recently identified and analyzed by Joel Garreau,[1] for example, are an attempt to explain emerging growth patterns in metropolitan development.

Several types of development patterns have become fairly standard in planners' analyses of urban form:

- The traditional centrally oriented urban area with a strong downtown core, distinct industrial areas around it, and gradually less dense residential neighborhoods in outer bands surrounding the center, bounded by a distinct rural edge—the "centralized" or "concentric circle" form of development.

- The "sector" model, a more accurate description of most cities' development patterns formulated by Homer Hoyt, a noted land economist, who defines sectors of specific land uses radiating from the center city.[2]

- The "satellite city" model that postulates development of a series of distinct towns or cities interlinked with the central city but separated from each other and the central city by a "greenbelt" of rural land.

- The newer "multinodal" urban pattern that consists of a traditional center supplemented by a series of outer concentrations of commercial and industrial development, some of which may be more significant than the center, with no distinct rural edge—the typical metropolitan area of today.

Scholars argue that some of these forms are more efficiently served by infrastructure systems, or provide a more convenient and pleasing living environment, or better preserve rural land. The nineteenth century advocate of satellite "garden" cities, Ebeneezer Howard, propounded the virtues of fresh air and open space that greenbelts and new towns in the countryside could offer. Advocates of reducing automobile travel in favor of greater use of transit understand that transit must link strong concentrations of development to work efficiently. What is unarguable, however, is that Americans' love of cars and living space has transformed the traditional centralized city with a distinct edge (still visible around European cities) to the multinodal urban areas of today. Many community plans and zoning ordinances, however, continue to reflect a strong interest in retaining many of the attributes of the traditional centralized model. Lincoln, Nebraska's comprehensive plan, for example, until recently was consciously based on maintaining a concentric circle of development, including policies to promote development in underdeveloped sectors of the circular city form.

These understandings of the importance of urban form play a role in continuing public interest to prevent development from sprawling into the countryside and to promote more compact growth.

The Case for (and against) Compact Urban Development

For many people concerned with the quality of urban life, the continuing outward explosion of urban growth poses troublesome concerns. The traditional tight-knit fabric of urban living has given way to greater physical and, some believe, social separation between individuals, families, and groups, lending support to "us and them" outlooks. Similar physical separations have taken place between locations central to daily living, such as residences, shopping, and working places, requiring travel that takes time and energy. Thus, while the automobile may provide many people more choices and opportunities for where and how to live and work, those choices have social and economic costs that some people cannot afford.

Another major issue is that the spread of developing and developed areas occupies more land that otherwise might be left available for farming, forests, and scenic open space or protected from disruption or destruction of environmentally sensitive resources. Development on the edges of metropolitan areas across the nation is consuming two or three times as much acreage per household as was the case in earlier decades. Land thus occupied is difficult to develop further as the population grows. People living in urban areas must travel longer and longer distances to reach the open countryside. The dependence on automobile travel for almost every function of daily living aggravates both traffic congestion and air quality throughout the region.

The trend toward scattered development dependent on automobiles raises two more quantifiable concerns. One is the cost of extending and expanding infrastructure systems that provide the necessities of daily living—the roads and highways, water and sewer lines, schools and libraries, telephone and power lines, and other common facilities and services. These costs tend to increase for each unit of development as densities of development decrease. Furthermore, as people move out of settled areas to new ones, they leave behind major investments in infrastructure that cannot be properly maintained by the remaining population.

City planners long have maintained that compact development saves capital and operating costs for infrastructure systems. A major study of these factors was commissioned in the early 1970s by the U.S. Department of Housing and Urban Development, the Council on Environmental Quality, and the Environmental Protection Agency. The study, called _The Costs of Sprawl,_ remains the principal study supporting the concept that sprawl costs more to serve by urban systems than compact development.[3] Although its methodology has been criticized, the research found that low-density development required more extensive and therefore more costly infrastructure systems than higher-density development. Other analyses, including one by the National Association of Home Builders, found similar results.

In a 1989 summary of cost-of-sprawl studies to date, James E. Frank concluded that capital costs of streets, sewers, water, storm drainage, and schools for a typical subdivision of three houses per acre can be reduced at least one-third by developing near basic public facilities and employment centers, at densities averaging 12 houses per acre (assuming a mix of housing types).[4]

Most of such studies assume that all development will be served by urban-type facilities. Much rural development, however, relies on unimproved roads, water wells, and septic tanks rather than more expensive facilities. Those private infrastructure costs, plus the lower land costs typically found in outlying locations, have not been factored into the studies cited above. Nevertheless, several factors tend to affect such cost savings:

- The costs of many nonprivate facilities such as schools (including bussing), fire stations, police protection, and road maintenance are increased by scattered development.

- Initial low-cost infrastructure in low-density areas must be replaced at substantial cost when more intensive urban development occurs in the area.

- The dependence of scattered development on wells and septic tanks almost inevitably leads in the long term to maintenance problems and potential impacts on water quality.

The upshot of all analyses to date is that the fiscal case for or against compact development remains unclear. Recent research by Robert Burchell and Paul Tischler, two of the nation's preeminent specialists in fiscal studies, concluded that sprawl development increases some infrastructure costs by relatively small amounts—about 25 percent for local roads, 15 percent for water and sewer systems, and 5 percent for schools.[5] Local road improvement costs, however, are often funded by developers; water and sewer costs are often funded by raising water

Fiscal Issues in Managing Growth

Paul S. Tischler

A program for managed growth will not be implemented unless it is fundable. Fiscal analysis techniques can evaluate the fiscal reality of various land use plans and other managed growth scenarios. The bottom line for fiscal impact analyses is the cash flow to the public sector from prospective development. To determine cash flow, three components must be considered: revenues, capital costs, and operating costs.

From a fiscal perspective, several important issues arise in evaluating growth management proposals. One is the overall concept of fiscal impact analysis. Unfortunately, fiscal analyses too often consider only potential capital costs, which can lead to erroneous conclusions. Urban sprawl costs more than concentrated development in almost all cases when only capital facility costs are considered. Longer lengths of pipes and roadways, as well as school bus routes, make low-density development more expensive to serve with urban facilities. However, capital costs make up only 10 to 20 percent of most jurisdictions' budgets, making operating costs a major consideration. For some services operating costs may not vary significantly due to development patterns. For others, such as fire protection, marginal-cost fiscal impacts based on case studies usually indicate significant operating cost variations. For that reason, infill and contiguous new development are likely to produce lower fire protection costs than for "leap-frog" development.

Probably the most important component of fiscal analyses is revenues. Depending on specific state and local revenue mechanisms, it is possible that lower-density, high-value market values will generate higher net revenues than more compact development, even after accounting for higher capital and/or operating expenses. Growing jurisdictions in Maryland, for example, generate most of their revenues from property and income taxes and transfer fees, all related to the market value of development. Residential market values generally increase as densities decrease. These kinds of findings must be understood as part of the decision-making process for managing growth. They may add significance to nonfiscal impacts of growth on the environment, quality of life, and other factors.

Other fiscal factors pertain to the timing and geographic distribution of projected development. Once facilities and services have been extended to urbanizing areas, rapid development of those areas usually produces the best fiscal results. Debt service and other costs for new facilities benefit from steep increases in revenues from new development. Similarly, understanding fiscal implications of development in various parts of an urbanizing area can assist planners in optimizing both geographic location and timing of future development.

A candid assessment of fiscal impacts of different development scenarios will lead to a more realistic, fundable, implementable growth management program.

rates. However, other evidence suggests that sprawl development may impact important environmental qualities and generate longer commuter travel. The most conclusive test may be Americans' increasing concern over the amount of open space and environmentally sensitive land being consumed by development.[6]

These concerns have led many communities to adopt strategies for directing growth to certain areas and discouraging it in others, and for encouraging more concentrated, contiguous development that can be efficiently served by infrastructure systems and is less land consumptive. To assist in limiting the outward march of growth, communities also focus more attention on retaining and improving existing developed areas.

Limits on Urban Expansion: Urban Growth Boundaries, Development Policy Areas, and Growth-Area Designations

Urban growth boundaries and similar legislative limits on the location of growth are intended to demarcate areas expected to undergo development from those in which development will be discouraged. Other terms used to describe similar intentions are urban service limits (restricting infrastructure extensions), urban limit lines, urban/rural limits, development policy areas or "tiers," and designated growth areas.

Urban service limits and similar boundaries focus on defining areas easily and inexpensively served by infrastructure systems. Such definitions were quite common for areas to be served by water and sewer facilities, even before the growth management concept emerged. Variations on the theme are numerous. One Virginia city established a "green" line to delineate its urban service boundary; Boulder, Colorado imposed a "blue" line signaling the limit of development on the surrounding mountainsides based on capabilities for extending water service.

Boundaries on urban development in general are more recent and increasingly employed. The two states that imposed the most rigorous standards for community regulation of development, Oregon and Florida, require or strongly encourage local governments to adopt urban growth boundaries. Oregon's state law in 1973 mandated boundaries for all municipalities; the resulting local boundaries have been in effect for almost two decades. Florida's growth management act in 1985 did not mandate growth boundaries but it required all cities and counties to adopt comprehensive planning policies that curb urban sprawl.

Two other states, Washington and Maryland, have growth management acts that require all communities to designate urban growth areas in their comprehensive plans, which effectively establishes urban growth boundaries. As of 1996, many communities are still attempting to comply with those requirements. Charles County, Maryland, however, illustrates the concept: Its current plan designates about one-third of the county for urban development (and within that area, gives priority to areas served by water and sewer); the plan establishes a target of 75 percent of future county development to occur in the designated growth area.

In four states, therefore, all or many communities have established boundaries to define development areas, and many other communities across the nation have adopted this technique.

Another variation on growth boundaries is establishment of distinct development policy areas, sometimes termed "tiers," that provide for gradations of development. They function much like super-zoning categories to define general expectations for development. The small city of Largo, Florida, in the Tampa/St. Petersburg area, for example, established four types of areas: downtown, redevelopment (inner areas), management (developing areas), and environmental conservation. The city's development code spells out general standards and prohibited uses in each area as the basis for more detailed zoning requirements.

One of the best-known examples is San Diego's tier system. Adopted in 1979, it defines urban, urbanizing, and urban reserve areas, each with its own set of development standards. The city also tied its infrastructure funding policy to the areas, levying impact fees in urbanizing areas but waiving them in urban areas to stimulate redevelopment of older areas.

More recently, Kane County, Illinois, one of Chicago's suburban ring of counties, adopted a comprehensive plan in 1996 that divided the county into three sections from east to west: urban, suburban, and future urban. The urban section incorporates the older towns and cities along the Fox River corridor, while the suburban section comprises areas undergoing development. The future urban section, almost entirely agricultural, will be protected from development until the suburban section is mostly developed.

These methods establish highly visible policies for focusing development, above and beyond traditional plans and zoning ordinances.

Establishing Boundaries

The concept of drawing a line around a developing community, within which all urban development will take place, is appealing in its simplicity and directness. It is highly saleable to voters upset by growth and to environmentalists concerned with protecting rural areas from suburban sprawl. A boundary suggests order, organization, discipline, and rationality. Nevertheless, boundaries present complex technical, political, and legal issues that can generate controversies and conflicts.

All these issues come into play in the act of establishing and maintaining a boundary. The *technical problem* is defining a rationale for drawing a boundary line—not more difficult than depicting a comprehensive plan map, but more potent in its implications. If the boundary is to designate the area within which a jurisdiction intends to deliver urban services, the potential extent of the major systems must be determined. This analysis will include projections of expected types of development and judgments about standards or levels of service and the most efficient areas for delivering those services. Sewer and water lines, for example, are most easily and inexpensively extended throughout a watershed; major roads must link to the regional road network; other service areas will be constrained by geographic features or jurisdictional limits.

The regional urban growth boundaries established by both the Portland, Oregon and Minneapolis/St. Paul regional councils were largely based on existing and projected service areas for the metropolitan sewer systems, which effectively identified the areas expected to undergo urban development.

Another approach to defining boundaries is determining the amount of land area that will be required for anticipated future development and the specific areas in which development should be encouraged. Usually, planning agencies will project the land area required to accommodate about 20 years' growth, which is the traditional planning period for comprehensive plans. Periodic boundary revisions are supposed to maintain that 20-year supply of land within the boundary.

Several types of estimates are necessary to determine future land needs:

- Projections of future increases in specific types and densities of land uses, translated into land requirements.

- Judgments about expected redevelopment and more intensive development of underutilized land that might reduce needs for use of undeveloped land.

- Determinations of appropriate directions of urban expansion based on infrastructure systems, environmental factors, land ownership patterns, and other considerations.

- Consideration of jurisdictional boundaries, annexation policies and possibilities, and other political constraints.

The environmental factors mentioned in the third point present an especially significant concern in determining not only the amount of land required but the location of future development. Approaches to defining lands *not* to be developed are fully described in Chapter 4. These estimates and analytical procedures are usually employed in preparing comprehensive plans and therefore are familiar processes for most planning agencies.[7]

Drawing boundaries, however, is not a failsafe procedure. Portland, Oregon's regional agency, Metro, discovered that during two decades a substantial amount of residential development on large lots had occurred on the outside edge of its urban growth boundary. Proposals to expand the boundary and extend urban services to potential development areas beyond the low-density settlements met with stiff opposition from residents. Boundary setting around Hagerstown in Washington County, Maryland proved worthless: The boundary incorporated more land than could be developed in 50 or more years; the line was so crudely drawn on the map that it covered several hundred feet of territory, making interpretation of its location almost impossible; many areas within the boundary were not scheduled for sewer service but some areas outside the boundary were already sewered.

Political issues enter the process in determinations of types of future development to be accommodated, the specific areas to be included within the boundary, and periodic reviews and revisions to the boundary. Densities of expected development, for example, can be influenced by public policies that encourage higher or lower numbers of dwelling units in certain areas, or favor development of intensive industrial development rather than low-density business parks. Public policies also can encourage development in underutilized areas of existing development rather than promoting fringe-area growth. The determination of estimated densities, of course, should take into account the degree to which such policies can affect market forces.

The 2040 plan for regional development adopted in 1994 by the Metro organization of Portland, Oregon represents one of the most ambitious attempts to set public-policy constraints on boundary changes. A major concern of the 50-year plan was to define the future boundary for regional development, which local planners believed would establish the basic urban form of the Portland region. Planners evaluated four alternative concepts: (1) one that assumed existing trends, (2) a more compact form, (3) a highly concentrated form that assumed no expansion of the boundary, and (4) a plan that assumed that one-third of future growth would take place in satellite cities. The plan selected by the Metro council, a regional elected body, calls for most future growth to take place within the existing boundary, including intensive development and redevelopment in and around existing nodes of development. The existing boundary, drawn in the 1970s to accommodate 20-years' growth, expanded slightly during that period, and will expand relatively moderately over the next 50 years of development.

Market forces, of course, may not cooperate with those public policies. The 1981 comprehensive plan for Sarasota County, for example, made only modest changes in the boundary set in 1975. Planners proposed promoting more intensive development, thus requiring less land for future development. The new plan included higher-density centers and optional high-density residential development areas. In fact, the analyses for the 1989 plan found that development densities had decreased rather than increased, thus necessitating significant expansion of the boundary. (See Figure 3.1.) Public officials had undercut their own density policy by consistently turning down higher-density development proposals due to opposition by project neighbors with a not-in-my-backyard (NIMBY) attitude.

The proposed boundary changes in Sarasota County set up a storm of complaints by environmental groups and civic activists, an occurrence

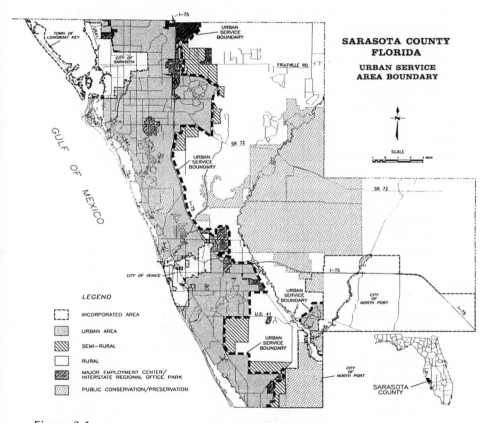

Figure 3.1

Sarasota County plan, 1989. Sarasota County's growth boundary established in 1975 still restricts the spread of development eastward into rural lands, although it has been expanded with each revision of the comprehensive plan. (Courtesy of the Sarasota County Planning Department.)

in many communities that have established growth boundaries. Belying Robert Frost's observation that "good fences make good neighbors," boundaries, once set, seem to generate conflict rather than resolve it; they become political lighting rods for controversies over growth and development. Developers in Portland, for example, claim that sites for business parks that would generate economic gains are becoming scarce. Homebuilders in Portland, Boulder, and other cities routinely complain that restrictions on land supply drive up housing prices.

Meanwhile, citizen activists and environmental groups concerned about the rate or amount of development consistently oppose boundary expansions. Citizens in Sarasota County petitioned an initiative in 1990 calling for a two-year moratorium on development until a revised plan limiting boundary changes could be prepared. Although defeated by a three-to-one vote, community tension over the issue continues to this day. San Diego's experience was even more dramatic. Its "urban reserve" was intended to be opened up for development as urbanizing areas became fully developed. Instead, the 12,000 acres took on a new meaning for many San Diego residents as the last vestige of once-plentiful open space in the city. After several attempts by developers to redesignate the area for development, a citizen's initiative was approved that requires a public vote on any change in the reserve. Meanwhile, development long ago jumped over the urban reserve to fuel growth in other rapidly growing communities in San Diego County.

Legal Concerns

Communities implement growth boundaries through zoning and other policies that promote urban types and densities of development within the boundary and discourage development outside the boundary. The key issue in most cases is reducing growth outside the boundary where landowners often wish to retain rights to development. Zoning for these outer areas usually establishes minimum lot sizes large enough to discourage residential development—at least 10 acres outside the Lexington/Fayette County, Kentucky boundary, 20 acres outside Portland's, and 40 acres in lands designated for agriculture outside the Twin City urban service area. McHenry County, Illinois set a 160-acre minimum lot size for its agricultural area. Zoning also permits only activities associated with rural areas: various types of farming, forestry, and so on. (A detailed discussion of techniques for protecting open space, agricultural areas, and other rural areas from development is found in Chapter 6.)

Outside the boundary, however, landowners just a few feet from properties that may be developing are told that they cannot develop unless the boundary is shifted. Meanwhile, their property values and development dreams are put on hold. Irate and frustrated by these constraints, landowners frequently view them as taking their properties without compensation.

Some communities address this problem by labeling the area an "urban reserve," implying that development will be approved at a future date and is simply being staged over time. Other communities make the case that agriculture and natural resources such as forests are significant economic resources that should be protected from potential impacts of scattered development. Oregon's requirement for urban growth boundaries around every community was based in large part on the immense value to the state's economy of the rich Willamette Valley croplands and the surrounding forests that produce so much timber.

Courts generally have allowed local governments to restrict development if the public purpose is clearly defined. Regulations that merely reduce property values or dampen their potential increase are seldom held to be a taking of property. To protect themselves against a takings suit, however, governments should carefully establish the necessity and desirability of imposing boundaries on urban growth. Studies that demonstrate the value of retaining farmland or natural resources and detailed programs that indicate the orderly expansion of infrastructure systems to developing areas help to make the case. In addition, allowing some development to take place, such as one-family homes accessory to farms and provision of appeals processes that consider hardships, demonstrates the government's good faith in restricting development.

Unexpected Consequences

After more than 20 years of community experience with regulating development in and out of designated growth areas, two issues appear to determine the effectiveness of boundaries in guiding community expansion. One is the type of growth that occurs *within* the boundary. Most communities that have adopted some type of growth boundary have not succeeded in promoting truly compact development within it. The example of Sarasota County previously discussed, where continued low-density development within the boundary generates constant pressures to expand it, is typical rather than unusual. Planners at the Metropolitan Council in Minneapolis/St. Paul acknowledge that development in most of the area within the regional boundary established decades ago could be characterized as urban sprawl. Only the extensive amount of land within the original boundary and the relatively moderate pace of regional growth has limited needs for expanding the boundary.

For most communities, it appears that boundaries have been fairly effective in reducing scattered development in rural areas but not successful at curbing sprawl in urbanizing areas. Portland's Metro organization addressed the problem of sprawl within the boundary by legislating minimum density targets for all communities in the region. Normally, zoning establishes maximum densities that proposed development should not exceed. Portland-area communities, in addition, are assigned threshold densities that development should reach or exceed, as a means of ensuring compact development and producing affordable housing. (More discussion of this program can be found in Chapter 8.)

The second issue of concern in using growth boundaries is the "leaking" of development *outside* the boundary line. A 1991 study of Oregon communities' experience with growth boundaries found that a considerable amount of development is occurring outside the mandated boundaries.[8] In one small town, more development had taken place outside than inside its boundary. Such development was taking place on lots recorded prior to the establishment of the boundary or on "exception" lands determined to have low value for agricultural or forestry use. About one million acres of Oregon land are now in the exception category; applications for designation of other lots average about 4000 a year.[9]

In the Portland area, thousands of lots have been developed outside the official urban growth boundary—about 9 percent of all new housing units in the region. Local residents call many of them "hobby" or "martini" farms because their owners purchased large lots and declared their intention of using most of the lot for raising horses or planting gardens. (These are the low-density developments that plague planners attempting to expand the Portland boundary.) But Portland has another problem as well—Vancouver and Clark County across the state border in Washington, an area not controlled by Portland's boundary. Portland-area observers believe that a substantial amount of regional development has taken place there rather than within the boundary.

Other growth-boundary jurisdictions have experienced similar leakage or leapfrogging. Developers and builders kept out of San Diego's urban reserve are building instead in the booming towns and cities in the northern part of the county. Lexington/Fayette County's urban-limit line has protected the horse farms outside its boundary but a considerable amount of development has occurred north and west of the city in other jurisdictions. This experience emphasizes the reality that a growth boundary is fully effective only if it controls most of the region's highly desirable, developable land.

Urban limit lines have their limitations. Like other growth management tools they can lead to unintended consequences. They tend to become political pawns, symbols of broader community conflicts. They may curb urban sprawl but in themselves will not provide a cure-all for urban development ills. They cannot control all external development. Critics also claim that limiting growth to certain areas reduces the supply of land available for development and therefore drives up housing prices; this issue is fully discussed in Chapter 9. In fact, Randall Arendt and James Constantine argue in a recent article that urban growth boundaries are not necessarily the best approach to preserving rural areas and open space. They propose use of alternative methods such as focusing development in corridors, nodes, and clustered developments, preserving green wedges and rural edges through the use of conservation plans tied to clustering, development exactions, and the purchase of open lands.[10]

Communities evaluating the concept of boundaries might consider the following guidelines:

- Growth boundaries should build on and logically link to comprehensive planning policies, zoning requirements, and infrastructure programs, rather than substitute for adequate planning.

- Growth boundaries should be based on realistic projections of growth and types of activities to be accommodated.

- Calculations of future land requirements should consider not only amounts and densities of various land uses but also conditions of land ownership, site development, geographic constraints, and other potential restrictions on the supply of land for development.

- Boundary proposals should include procedures for periodic review and adjustment of boundaries, with specific provisions for maintaining an adequate supply of developable land within the boundaries.

Managing Development Outside the Jurisdiction

Controlling urban expansion by use of growth boundaries and similar techniques is a relatively straightforward process if the boundary is entirely within the jurisdiction exercising control. Most of the examples described in the preceding section consist of regional agencies or large counties that have plenty of space to allow for both urban development and protected rural lands. Most local governments, however, must cope with the fact that much of their growth may be initiated and even continue to exist outside their jurisdictional boundaries. Their ability to influence the location and quality of this development may be critical to the economic and social viability of the community.

Recognizing this problem, many states have given cities and towns tools to manage, at least to some degree, development occurring outside their borders. These tools may include extraterritorial jurisdiction and annexation. In addition, cities that operate essential public facilities, such as sewer and water systems, have discovered the value of controlling service extensions to influence the character of development in urbanizing areas. Interlocal agreements is another useful tool.

Extraterritorial Jurisdiction

Municipalities in many states are given powers to oversee planning and zoning for development in a circumscribed area around their boundaries. These powers vary widely from state to state: "Oversee" can mean total control over setting development standards, simply the right to review and comment on rezoning and subdivision proposals, or to prepare plans for the areas involved. North Carolina gives local governments planning and zoning jurisdiction over areas up to three miles outside their boundaries. (Municipalities negotiate interlocal agreements to work out overlapping jurisdictions.) Raleigh, North Carolina, for example, has used this power for many years to establish development standards for urbanizing areas outside the city. In addition, the state lets municipalities exercise annexation to expand city boundaries as development densities reach urban levels. In 1988, the state authorized interlocal annexation agreements that allowed cities such as Raleigh to negotiate interlocal agreements to establish "spheres of influence," or boundaries for future annexation. With these powers, Raleigh could exert a considerable amount of control over development on its fringes.

California and Idaho cities also can establish spheres of influence that indicate where urban expansion can take place that ultimately may be annexed to the growing city. Cities can plan for extending infrastructure systems to those areas and establish standards for the type of development that will be allowed. Fresno, California, as an illustration, adopted an ordinance designating an "urban growth management area" outside its corporate limits, the area that is expected to become urbanized over the next 20 years. Following California law, Fresno prepares plans for infrastructure systems in this area and, as development takes place, annexes territory in which it provides urban services. Perhaps the most significant potential control over future development is given to New Mexico municipalities, which are authorized to control zoning in a five-mile area outside their boundaries.

In many New England, Mid-Atlantic, and Midwestern states, however, extraterritorial jurisdiction is not authorized. States such as Massachusetts, New Jersey, and Michigan have divided their entire area into towns, townships, or municipalities that can exercise planning and zoning, leaving no territory without those powers. In states like Maryland and Virginia, powerful counties can control growth management in unincorporated areas, acting much like super-municipalities. In other states, such as Colorado, counties are given little authority to guide development and municipalities are allowed to negotiate agreements with surrounding counties about development controls discussed at greater length in a later section.

Annexation

Most states authorize their municipalities to annex territory to retain some control over urban development. The political possibility of exercising this power, however, varies from state to state. Some states, such as North Carolina and Texas, require only that the city provide or commit to providing urban services in the area annexed. A number of states require reviews of annexation proposals by courts, special quasi-legislative bodies, or even the state legislature. Other states have established elaborate annexation procedures that require affirmative votes from residents of the annexing jurisdiction, the jurisdiction losing territory, and the residents of areas to be annexed—a difficult test in many growing urban areas.

Where annexation is feasible, some local governments prepare detailed plans and appropriate zoning that becomes applicable when annexation takes place. Tracy, California is one of a number of California cities that takes advantages of the "specific plan" process permitted by state law. Tracy officials worked with local landowners and developers to prepare detailed plans, including infrastructure needs, for developing areas as a condition of annexation.

Cities forego annexation opportunities at the risk of losing control over future development. City officials in Blacksburg, Virginia, a university town in western Virginia, decided not to annex a developing area along the principal highway. Within a few years, the area had developed with a hodgepodge of uses with inadequate public facilities, creating a tacky entrance to the community and congesting the highway. When Florida officials in Sarasota and Venice declined to annex developing areas, the county was forced to play catch-up in developing the administrative skills, funding sources, and facilities to support urban growth.

Annexation processes are further complicated by the degree to which the state encourages the incorporation of new municipalities and/or organization of special taxing districts. In states such as Oregon, Arizona, and Illinois, residents of developing areas can incorporate new municipalities rather easily, providing a potentially attractive alternative to being annexed by the city next door. Residents of two urbanizing areas in the Portland, Oregon region, for example, voted to incorporate to prevent potential development of multifamily housing in their areas. Developers and residents of urbanizing areas in many states can also form special taxing districts to provide essential services, thus removing a major incentive for annexation to adjoining cities. (See the discussion of special districts in Chapter 6 for more details on this process.)

Unfortunately, the primary way in which individual municipalities can control their growth in many states is through negotiating annexation deals with developers for more permissive zoning than allowed outside the municipality. Illinois towns, for instance, regularly compete for development, especially commercial and business development that would increase tax bases, by negotiating annexation agreements that promise desired zoning in return for being absorbed by the municipality. That type of deal making—zoning for sale, in effect—occurs in many states, virtually eliminating opportunities for growing cities to retain control over the quality of future development.

Service Extensions

Most cities and towns perform basic governmental functions in managing services essential to the entire community, such as police and fire protection, road construction and maintenance, sewage collection and treatment, water treatment and distribution, and libraries. Some of these services may be provided in other ways: Fire protection may be provided by volunteer groups, for example, and some services may be provided selectively by other levels of governments, private companies, or special districts formed for that purpose.

To the degree that local governments provide desirable services unavailable from other service deliverers, however, these services can be an instrument for managing growth. Earlier in the chapter the importance of metropolitan sewer service as a means of managing growth by regional agencies in Portland, Oregon and the Twin Cities in Minnesota was described. In most cases, growth boundaries are employed in company with policies for extension of urban services to determine the location and quality of future development. As demonstrated by Raleigh's experience, the effective use of extraterritorial jurisdiction and annexation powers depends on capabilities for extending desired urban services to developing areas.

Local governments sometimes fail to take advantage of this means of managing development. Local managers of semi-autonomous sewer and water agencies, for instance, frequently act like private enterprises interested in maximizing their service areas rather than serving other public purposes such as growth management. In King County, Washington, in the Seattle area, for example, county officials spent decades attempting to reach agreements with the regional sewer agency to limit sewer extensions to planned-growth areas. In other cases, state laws or court decisions limited the ability of local governments to direct services to selected areas. Boulder, Colorado's intentions to limit expansion of water and sewer service outside its borders as part of its growth policy were dashed by a Colorado Supreme Court decision declaring that such services were public utility enterprises that should not be constrained by other policy concerns of the city.[11]

The fly in this particular ointment is that the services must be viewed as desirable or necessary by residents of the areas proposed for service extensions—who probably will pay new fees, charges, and taxes for the services. Sewer service extensions, for example, are considered necessary where private septic tanks are not feasible alternatives. In both Raleigh and the Minneapolis/St. Paul areas, an essential part of their growth management programs was based on the inability of large areas in the path of potential development to pass soil percolation tests, so that the lack of sewer service effectively limited development. In Lexington/Fayette County, Kentucky, the capabilities of the urban limit line to protect rural areas is reinforced by the state health department's requirement for a minimum of 10 acres for the use of septic tanks.

However, where septic tanks and water wells can function, residents, who are located in those areas to avoid expensive city services, can and often do oppose annexation or extension of urban services. The problems rural residents have caused in resisting changes in Portland's growth boundary are just one example of many. Recently in the Phoenix area, development of an upscale project complete with all urban services and amenities was opposed by neighboring landowners content with wells that produced intermittently, failing septic tanks, and unpaved streets but concerned that more development would ruin the neighborhood.

Interlocal Agreements

As indicated in the preceding sections, interlocal agreement plays an important role in securing guidance over development outside jurisdictional boundaries. Although specific forms vary from state to state, most local governments throughout the nation are empowered to enter into cooperative agreements with other local governments, state agencies, and special taxing districts. In general, agreements can commit the signatories to cooperative actions that each of the parties to the agreement is permitted to do individually. Interlocal agreements may be made informally, through such mechanisms as advisory groups, or by formal, signed agreements or compacts, or by contractual understandings for specified services.

Interlocal agreements to manage development outside local governmental boundaries are fairly common—the experience of Raleigh described earlier is typical. Another example is Boulder's long-standing agreement with Boulder County on managing growth outside the city. Both city and county adopted a jointly sponsored comprehensive plan for Boulder Valley in 1970, and the city continues to control the planning and zoning process in that area. Another nearby example is Fort

Collins, which in 1980 executed an agreement with Larimer County and Loveland, a city to the south, to define an urban service boundary. The agreement establishes the policy that Fort Collins may annex developing areas as appropriate and sets urban standards for interim development of those areas prior to annexation, including a *minimum* density requirement. The agreement, therefore, assures that the city can control the extension of services and the quality of urban development for the foreseeable future.

A number of cities and counties have entered into interlocal agreements to form joint planning and zoning commissions as a means of coordinating development across city boundaries. Among them is Lincoln/Lancaster County, Nebraska, whose growth management program is founded on the skillful combination of many of the growth-managing approaches discussed earlier.

Putting It All Together: Lincoln, Nebraska's Growth Management Strategy[12]

Lying about 40 miles southwest of Omaha, Lincoln is the last city west of the Missouri River until one reaches Denver, some 450 miles away. Founded in 1867 as the capital of the new state of Nebraska, Lincoln is first and foremost the state's center of government and home of the state university. With a population approaching 195,000 in 1996, Lincoln's growth has been steady and consistent for decades. Lincoln is a white-collar town, home to a substantial cadre of professional and civic leaders with a long-standing commitment to "good government."

Lincoln has a rich history of planning endeavors, made more significant by its relative isolation in the farmlands of the plains states. As early as 1912 a municipal planning commission proposed the first city plan. Although it was not adopted, in 1924 the city succeeded in adopting its first zoning code; in 1929, responding to local leaders' concerns for controlling future development, the state legislature gave the city zoning jurisdiction over a three-mile area outside the city borders. The city's first comprehensive plan was developed and adopted between 1948 and 1952. A joint city–county planning commission was formed in 1959, and a regional comprehensive plan was adopted in 1961. City–county plans were updated in 1977, 1985, and 1994.

The Comprehensive Plan

The cornerstone of Lincoln's growth management program is the comprehensive plan, which outlines planning goals, establishes growth patterns, and provides a policy framework for implementation tools such as zoning, capital and transportation improvement programs, design standards, and protection of the natural environment. (See Figure 3.2.) Versions of the plan through the years have emphasized several policy areas of particular concern to Lincoln citizens. One was guiding the physical pattern of growth—specifically, attempting to contain growth within a concentric pattern outward from the established core of the city. Each plan emphasized the importance of contiguous development as a means of retaining a vibrant community and providing efficient urban services. Allied with this interest are other concerns for maintaining and revitalizing the downtown area and maintaining the quality of life and physical condition in older neighborhoods, a direct outgrowth of the city's interest in containing development.

The city's attempts to encourage a steady pattern of concentric growth, however, ran athwart of market forces. The city's natural growth has pushed toward the southeast and demand for housing and commercial development in that sector remains strong. City efforts to promote more growth in the northwestern and southwestern parts of the city generally have been ineffective, although some development has occurred. As one local attorney said, "you can't turn off the spigot in one area and expect it to turn on in another." During the mid-1980s when housing prices rose rather steeply, some developers and builders claimed that design standards and shortages of land supply in desirable areas (i.e., the southeast) resulted in more costly housing. A city decision to permit major development on a northwestern site outside the city proved disastrous as the project failed, heightening perceptions that the western areas are less desirable for development.

Nevertheless, aided by its strong annexation powers, Lincoln has assimilated new growth as it occurred. Nearly 95 percent of the county's population increase during the 1980s took place within city boundaries. The 1994 comprehensive plan, although less wedded to the concentric circle ideal, is still predicated on continuing a pattern of urban expansion that keeps new development contiguous to the existing urban edge.

Control over Future Development Areas

Some important state and local legislation forms the structural basis for successful implementation of Lincoln's comprehensive plan. First, as indicated earlier, the state authorized the city to maintain zoning powers over development in the area three miles beyond the city limits. Second, state laws also prohibit incorporation of municipalities within five miles of the city limits without city consent and provide a relatively easy annexation procedure. Third, through an intergovernmental agreement, many city and county functions are combined, including the departments of planning, health, employment, and human services. Finally, the

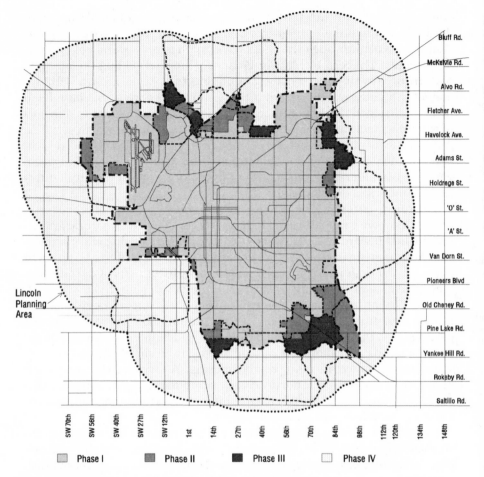

| ■ Phase I | ■ Phase II | ■ Phase III | ☐ Phase IV |

SUMMARY OF PHASES IN PLAN

Phase I—Areas designated for immediate development will generally be contiguous to existing development with some or most of required infrastructure in place.

Phase II—Areas designated for near-term development will be contiguous to existing or planned development but lacking one or more major items of infrastructure, such as arterial road, park, or trunk sewer.

Phase III—Areas designated for mid-term development will be contiguous to existing or planned development, lack most infrastructure required to support development, but might reasonably be excepted to develop within the planning period.

Phase IV—Balance of city of Lincoln's land use jurisdiction shall be held as an urban reserve. Falls within community's growth area but beyond the planning period.

Miles

0   1   2   3

—·— Anticipated Year 2015 Service Limit

Figure 3.2

Lincoln, Nebraska plan. Lincoln, Nebraska's firm control over utility extensions is demonstrated in this phasing plan for future development around the city, which follows the long-established policy of promoting contiguous, compact development. (Courtesy of the Lincoln City/Lancaster County Planning Department.)

municipality controls most of the utilities necessary for growth, includ-ing water, sewer, and electric services. (The city also provides electric service outside the city limits.)

These powers, lacked by many American cities, give Lincoln almost total control over development of its urbanizing fringe. Lincoln has taken utmost advantage of these powers to direct development both within and outside its borders and to ensure a balance between maintaining exist-ing neighborhoods and commercial areas and newly developing areas.

Intergovernmental Coordination

In addition to city controls over development outside its boundaries, the city and Lancaster County have worked together for years to coordinate development policies. In 1959 a joint city–county planning commission was formed. Since then, the city and county have worked closely in the formulation of a series of joint comprehensive plans. The 1994 plan in-cludes, for the first time, a unified land use plan illustrated on a single map. The joint planning process allows the city–county plan to recog-nize, in its words, "the relationship between urban and rural areas and creates a document that reflects the needs of both settings."[13] Needs for protecting natural features and maintaining the vitality of 12 municipal-ities and rural settlements outside the city are also addressed.

Intergovernmental coordination has been aided by the long-term con-tinuity of planning leadership in Lincoln. The current planning director, Timothy Stewart, is only the third director in the department's history.

Citizen Participation

A well-educated, professionally employed polity has helped ensure well-informed community involvement in planning and implementation processes. The latest comprehensive plan evolved over four years of ef-forts that included rethinking of downtown's future development, con-vening of a "Community Congress" to define community goals and ob-jectives, adoption of a 150-goal statement by the city and county, and task force consideration of five key issues.

The initial draft plan issued in mid-1993 received mixed reviews. The new plan was adopted in 1994 after what planning director Tim Stewart called a "painful" adoption process, with extensive citizen and official re-views and revisions. Traditional plan concepts, including the concentric growth policy, were reconsidered and reframed. Now the planning de-partment is moving to further define implementation efforts and consid-ering a longer look into the future, perhaps toward a 50-year horizon.

Many benefits resulted from both city policy and state legislation. Growth remains orderly without the leapfrogging that places inordinate demands on service delivery. City boundaries have kept pace with development and stayed within the existing watershed. Lincoln's downtown has remained as vital as can be found in any city its size. In addition, the quality of commercial development is high and municipal services are considered excellent.

Limits on Growth: Stopping or Slowing Expansion

The growth management concept gained widespread attention during the early 1970s when towns and cities began imposing limits on the amount or pace of development. Even today, some people associate growth management with those early efforts to curb growth rather than accommodate it. And even today, some communities continue to limit development. Although the City of San Diego dropped limits after a brief period, most of the 17 other cities and towns in San Diego County have adopted caps to annual development. In the Denver area, four cities (Boulder, Golden, Louisville, and Westminster) limit the amount of annual growth and others, including Fort Collins, are considering limits. California and Colorado communities are more apt to impose limits than communities in other states; in fact, it is probable that those two states account for more local growth-limiting programs than all other states combined. The combination of residents' reactions to long-term rapid growth, legal restraints on raising revenues for infrastructure, and permissive local and state laws appear to stimulate this type of approach to growth management.

Approaches and Techniques

Several approaches are used to limit growth. The most common is setting a limit on the number of residential building permits that the local government may issue each year. Typically, the limit is based on average growth rates over some period of time prior to the most recent surge of construction activity. Boulder limited development to a rate of 1.5 percent or about 450 units a year after several years of 5 to 10 percent annual growth. Westminster, Colorado employed a variation based on its rationale for growth control, available water supply. It limits annual residential service connections. Carlsbad, California determined the number of units that would ultimately "build out" the community, related that number to a schedule of facility construction, and arrived at an annual average number of housing units it would approve.

Other communities find other ways to limit growth. A number of California cities, including Santa Barbara, have refused to plan and fund increases in water supply, thus instituting a de facto limit on growth. At one time a few years ago, many of the towns around Boston were issuing no new sewer hookups unless developers paid for expensive system improvements. Still other communities enacted an adequate facilities requirement, then failed to schedule public facility construction at a rate that would have kept up with growth. Many growing suburban communities react to growth by restricting development of multifamily housing and/or rezoning large areas for very low-density development, thus reducing growth rates if not the root causes of growth problems.

Communities that do impose growth limits must then determine a means of selecting developments, assuming that more requests for approval will be submitted than permitted by the limit. Petaluma and Boulder both instituted "point" or "merit" systems for that purpose. The systems were used to rate proposed projects according to stated criteria such as the availability of public services to provide for needs of project residents, the quality of architectural and site design, and provision of amenities such as bicycle and foot paths. The systems encouraged developers to "donate" facilities and amenities to win more points. Petaluma's system was applied to all applicants; Boulder's went into effect when the semi-annual allocation of permits was exceeded. Ironically, because growth rates in both cities remained generally lower than the limits, the systems were discarded as a means of allocating permits, although Boulder still uses its system to evaluate projects.

Other communities use existing subdivision regulations to evaluate projects but still must determine whether to award permits on a "first-come, first-served" basis or by prorating available permits among all applicants. Most communities also set up special quotas for types of housing considered especially desirable, such as low-cost housing or infill development. Administration of such processes can become quite complicated. Tracy, California discovered that its permit award system resulted in certain developers of large subdivisions acquiring most of the allowable permits, creating monopoly conditions and opening the door to sale of permits among developers.

Growth limits can also be applied to specific areas. In applying adequate facilities requirements, for example, as detailed in Chapter 6, inadequate facility capacities can lead to de facto limits or moratoriums in certain areas until facility capacities are increased to allow continued development. In addition, a number of local governments instituted limits on development of downtown office buildings in the development boom of the late 1970s to mid-1980s. Seeing huge developments changing the face of their central business districts, local residents pressed for slowing development and making it more compatible with the existing downtown environment. San Francisco's program was best known. It limited office development to 475,000 square feet per year and required special attention to design details and amenities. Seattle adopted similar restrictions and requirements. (Both of these cities and others also adopted "linkage" programs that required downtown developers to contribute to housing programs, described in Chapter 9.) These downtown growth limits are practically irrelevant in today's market, although they are still on the books.

Limits on growth also have been considered for metropolitan areas, rather than individual communities. In both the San Diego and Portland regions, some citizens' groups were concerned enough about rapid growth to press for slowing it down. After studies pointed out the difficulties and potential consequences of actions that would cause development to decline, the notion was dropped as a viable strategy.[14]

Moratoriums

Development moratoriums are temporary growth limits, usually halting all further issuances of building permits for a specified period of time. The moratorium can postpone all development or development of a particular type or in a particular area, such as any residential construction, commercial construction along a congested highway segment, or development in a certain school district. It can be a few months in duration or several years.

Communities adopt moratoriums to allow a catch-up period for responding to critical problems—mounting concerns about critical public facilities or failing development policies. Calvert County, Maryland adopted a six-month moratorium in 1995 on issuing permits in three antiquated subdivisions that quite suddenly were attracting hundreds of new families with children, quickly overloading available school capacity. The unexpected spurt of students was one problem; the other was that the county's impact fee did not apply to these subdivisions platted some 30 years in the past. In the boom-development days of the mid-1980s, Nashua, New Hampshire imposed a one-year moratorium on further commercial development on a major highway to prepare plans that would alleviate traffic congestion. San Diego adopted an 18-month "interim growth control ordinance" that allowed substantially fewer permits for residential construction than the previous rate of issuance while the city's planning and growth management policies were reconsidered.

The legality of moratoriums has been well established in the courts. Generally, moratoriums are considered within the rights of local governments if they

- are intended to deal with a defined problem that will be created or worsened by development; and

- extend for a reasonable time during which local officials take steps to find solutions to the problems triggering the moratoriums.

Local governments, in other words, must demonstrate a health, safety, or welfare basis for halting development and then move to determine a solution that will permit development to resume. Daniel Mandelker, one of the nation's foremost land use attorneys, comments that courts usually "take into account the purposes served by the interim control and the restrictions it imposes. The courts will strike down interim controls that clearly serve improper regulatory purposes." The courts, he states, "view the interim control as a necessary measure to protect the municipality from development" that might be inconsistent with new policies and ordinances.[15]

Moratoriums have their downsides, however. Most significantly, short-term moratoriums seldom affect the current pace of development. In most communities, enough development has received permits or commitments (by subdivision plat approval, for example) to keep the development pipeline flowing for some time. That problem is heightened by the permit rush that typically occurs when builders learn that local officials are considering a moratorium. In Calvert County, for example, builders obtained hundreds of permits just before the moratorium took effect. Although many of those permits were not translated into construction, the development process was thrown into disarray.

Long-term moratoriums create other problems in disrupting the development process, generating political conflict and often litigation, and allowing monopoly conditions to inflate land and housing prices. Furthermore, one commentator observes that

> if jurisdictions merely pause without seriously reconsidering and reforming their approach to land use regulation and growth management, moratoriums may do more harm than good. They can disrupt local economies, increase unemployment, and inflate real estate prices, possibly with effects that persist and outlast the term of the moratorium.[16]

In addition, moratoriums are a visible reminder that the local government has not kept pace with growth, that its past actions have been too little and too late. A moratorium is an admission of failure on the part of government officials. Eric Kelly, a noted land use attorney, observes that "a moratorium is a worst-case result for all parties."[17] Not only are developers stopped from pursuing plans that may have received approval and in which substantial investments have been made, but city officials are forced to forego potential revenues from that development. Kelly cites the instance of Westminster, Colorado, which found in 1978 that it had approved far more development than its water and sewer system could serve. The city needed connection fees from new development to amortize bonds issued to pay for existing utility lines. The brief moratorium it imposed caused headaches for both developers and city officials, something that might have been avoided by "planning ahead."[18] Politically, however, citizens upset by development trends find moratoriums a satisfying response to current crises, if not long-term solutions.

Conclusion

Techniques that allow communities to manage the direction, quality, and pace of growth offer some of the most potent regulatory approaches in the arsenal of public policy affecting development. Growth boundaries and similar methods for determining the location of future development establish strong guidelines for the development process, providing a framework for zoning and other regulatory actions as well as for private development decisions.

Similarly, local powers to control growth in developing areas outside existing jurisdictional boundaries are essential to managing community development. Without those powers, communities are unable to guide their destinies and are vulnerable to the potentially damaging effects of development decisions outside their control. In combination, as we see in the experience of Lincoln, Nebraska, these growth management tools can provide highly effective approaches to responsible growth management.

4

Protecting Environmental and
Natural Resources: "Where Not to Grow"

In his seminal work, *Design With Nature*, Ian McHarg writes of the interaction of man and nature:

> A single drop of water in the uplands of a watershed may appear and reappear as cloud, precipitation, surface water in creek and river, lake and pond or groundwater; it can participate in plant and animal metabolism, transpiration, condensation, decomposition, combustion, respiration and evaporation. This same drop of water may appear in considerations of climate and microclimate, water supply, flood, drought and erosion control, industry, commerce, agriculture, forestry, reaction, scenic beauty, in cloud, snow, stream, river, and sea. We conclude that nature is a single interacting system and that changes to any part will affect the operation of the whole.[1]

McHarg makes us aware that human and natural systems are intricately bound together. Cities, he believes, exist in natural settings whose qualities are essential to maintaining life.

The currently popular concept of sustainable development builds on McHarg's insights. It calls for maintaining the integrity of complex ecological systems while promoting economic viability and social equity. Although development is necessary to further economic and social ends, it should be undertaken in ways that minimize impacts on the natural functions of landscapes. Development should be designed to maintain

83

sensitive lands and habitats, to minimize its footprint on the land in order to retain natural features, and to make use of natural resources rather than engineered facilities wherever possible.

As John Rogers and B. Fritts Golden state, "in the struggle to find effective strategies to maintain a stable and sustainable environment, managers, policy makers, and the public are discovering the limitation of a philosophy based on subduing the earth and making economic use of all resources."[2] They suggest that managing ecosystems to retain multiple biological species as part of an integrated natural community not only protects species but also provides natural functions that benefit humans, such as retarding floods and filtering nonpoint pollution. Urban historians Christine Rosen and Joel Tarr add that "the natural and built environments evolved in dialectical interdependence and tension," in which the built environment, "through its effects upon and interaction with the natural environment, is a part of the earth's environmental history."[3]

Together with the new focus on sustainable communities, McHarg's vision in 1969 of the intrinsic values of regional landscapes in shaping and supporting human settlements remains a powerful force in managing community growth. The concepts of "design with nature" are embodied in countless planning policies, zoning and subdivision provisions, and growth management techniques in use today. Communities and regions throughout the United States are managing growth to preserve valued natural qualities.

Planners usually begin their analysis of future development patterns by identifying significant natural features that ought to be conserved. McHarg identified eight natural features that should be respected in planning future development: surface water, marshes, floodplains, aquifers, aquifer recharge areas, steep lands, prime agricultural land, and forests and woodlands. These features, he taught, form natural systems that are an essential component of our living environment. Land, in other words, is not simply a commodity awaiting development, and stream valleys are not just handy places to dump trash. Prime agricultural land is a finite resource that should not be indiscriminately covered with concrete. Marshes and floodplains perform valuable functions for humanity's benefit as well as for the natural order.

The state of Florida, for example, requires a conservation section in all comprehensive plans that addresses needs

> for the conservation, use, and protection of natural resources in the area, including air, water, water recharge areas, wetlands, waterwells, estuarine marshes, soils, beaches, shores, floodplains, rivers, bays, lakes, harbors, forests, fisheries and wildlife, marine habitat, minerals, and other natural and environmental resources.[4]

In addition, subdivision regulations now routinely require stormwater retention measures to control erosion, setbacks to buffer stream valleys, protection of floodplains, and other measures. Zoning ordinances frequently incorporate conservation, agricultural, and open space districts to protect valuable natural areas.

By identifying and planning for protection of these resources, communities are determining "where not to grow." Implementing these plans, they use a variety of regulatory, funding, and programmatic approaches to guide and restrict development in open areas. In this endeavor, local governments are supported by an array of powerful federal laws that call for protecting essential environmental qualities.

The Framework of Federal Laws

Beginning in the 1960s, environmental activists backed by a broad constituency of concerned citizens persuaded the U.S. Congress to enact a multitude of ambitious laws to recognize the public responsibility to protect vital environmental qualities. (Not coincidentally, they relate to McHarg's eight important features of the regional landscape.) The principal laws, listed by date of enactment, are described in the accompanying feature box.

Many states also passed environmental laws, including acts modeled after the National Environmental Policy Act (NEPA), that require evaluations of environmental impacts caused by state actions and, in some cases, by major private development projects.

These laws, in general, require federal or state agencies to determine that proposed projects will have little or no impact on environmental qualities or that actions will be taken to avoid, reduce, or compensate for impacts before permits can be issued. In addition, the NEPA process provides many opportunities for public review and comment on proposals and for litigation on both the substance and procedures of environmental impact reviews.

In two significant ways, however, the federal and state environmental laws fail to respond to McHarg's call for respecting nature. First, permitting procedures generally deal with individual project applications rather than areawide environmental concerns. The possible cumulative effects of many projects, over time, are not evaluated. Relationships between permits for different purposes are never established. In many cases, opportunities are missed for reconciling competing objectives or making trade-offs for securing better conservation.

Second, federal permitting procedures operate virtually independently of regional and local planning processes. Federal agencies view their role as regulators, administering laws and rules in a top-down man-

Major Federal Environmental Laws

Douglas R. Porter

Clean Air Act: Adopted in 1963 and administered by the Environmental Protection Agency (EPA), the act seeks to prevent and control air pollution by requiring conformance with clean air standards within metropolitan areas. EPA sets emission standards for major pollutants emitted by stationary sources, such as industries, and utilities and for mobile sources, such as vehicles. Deadlines set by Congress for attaining standards have been reset time after time; in 1990 Congress mandated a system of graduated controls and staggered deadlines for compliance. Proposals for achieving standards include reductions in urban sprawl and greater use of transit and other alternatives to single-occupancy vehicles.

National Environmental Policy Act: The overarching environmental act passed in 1970 requires federal agencies to consider the potential environmental effects of their programs by preparation of environmental impact statements (EIS) for "all federal actions significantly affecting the quality of the human environment," including highway construction, subsidized housing, and other assistance in development projects. Statements must analyze potential environmental impacts, identify unavoidable adverse impacts, evaluate possible alternatives, and define commitments of resources. Many states have adopted similar requirements governing state actions.

Clean Water Act: Intended to "restore and maintain the chemical, physical, and biological integrity of the nation's waters," this act of 1972 establishes procedures to reduce or eliminate discharge of pollutants into navigable waters and to protect fish, shellfish, and wildlife. Perhaps best-known is Section 404, which requires permits for filling or dredging in wetlands. The permits are issued by the U.S. Army Corps of Engineers but the EPA may review Corps decisions and veto them if appropriate. Current policy gives priority to avoid-

ner. They make little attempt to ensure that permits make sense in the context of local planning and policies. A report by the Maryland Office of Planning makes the point: "The regulations may treat matters in isolation but nature does not." It goes on to observe that "a more ecological approach to regulation, one that looks at the relationship of all the pieces, would prevent some of the defects in the present system."[5]

Local governments, therefore, often have a difficult time applying federal environmental mandates in their attempts to respond to McHarg's recommendations for environmental planning. Nevertheless, local governments must seek to reconcile environmental objectives with specific development needs and a multitude of individual projects. To accomplish these ambitious ends, they employ techniques to define, in ad-ing any development of wetlands but allows some use of wetlands if mitigation measures are taken to avoid any "net loss" in wetland resources.

Coastal Zone Management Act: Also enacted in 1972, this legislation encourages wise management of coastal areas by offering federal financial assistance to states that voluntarily agree to participate in conservation of coastal resources. State programs coordinate and guide actions of federal, state, and local governments that affect coastal areas.

Endangered Species Act: This 1973 law protects species of fish, wildlife, and plants threatened with extinction. Species listed as endangered by the U.S. Department of Interior and Department of Commerce are protected from any action that would harm them or their habitats. "Incidental takings" of endangered species may be permitted if a habitat conservation plan is prepared to provide commitments to habitat preservation and mitigation.

Resource Conservation and Recovery Act: This 1977 act promotes improved management of solid waste by state and local governments. It promotes recycling, prohibits open dumping of solid waste, and controls generation and management of hazardous wastes.

Superfund Act: Officially entitled the "Comprehensive Environmental Response, Compensation, and Liability Act of 1980," this act provides for liability, compensation, cleanup, and emergency response for hazardous substances released into the environment and the cleanup of inactive hazardous waste disposal sites. → Exxon Valdez

Coastal Barrier Resources Act: Intended to preserve the barrier islands lying off the continental coastlines, this act of 1982 prohibits federal expenditures for flood insurance, bridges, airports, sewers, roads, and other grants and loans for facilities in undeveloped coastal areas.

vance of development, resources that should be conserved and to establish measures to acquire, protect, or minimize adverse impacts on those resources.

Identifying Resources

The obvious first step to conserving environmental and natural resources is identifying what and where they are. Many local planning offices expend a considerable amount of time and effort to determine the location and characteristics of specific resources in areas that may be affected by development. By identifying and evaluating resources they help to establish priorities for their conservation. In many cases, they employ a McHargian technique of overlaying resource maps to define areas that are of greatest value for natural conservation. In addition, local planners may undertake a "carrying capacity" analysis, also a technique employed by McHarg, to determine areas (e.g., floodplains, steep slopes, prime farmlands) that should not be developed, areas that may be developed with special care to avoid adverse impacts, and areas suitable for development. The capabilities of underlying geology and soil conditions to sustain development are evaluated, including acceptability for use of septic tanks. A carrying capacity analysis does not provide an absolute measure of land to be conserved (other factors such as technical means of overcoming limits on suitability can affect that determination) but can offer a useful initial definition of natural constraints on development.[6]

Large-Scale Planning for Conservation

Community planners can conduct analyses for areas in the path of development to help in demarcating growth areas from conservation areas. In the broadest approach to conservation planning, they may focus on delineating significant ecosystems that have particular attributes for supporting plant, aquatic, and animal life—rivers, wetlands, ponds, and forests, for example, that help to maintain biodiversity. Increasingly, environmentalists are encouraging conservation planning that encompasses entire watersheds incorporating many of the ecosystems common to an area.

The Chesapeake Bay forms a very large watershed that has been subject to regional and local conservation efforts over many years, as described in a later section of this chapter. Other examples are the New Jersey Pinelands and Lake Tahoe in California and Nevada, which have been subject to special planning efforts described in Chapter 8. A recent example of large-scale conservation planning is the Natural Communities and Conservation Program (NCCP) of the state of California being applied in southern California. The NCCP promotes voluntary, collaborative efforts among landowners, local governments, and state and federal agencies to preserve endangered habitats or ecosystems. The program's first goal is to preserve the coastal sage scrub ecosystem in more than 6000 square miles of Southern California. The ecosystem is home to about 90 potentially threatened or endangered species in an area that has been rapidly growing for decades. Counties and cities within this area have worked with state and federal agencies and landowners to identify key habitat areas and corridors, characterized by a range of soils, terrains, slopes, and other landscape features, that will accommodate a wide variety of species. Just a few years into the program, over half of the scrub habitat are protected by voluntary commitments of 31 local governments and 37 private landowners and developers. The planning process also has identified developable lands outside habitats for future urban growth.

San Diego's Association of Governments (SANDAG), a cooperative relationship among 18 municipalities and the county government in San Diego county, has played a significant role in the Southern California NCCP process. SANDAG cooperated with several constituent jurisdictions and key organizations to undertake a series of habitat protection planning efforts to identify, in advance of development, major habitat conservation needs throughout the county. The Multi-Species Comprehensive Plan (MSCP) for the southern part of San Diego County, for example, is a remarkable effort to proactively plan for reconciling habitat protection with future development, thereby improving the certainty of the development approval process in that fast-growing area. The plan calls for conservation of about 85 percent of the 109,000 acres of privately owned habitat and 96 percent of the 75,000 acres of publicly owned habitat in the study area.

An economic impact analysis of the plan demonstrates that the multispecies protection approach will produce measurable economic benefits in comparison to "business as usual" project-by-project habitat protection efforts. The analysis shows that a functional, multispecies habitat preservation program will ensure the region's economy against large and persistent development disruptions that would otherwise occur due to ad hoc planning and conflicts over funding habitat protection. Such disruptions could result in fewer jobs and lower resident incomes. The study estimated that the MSCP plan would generate 5000 additional jobs, over 46 percent of which would be in the construction industry. The added jobs would lower the unemployment rate and increase personal income in the region by about $184 million, or an amount of $78 per household. On the cost side, even the high-acquisition alternative (requiring major public outlays for habitat purchase) would require only about $15 to $20 per household per year. In the absence of the MSCP, the study estimates that individual project planning and permitting for habitat protection would delay project starts by an average of three years and would probably require greater mitigation and increase habitat maintenance costs.[7]

In the northern part of the county, the city of Carlsbad was one of the first local governments to enroll in the NCCP and undertake development of a citywide conservation plan. (See Figure 4.1.) In the first stage of the plan, final approval was granted for a habitat conservation plan for three large tracts of land totaling 2300 acres in Carlsbad owned by a developer.[8] About 950 acres is covered by coastal sage scrub inhabited by the California gnatcatcher, a species listed as threatened by the U.S. Fish and Wildlife Service. About 33 other sensitive species inhabit the prop-

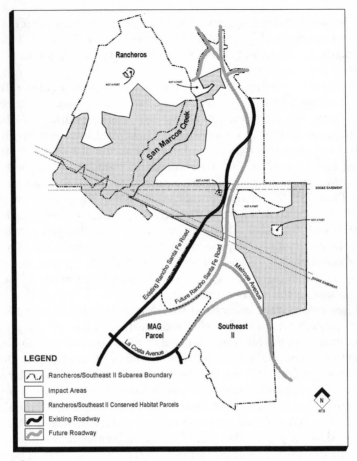

Figure 4.1
Carlsbad habitat conservation plan. Carlsbad's planning process focused first on identifying conservation planning areas and then, within those regions, defining specific preservation areas. The plan for the Southeast Area identifies preservation areas and related development (including new roads) that are incorporated into the adopted habitat conservation plan. (Prepared by Hofman Planning Associates.)

erty, of which as many as 16 may be listed as endangered in the next few years.

The city, developer, local environmentalists, and state and federal resource agencies were all concerned with the prospect of development on the three sites. The Fieldstone Company, an Irvine-based developer, purchased the property in 1988 and anticipated moving ahead with development in a predictable manner. The city wished to complete a long-planned road that would cut through the tracts and across prime coastal sage scrub lands, and that could be financed only by development of bordering lands. Environmentalists knew that outright purchase of the habitat for conservation was not feasible given the price tag of $150,000 or more per acre.

A collaborative planning process began in 1989, laying the groundwork for working relationships among the development firm and environmental agencies. In January 1992 the city formed a planning committee comprising representatives of all interests; by December 1992 the habitat conservation plan was formally submitted to state and federal agencies. It was approved by the Department of Interior in 1995. The plan sets aside about 700 acres of habitat on the sites and up to 240 acres to be acquired by the developer off the sites. Most of the reserved land forms a broad wildlife corridor bisecting the sites. The developer clustered planned development on the remaining land and agreed to stringent revegetation requirements. The city revised its road alignments and road financing program and gave conceptual approval for density transfers for planned development areas. Efforts are now underway to define a long-term management program for the reserved habitat areas and to complete planning for the remainder of the city.

This conservation planning process took place within the city's framework of growth management efforts. Not only did it resolve long-standing conservation issues but its detailed planning helped to define future development patterns for the city.

Another planning effort that has helped to identify key conservation needs is the recent "Desert Spaces Management Plan" prepared by the Maricopa Association of Governments for the Phoenix, Arizona region. (See Figure 4.2.) The plan identifies (1) public and private lands with outstanding open space values that should be protected from development; (2) public and private lands with high open-space values whose environmental features should be retained through sensitive development; and (3) existing or designated parks, wilderness, and wildlife areas. The plan recommends acquisition of the first category of lands, some 1.5 million acres, through a combination of regulatory restrictions, reservations through the subdivision exaction process, donations by individuals and conservation groups, purchase of easements, or acquisition. The second category, about 2.2 million acres, is expected to be managed through zoning and subdivision approval processes that could secure reservations of important natural features in development plans.

The real significance of the plan, however, is its identification of the major natural areas worthy of preservation as a guide to the future actions of governments, landowners, and conservation organizations in the area. The plan provides a target for future conservation through a vari-

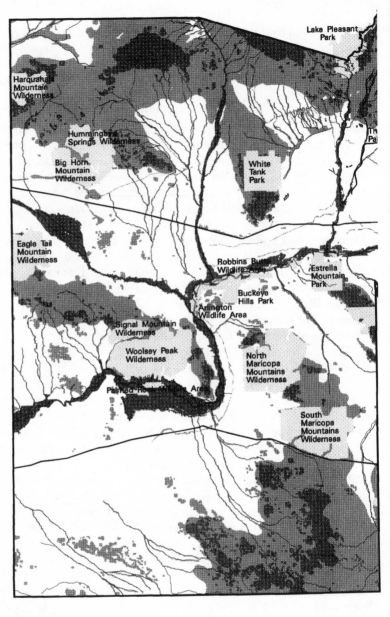

Lake Pleasant
Park

Harquahala
Mountain
Wilderness

Hummingbird
Springs Wilderness

Big Horn
Mountain
Wilderness

White
Tank
Park

Eagle Tail
Mountain
Wilderness

Robbins Butte
Wildlife Area

Estrella
Mountain
Park

Buckeye
Hills Park

Arlington
Wildlife Area

Signal Mountain
Wilderness

Woolsey Peak
Wilderness

North
Maricopa
Mountains
Wilderness

Painted Rock State Area

South
Maricopa
Mountains
Wilderness

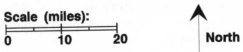

Scale (miles):

0   10   20

North

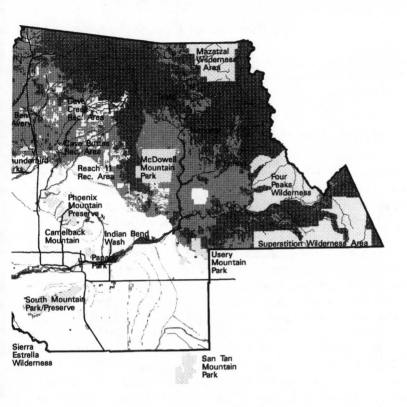

Legend:

Conservation Areas: 962,244 acres

Public and Private Lands with outstanding
open space value. Recommended for
protection from development and its
effects through policy amendment,
easements, restrictions, and/or
acquisition.

Retention Areas: 1,419,265 acres

Public and Private Lands with high open
space value. Recommended for sensitive
development regulation.

Secured Open Space: 645,798 acres

Designated Parks, Wilderness, and
Wildlife Areas.

Figure 4.2

Maricopa County open space plan. The Desert Spaces Management plan for
the Phoenix region identifies key features to be protected from development
and specific roles for public and private sectors in protecting them. (Courtesy
of the Maricopa Association of Governments.)

ety of means, including the kind of approach used by Scottsdale, Arizona described later in this chapter. The Maricopa County open space plan was adopted by the Association of Governments in 1995.

Federal and State Planning Efforts

Other planning processes to identify conservation needs for large areas, such as watersheds, are frequently carried out in connection with federal permitting procedures. In accordance with the 1980 amendments to the Coastal Zone Management Act, the U.S. Army Corps of Engineers can develop Special Area Management Plans (SAMPs) in conjunction with federal, state, and local resource agencies. The plans provide both natural resource protection and reasonable coastal-dependent development for designated areas. Similarly, the Endangered Species Act allows landowners, governmental agencies, and environmental groups to participate in preparing Habitat Conservation Plans (HCPs) to identify habitats to be conserved as well as areas that may be developed. Approval of such a plan allows minor incidental "taking" of low-priority habitat in return for assurances of protection and maintenance of high-priority habitats. The EPA and the Corps can also carry out studies to provide Advanced Designation of Wetlands. The studies, by designating wetlands as suitable or unsuitable for disposal of dredged or fill material, reduces conflicts between landowners and the agencies in securing Section 404 permits.

All of these federally supported planning efforts provide stakeholders an opportunity to participate in planning, improve the predictability of the federal and state permitting process, and provide more flexibility to address environmental/development conflicts in the regulatory process. The planning processes are time-consuming, however, and except for HCPs carry no assurances that the plans, once completed, will be fully supported by later agency actions.

Many states have encouraged conservation planning in key areas by designating critical areas in which conservation of important natural features and resources (including coastal resources) are threatened by continuing development. The Florida Environmental Land and Water Management Act of 1972 allows the state to designate areas with resources of national or statewide significance as "areas of critical state concern." When the governor and cabinet identifies a critical area, a "Resources Planning and Management Committee" composed of representatives of all interests is appointed. The committee studies area conditions and needs and recommends management principles for guiding development. Local officials are responsible for modifying their comprehensive plans and development regulations to implement the principles. If they do not accept that responsibility, the governor and cabinet may formally designate the area as a critical area, subject to legislative confirmation, and may prepare and adopt local plans and regulations to implement the principles. To date, four areas have been designated: the Big Cypress Swamp, the Green Swamp, Apalachicola Bay, and the Florida Keys.

The Maryland Chesapeake Bay Critical Areas Law, enacted in 1984, created an innovative program to improve water quality, preserve sensitive habitat including wetlands, and limit the extent and character of growth in and around the Chesapeake Bay and its tidal tributaries. Its ambitious efforts portray the kinds of applied techniques in use in many critical areas.

The largest estuary in the United States, the Chesapeake Bay stretches some 195 miles from north to south and drains an area of 64,000 square miles, including most of Maryland, Virginia, Pennsylvania, and the District of Columbia, and parts of Delaware, New York, and West Virginia. The watershed is rich in wetlands, of which 1.2 million acres remain, one quarter in tidal wetlands. The impacts of population increases in the Bay region during the 1960s and 1970s began to cause dramatic declines in fisheries, waterfowl population, and general water quality, as well as submerged aquatic vegetation.

Mounting concerns over the Bay's condition stimulated conduct of a seven-year EPA study. Completed in 1983, the study identified point and nonpoint sources of pollution that increased nutrient and sediment loading of Bay waters and as sources of increased toxic pollutants. Post-war industrial and residential development, and expanding agricultural activities, were producing negative impacts on water quality. Following the study, the states of Maryland, Pennsylvania, and Virginia, plus the District of Columbia and EPA, signed the Chesapeake Bay Agreement that committed each party to take immediate, substantial measures to restore and protect the bay. One of the most dramatic commitments came from Maryland, which enacted a series of initiatives in 1984, including the Chesapeake Bay Critical Area Law (Maryland Natural Resources Code Annotated, Section 1801, et seq.).

The new legislation defined a critical area consisting of the water of the bay, tidal wetlands and tributaries, lands under these waters, and 1000 feet of upland adjoining the water boundary. A 25-member commission was established to develop criteria to guide the plans and actions of the 16 counties and 45 municipal governments within the critical area. The law required the criteria to address ways to minimize adverse impacts of pollutants on water quality, conserve fish, wildlife, and plant habitat, and establish land use policies that would accommodate growth but control growth-related pollution.

After many meetings, discussions, and hearings, and approval by the state Senate and General Assembly, the criteria were enacted into law in May 1986. The criteria placed strict limits on growth in undeveloped areas and defined three categories of land and standards for development in each of them:

- *Intensely developed areas,* where little natural habitat remained, in which local governments should adopt strategies to lower pollution loadings from new or redeveloped uses, as well as improve the quality of runoff water, encourage retrofitting of stormwater facilities, and minimize impacts on habitat protection areas.

- *Limited development areas,* currently developed in low- to moderate-intensity uses and with public sewer and/or water service, in which habitat protection areas should be preserved, wildlife corridor systems preserved or created, wooded areas preserved to maximum extent possible, impervious surface limited to 15 percent of a developed site, and cluster development of housing encouraged.

- *Resource conservation areas,* mostly natural in character, in which natural areas should be preserved and further development of housing could occur at densities not exceeding one unit per 20 acres, although local governments could establish minimum lot sizes within the overall density limit; generally, no new industrial or commercial development is permitted.

After intense lobbying from developers and rural jurisdictions, the standards for resource conservation areas were relaxed to allow 5 percent of such areas adjoining other areas to be developed. Grandfathering provisions also accommodated existing projects and approved plans, and intrafamily land transfers were allowed provided the one-unit/20-acre standard was maintained.

Other criteria were spelled out for specific types of activities and areas, such as shore erosion works, forests and woodlands, wetlands, and agriculture.

The commission called for local governments to prepare plans adhering to the approved criteria and submit them for commission approval. Planning funds were provided and technical staff issued guidance papers to explain applications of the criteria. Over 18 months, commission staff worked with counties, cities, and towns to secure approval of plans. Eventually, all local plans were approved, after delays and conflicts caused by misinterpretations of the criteria and the reluctance of some jurisdictions to respond to the commission's mandates. A considerable amount of negotiation took place over the flexibility of the criteria in local applications, and the grandfathering waiver dissatisfied many program supporters as the extent of preapproved lots became known. Nevertheless, the commission succeeded in forcing local jurisdictions to account for environmental factors in planning for development; substantial preservation efforts are now in place on the shores and waters of the bay.[9]

The Chesapeake Bay critical areas program exemplifies the ways in which identification of specific natural resources over a large region, formulation of standards and criteria for preserving them, and application of those measures through a coordinated state/local governmental process can produce effective preservation results. Similar programs in other states are demonstrating that conservation planning can work.

NB

Local Planning Processes

Like Carlsbad, described earlier, many local governments adopt plans for conserving important natural features and resources as part of state and federal planning efforts. Others carve out their own approaches based on local concerns and interests. Larimer County, Colorado recently completed an open space conservation plan for the region between the cities of Loveland and Fort Collins. (See Figure 4.3.) The Larimer County Policy Plan adopted in 1977 defined the preservation of physical and visual

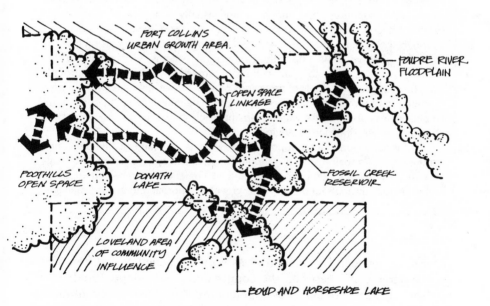

Figure 4.3

Larimer County greenbelt plan. To conserve community identity and the northern-front range landscape, Larimer County sponsored an intergovernmental planning effort to define critical open space connections and other design attributes of the region. Open space within a corridor can provide linkages as well as community separation. (From *A Plan for the Region Between Fort Collins and Loveland*, prepared for the cities of Loveland and Fort Collins and Larimer County by BHA Design, Inc., April 1995, p. 42.)

Strategies for Metropolitan Open Space

Larry Orman

How do you know when you're out of the city? For the 30 or so large metropolitan regions that are home to half of America's citizens, it's often hard to tell. And it's a growing problem, because census data shows that major metropolitan regions are urbanizing far more land per person now than was the case two decades ago. This profligacy is driven by the suburban office boom, the search by land markets for new, cheaper supplies of land, lax growth management laws and policies—and our failure to come to grips with metropolitan forces that go beyond city and county boundaries.

The toll of this renewed pressure on open lands surrounding our urban regions is huge. High-quality farmland is under serious threat, with the loss of much high-value, specialty agriculture close to urban markets. Extensive biotic systems that ensure diversity and thus health in plant and animal communities are also vulnerable. So are riparian corridors and their watershed, sites for future parks, and historic places. In many cases, these threats affect the very landscape that gives metropolitan regions their identity.

Responding to these issues one at a time is unlikely to be effective. Most open space has more than one value and usually is part of a larger system whose integrity is vital for survival. In contrast, most regions are governed through scores of local governments, each with independent decision making often at odds with the imperatives of natural systems. Our piecemeal responses over many decades fall well short of meeting challenges to metropolitan open space. Hundreds of thousands of acres are at stake, requiring a next generation of growth management solutions. The emerging techniques in the multispecies habitat conservation plan approach show promise, but it is worth looking further for broad strategies.

First is the vision that metropolitan open space—the large-scale open lands at the edge of a region's cities—should be seen as a system. This is the longstanding "greenbelt" concept originated in England and repeated in some other regions throughout the world. A greenbelt approach to growth manage-

separation between the two cities as a public policy goal. Intergovernmental agreements between the county and cities adopted in 1980 established a "rural nonfarm development area" intended to maintain that separation. Since then, both cities have continued to grow. However, believing that continued development of two-acre lots was not a satisfactory solution, a diverse group of staff and elected officials from the cities and county began working with property owners and citizens in 1988 to develop a workable strategy for preserving open space.

The plan, encompassing an area of about 77 square miles, is intended to be "outcome friendly." It provides property owners and decision mak-

ment would help integrate protection strategies for the wide range of regional open space resources. It also gives the public a simple concept to relate to—as borne out in the popularity of regional greenbelt systems in England. The power of the strategy is clear from experience in other countries.

The second strategy is securing the inner edge of a regional greenbelt, using the urban growth boundary pioneered so successfully in Oregon. The beauty of a boundary, one based on firm 20-year growth lines and compact development patterns, is its engagement of all major interests in debates about metropolitan development and conservation, which forces a mutual accounting of the variety of interests. The simplicity of the idea makes it immensely appealing to the public and easy for political leaders to accept. The 2040 regional plan in Portland, the city-by-city strategy of the Greenbelt Alliance in the San Francisco Bay area, and the new statewide planning process in the state of Washington all testify to its power.

Finally, more and more of us are coming to understand metropolitan open space as an interweaving of broad sweeps of rural landscape with webs of green inside urban areas. These "greenspace" systems provide a framework by which to relate urban creeks to often distant watersheds, link regional agriculture to the burgeoning urban gardening movement and new markets for fresh foods, highlight the importance of urban forests, and engage people low on the income scale with greening and restoration in their own neighborhoods. A metropolitan greenspace strategy aids coalition building and public education. Showing how many different open space resources link to a central concept creates a far more receptive public and more effective constituency for a full range of open space conservation.

All of these approaches require a regional strategy. Most of them require significant regional decision making (not just voluntary cooperation). That is a challenge, given the political winds of recent years, but building that regional framework is a task that will take us into the next century.

ers with specific direction on desired achievements, yet incorporates alternative choices to recognize changes in conditions over time. It includes some development in keeping with a rural landscape but retains natural and wildlife areas and corridors, views of the foothills from developed areas, and significant agricultural areas. The implementation program advocated amending the existing intergovernmental agreements to incorporate policies of the plan, amending existing regulations and policy documents of the individual jurisdictions, establishing a continuing intergovernmental framework for implementing the plan, developing a specific property acquisition strategy, establishing a transferable development rights program, and continuing liaison with affected property owners. Soon after completion, the plan was adopted by both cities and the first steps in implementation undertaken.[10]

At a much smaller scale, the town of Lincoln, Massachusetts, a community of 7710 residents covering 15 square miles, established a conservation-centered plan years ago. Growth management in Lincoln has meant a careful stewardship of the land. Families in Lincoln still own and farm land deeded to their ancestors in the days of the Massachusetts Bay Colony. With the economic stimulus of development along the Route 128 corridor since the 1960s, however, steady growth threatened to erode the town's rural character.

Lincoln's leaders have established procedures to plan, prioritize, and manage open space acquisition while allowing carefully planned development. When Lincoln adopted its first master plan in 1958, almost 40 percent of the town's land was classified as "vacant," including wetlands, a buffer zone around the local reservoir, and other open spaces. That same year, local citizens established the Lincoln Land Conservation Trust to manage open space tracts already given to the town and to solicit new donations. In 1973, the town rezoned 1200 acres to preclude development of wetlands. Three years later it adopted a new open space plan that designated 1450 acres as "land of conservation interest," and issued a prioritized list of lands it hoped to acquire or preserve in some fashion. That open space plan, updated in 1983 and 1989, remains a core working document in guiding town actions for conservation. Among other attributes, it demonstrates how Lincoln's open spaces combine into a network of connected lands that provide for ecosystem and recreational needs.

Today, the town and Land Trust together own about 1700 acres of fields, woods, trails, and wetlands. Another 375 acres in private lands are protected by conservation restrictions, largely as a result of clustered development. In addition to 180 acres of town-owned farmland, about 350 acres of farmland are preserved under a state tax abatement program. Thus, of the town's 9000 acres, over 2200 acres are conserved as a result of town actions.

In summary, planning ahead to identify open lands that should be protected is one of the most important steps in conservation. Not only does the process define targets for subsequent conservation actions, but it helps to organize constituencies that can assist in conservation efforts.

Conservation Implementation Techniques

Communities and environmental organizations have used various forms of land acquisition and regulatory approaches to accomplish conservation. Often a number of techniques are used in combination. Specific techniques are selected in keeping with the community's resources and objectives.

Land Acquisition

Acquisition of land is the most certain means of preserving the land's environmental and open space attributes for future generations. The most direct and often-used means of acquisition is outright purchase of "fee simple" ownership by governments or by nonprofit groups that will hold it in trust for conservation purposes. Federal and state parks, wildlife refuges, wilderness areas, forests, and similar areas are acquired in this manner. A new federal program managed by the U.S. Department of Agriculture is providing $14.5 million in 1996 to organizations and local governments for acquisition of easements to protect farmland.

In addition, many states have voted new taxes or earmarked selected revenues to acquire lands for conservation. Nevada voters, for example, approved a parks and wildlife bond act in 1990 that would generate $47.2 million for land acquisition. Arizona and Colorado both use lottery proceeds for acquisition of conservation areas. In 1992, Alabama voters approved establishment of the Alabama Forever Wild Land Trust, a 30-year land acquisition and stewardship program using revenues from oil and gas funds.[11]

Governmental purchases often are augmented by lands acquired by environmental organizations, who leverage targeted purchases with donated lands. Over 1000 land trust organizations have been formed throughout the nation to hold donated or purchased land and easements for conservation purposes. Perhaps the best known organization is The Nature Conservancy (TNC), an international nonprofit group, which owns more than 1300 nature preserves throughout the world as of 1992. Almost half of the 6.3 million acres it protects in the United States were preserved in cooperation with federal, state, and local government agencies.[12] TNC and other similar organizations can act quickly to purchase options, obtain appraisals, or acquire properties in advance of governments' abilities. TNC negotiated a recent transaction, for example, to acquire a 3835-acre glacial bog in the Poconos wetlands area of Pennsylvania, with subsequent sale to the Pennsylvania Game Commission paid by federal funds over a two-year period.[13]

The Trust for Public Land, the Land Trust Exchange, and the Land Trust Alliance are other major organizations that form partnerships with public agencies to protect land and create parks. The Trust for Public Land, for example, negotiated an option on a 15-acre wooded property that harbors migrating birds near Provincetown on Cape Cod. Then the Trust worked with a grassroots citizens' group to promote Provincetown's decision to acquire the land for conservation. The Trust is assisting the town with an application for state funds and is raising additional funds privately.[14] At another level altogether, The Nature Conservancy of California, a regional branch of the international Nature Conservancy organization, is managing preservation and restoration of 17,000 acres of wildlife habitat in the Irvine Company's Open Space Reserve in Orange County.[15] Such nonprofit groups and their professional staffs provide valuable ways and means for engineering conservation agreements.

Local governments frequently pursue their own acquisition strategies to manage growth. Citizens in Boulder, Colorado, for example, voted in 1967 to levy a special sales tax of 0.4 percent to acquire mountain land around the city, hoping to retain its distinctive setting. By 1992, the city had acquired over 22,000 acres of open space with $59 million in revenues from bond issues secured by the tax. Some of the land is used for recreation and adjoins to mountain parks owned by the city and county. Other land is leased to farmers. Altogether, the open space acquisition program, combined with Boulder's "blue line" limit on development above a certain elevation, has created a virtual greenbelt around the city. The city's experience testifies to the power of a long-term acquisition program based on a relatively small tax.

Sarasota County, Florida, whose establishment of a growth boundary was described in Chapter 3, reinforced its constraints on rural development outside the boundary by acquiring thousands of acres to protect its major water supply aquifer. These lands, added to a state-owned park of 19,000 acres, will ensure preservation of a significant amount of open space in the county.

In Scottsdale, Arizona a citizens task force recommended, and the city established by resolution in 1994, the McDowell Sonoran Preserve. This act was followed in 1995 by a citywide vote to raise the local sales tax from 1.2 to 1.4 percent to raise funds for acquisition of 4000 acres of open space land in the preserve. A study is now being conducted to determine a means of funding required capital improvements, management, and maintenance of the acquired lands.

Local governments in most states also can establish special authorities with their own taxing powers to acquire and manage parks and other open spaces. The extensive forest preserve system in the Chicago region, for example, is managed by county authorities in Cooke and its surrounding counties. The authorities use earmarked increments of property taxes to acquire open lands and manage them for recreational and conservation purposes. Montgomery County, Maryland is part of the bicounty Maryland–National Capital Park and Planning Commission charged with expanding and operating all types of parks and recreational spaces. The commission has aggressively pursued an acquisition program to preserve large acreages for parks, wildlife refuges, and similar open spaces in the northern part of the county to assist in preserving its rural character.

Because outright acquisition of conservation land can be expensive, sometimes only certain rights are acquired. Easements may be purchased to allow use for certain purposes, such as passage over property for hiking trails. Development rights can also be acquired to prevent future development. Based on the legal division of property ownership into a bundle of rights, purchase of development rights from a certain property permanently removes the right to develop it. The price for development rights is significantly smaller than for all the property rights, and thus is an increasingly popular answer to needs for reducing development in conservation areas.

As an example, Anne Arundel County, Maryland initiated a program to purchase development rights from property owners in its agricultural preservation area. Once a rural area of scattered settlements oriented to its extensive Chesapeake Bay waterfront, with the colonial city of Annapolis its only urban center, Anne Arundel County has grown rapidly in recent decades as a suburb of both Washington, D.C. and Baltimore. In 1995 its population had reached 460,000. To retain a valued part of its rural character, the county's 1978 general plan established an agricultural preservation area in the southern half of the county, some 95,000 acres, and adopted zoning in 1981 to implement the plan.

The county's acquisition of development rights compensates owners for restrictions on development and supplements a statewide rights-purchase program. Funded by a state tax on property transfers, the program provides annual grants to counties for purchase of development rights in areas identified for conservation or agricultural preservation. (A similar approach, transferable development rights, is described in a later section of this chapter.) Another method sometimes used by land trust organizations is to work out agreements with property owners for long-term leases or rights to manage land for certain purposes. Environmental organizations also avidly seek donations of land, negotiating beneficial tax positions as incentives.

Regulatory Approaches

A number of regulatory approaches can reduce the impacts of development on rural areas targeted for conservation and preservation of open space, including subdivision exactions, impact fees, clustering and limited-development incentives, large-lot requirements, transferable development rights, and mitigation banks.[16]

Subdivision Exactions. Probably the most-used regulatory approach to preserving open space are requirements or incentives for conservation incorporated in subdivision regulations. These provisions require developers to set aside sensitive lands and features such as stream valleys, steep hillsides, wetlands, and floodplains. Typical provisions, for example, might require a 50-foot setback of developed land (or buffer) from a stream bed or wetlands, or prohibit development on hillside slopes that exceed 15 percent. Sometimes developers are allowed to build higher densities in return for those set-asides, sometimes not. The reserved lands are either assigned for management by a community association or dedicated to the jurisdiction. The "common" lands owned by the community association are understood to add value to the entire development. If conservation lands are required to be dedicated for public use, key issues are the magnitude of the lands involved or their intended public use. Developers can claim that they are unfairly burdened by public requirements, as evidenced by the many "takings" cases that have won attention in recent years. (See Chapter 2 for a discussion of these legal issues.)

Attempting to restrict development, Scottsdale, Arizona experienced these problems firsthand in the distinctive Sonoran Mountains in the city. With the city's tremendous expansion in recent years, the issue of mountain and desert preservation mounted in significance. In 1977 when the edge of development reached past the Central Arizona Project canal, once considered remote, to the McDowell Mountains, Scottsdale enacted a hillside protection ordinance to prevent development of the higher parts of the mountains. Landowners litigated, however, and in 1988 the Arizona Supreme Court ruled that landowners in the hillside district must be allowed some use of their properties.

In response, the city enacted the "Environmentally Sensitive Lands Ordinance" in 1991. The ordinance, based on zoning rather than subdivision regulations, established an overlay district for a 134 square-mile area in North Scottsdale. The zoning provisions imposed a sliding scale of development densities on slopes of 25 percent or greater, unstable slopes and soils, desert wash areas, unique natural landmarks, and exposed rocks. The lowest required density is one unit per 40 acres on slopes over 35 percent or unstable slopes. In addition, the regulations required set-asides of open space. Required open-space ranges from 20 percent on relatively flat terrain up to 80 percent on steep hillsides and even 95 percent on unstable slopes. The ordinance provides incentives to locate development in the most suitable areas, including density transfers and clustering development to retain open space. To avoid preventing development on existing lots, owners are entitled to build at least one single-family home.

Another form of exactions are _impact fees, paid by developers to offset impacts on community facilities,_ usually outside the specific development site. Such fees are often used to acquire large community parks that would not be appropriately located within a specific development. (Impact fees are more fully explained in Chapter 5, on infrastructure.) A few jurisdictions are levying impact fees, however, to acquire conservation lands. Riverside County, California, for example, levies an impact fee on all development to provide funds for acquiring wildlife habitats.

Clustering Development. For decades, planners, builders, and developers have united in promoting clustered development as a means of conserving natural resources as well as reducing infrastructure costs. Clustered development allows developers to plat smaller than standard lots on one part of a site to save the remainder of the site for permanent open space. The conserved area then may be used for common recreation space or protecting environmentally sensitive lands and/or agricultural uses. Generally, cluster provisions are written to allow the overall amount of development permitted on the entire tract to be concentrated in one area. In addition, clustering provisions often allow mixtures of housing types that offer more choices for living styles than standard subdivisions. In some cases, incentives to clustering permit more housing than would otherwise be allowed. Figure 4.4 compares clustered and nonclustered developments.

Clustered development provides an alternative to typical zoning and subdivision requirements for traditional lots with generous setbacks, side yards, and rear yards. Such conventional approaches to land development consume a great deal of land; rarely respect terrain variations, existing vegetation, and other natural features; and require lengthy streets and utility lines to serve each lot. Clustering is a less costly form of development. A study by the National Association of Home Builders in 1976 demonstrated that a clustered development with a variety of housing types was one-third less costly per unit than conventional subdivisions.[17]

Clustering, however, has a poor reputation in some communities because it places homes close together with smaller yards than in conventional subdivisions. If not well designed, these concentrations can be unsightly. In addition, some people object to small yards as virtually un-American; clustering in many communities is opposed by residents fearful of any form of development other than single-family detached houses on large lots. In 1973, Duxbury, Massachusetts, a small town on the coast south of Boston, adopted a new bylaw allowing cluster subdivisions. The bylaw required substantial reservations of open space in return for smaller lots. A special permit involving a negotiated site plan was required. Over a period of 10 years, during which most development willingly employed the optional approval process, the town's boards grew more and more finicky about design details, reflecting their unhappiness with completed projects. Eventually the approval process proved so

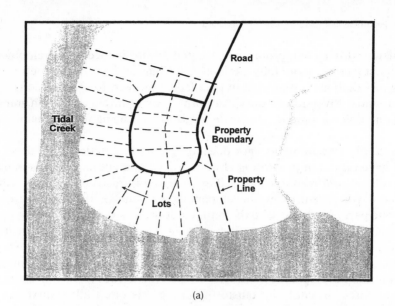

(a)

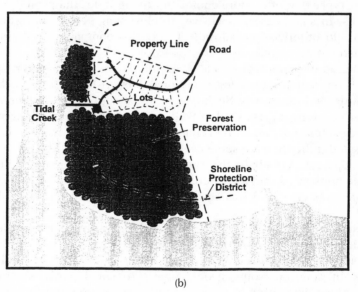

(b)

Figure 4.4

Cluster and noncluster housing comparison. The principle of clustered or limited development is depicted in this comparison of (a) a typical lot subdivision
in a waterfront area developed under conventional subdivision and zoning ordinances, and (b) a lot design that conserves both forested and shoreline areas
by using a cluster development plan. (From *Blueprint to Protect Coastal Water
Quality, A Guide to Successful Growth Management in the Coastal Region of
North Carolina*, prepared by the Center for Watershed Protection and Land
Ethics, Inc. for the Neuse River Council of Governments, 1995.)

time-consuming that developers reverted to building standard subdivisions.

Duxbury's experience demonstrates the ways in which clustering can prove troublesome. Due to the need to carefully review design characteristics of clustered housing, the approval process is less certain than for conventional subdivisions and can be quite lengthy, both of which increase development costs. In addition, the open spaces preserved in individual projects do not necessarily connect into an open space system that can optimize conservation and recreational benefits. The individual reservations in Duxbury subdivisions were left to small community associations to manage and were generally ignored. Clustering, to be most effective, should preserve spaces that are linked into a common network of open space.

Lincoln, Massachusetts managed to make those connections. Its conservation plan described earlier in this chapter functioned as a coordinating device for determining appropriate reservations of open space. The town also took a proactive role by approaching landowners before they were ready to sell or develop to work out ways to preserve open space. Sometimes this was accomplished by preserving entire tracts and other times through clustering development or promoting multifamily housing. In that way, says Robert Lemire, the chief local proponent for Lincoln's approach, "Lincoln has forged a relationship with its landowners" to accomplish compatible objectives, rather than alienate them.[18]

The town's efforts began in 1966, when a 109-acre colonial-era farm went on the market and town officials realized that they lacked the $300,000 purchase price to retain it as open space. Several citizens saved the day by forming the Rural Land Foundation, which purchased the property with a large bank loan (secured by $10,000 guarantees from 30 residents). The Foundation commissioned a development plan designed to preserve half the property, and then sold two existing houses and eight additional lots, deeded 56 acres to the Land Trust, and cleared $40,000 to be used in future endeavors. This hands-on action by concerned citizens has remained a hallmark of the Lincoln approach to growth management.

When several large tracts came on the market in the 1970s, town leaders sought ways to prevent sprawl without requiring town acquisition of open space. In 1971, they adopted the Open Space Residential District, which provided a two-for-one density bonus if the property owner left at least 70 percent of the property undeveloped. Initially aimed at a 100-acre tract slated for 40 single-family houses, the bylaw enabled the owner to build 80 condominium units on only 24 acres, requiring only a single road maintained by the condominium association. A year later, another property received an even larger density bonus in return for an assurance that half the units would be set aside for low- and moderate-income families. Part of the open space preserved on that tract is now a working farm managed by a civic organization.[19]

The clustering concept also can be employed at a larger scale to conserve land. The Bucks County, Pennsylvania planning commission, for instance, published model zoning provisions to promote clustered development in 1973. Over half the county's townships have adopted variations of the provisions, which has led to development of many clustered subdivisions throughout the county.[20] Calvert County, Maryland, which at one time promoted clustering as an option for conserving forests and farmlands in rural areas, recently mandated clustering in much of the county. In areas designated as Resource Preservation districts and Farm Community districts, 80 percent and 60 percent, respectively, of sites proposed for development must be set aside as preserved open space, with clustered development permitted on the remainder.

Some environmental organizations have appropriated the cluster concept to provide a means of financing conservation of valuable natural features—the *limited development* approach to conservation. Having acquired conservation land, they parcel off a small part of it for sale to people desiring to live in a natural environment. Proceeds from the lot sales help pay for the property. The Nature Conservancy, for example, helped form the Virginia Coast Reserve, a sanctuary that now includes 45,000 acres of beaches, marshes, and seaside farmland. With funding from foundations, corporations, local banks, and individuals, the corporation promotes acquisition of farm and village properties on the eastern shore, designs conservation easements to protect the watershed, and leases or resells properties to conservation-minded buyers. Rather than carve up acreage into 5- or 10-acre lots, the farms are held intact and residential lots are clustered.[21]

The clustering concept has been reinvigorated in recent years by proponents of *neotraditionalism* in development, also called "new urbanism." Urban designers such as Andres Duany and Peter Calthorpe have attracted wide attention throughout the nation with their calls for focusing development in more concentrated forms. Although they propound specific site and building designs, such as grid street patterns and pedestrian-friendly building relationships, their concepts employ clustering as a major theme for building urban villages and new towns. Such development forms inherently save land for conservation purposes.

Large-Lot Zoning. Communities intent on conserving open space can impose zoning that requires minimum lot sizes so large as to discourage development. Such zoning also is accompanied by provisions that permit only rural uses such as agriculture, forestry, and related development. Particularly if combined with delineations of growth boundaries or designated development areas, described in Chapter 3, large-lot zoning can effectively deter development for many years.

To provide a sufficient deterrent, lot sizes must be set large enough to make their purchase for residential use too expensive for most homeowners. Clearly, land prices depend on local land markets and pressures for development, and thus the appropriate minimum lot size will vary from place to place. Outside Portland, Oregon minimum lot sizes are five or more acres. Lexington/Fayette County, Kentucky precludes most development by requiring minimum lots of 10 acres. Montgomery County, Maryland requires 25-acre lots in its farmland preservation area; and Baltimore County, Maryland zones for minimum lots of 60 acres in its rural area. The agricultural zoning district in McHenry County, Illinois requires 160-acre lots.

Anne Arundel County, Maryland is one of several counties in that state that have established an agricultural preservation district. The zoning provisions in the district required lot sizes of at least 20 acres for areas of prime soils and limited the amount of development on nonprime soils to one-third of the site acreage. Unfortunately, development on nonprime soils became rather significant in subsequent years, especially for high-priced housing in subdivisions near major highways.

The 1986 plan revisions upgraded the policy on agricultural preservation, announcing that "the county will treat agricultural and forest land as an equal or preferred land use rather than as a temporary or residential use. . . ." Implementing that policy, the 1989 comprehensive rezoning retained 88,000 acres in rural zoning and abolished the development option for nonprime soils. The county's master water and sewer plan projects no extensions of service to these areas. In addition, the county adopted an easement purchase program to acquire development rights from farmlands and woodlands, designed to complement a similar state-funded program. The regulations issued in 1991 for purchasing easements established criteria for determining priorities for land acquisition. A tax credit program was also established to reduce property taxes on land enrolled as a county or state agricultural district for at least 10 years.

Anne Arundel County's program thus announces a firm preservation policy in its county plan, backs it up with restrictive zoning, and provides compensatory relief in the form of purchase of development rights and tax credits—a powerful combination of incentives. The results show up in several ways. From 1966 to 1993, the county reduced the area scheduled to be served by public sewer systems from 86 percent to 41 percent of the county's land area. From 1988 to 1994, 91 percent of the new building lots created in the county were located in planned development areas served by public sewers.

Less ambitious approaches to conservation are unlikely to be effective. In particular, local officials hoping to forestall development by zoning for one- to five-acre lots most often are whistling in the wind. Such lot sizes, carrying attractive prices geared to low development costs, frequently promote wide-scale development rather than discourage it. Crossing the urban service boundary in the Minneapolis/St. Paul area, for example, one finds somewhat larger lots but little diminution in development taking place. Development on those lots also occupies a great deal of land. In Charles County, Maryland, on the rapidly growing edge of the Washington, D.C. region, less than 25 percent of the county's growth is taking place on one- to three-acre lots in farm and forest lands outside its designated development area. Over the next 25 years, however, that rural growth is expected to swallow up some 25,000 acres (about 39 square miles). That acreage amounts to 50 percent more than the land expected to be consumed by three times the amount of development inside the designated area.[22]

Unfortunately, mid-size lots are viewed by many people as a very desirable form of development. In a highly contentious clamor over growth during the mid-1990s, for example, residents of communities in the fast-growing northern sector of the Phoenix, Arizona metropolitan area demanded retention of one-acre and larger minimum lot sizes to "preserve the desert environment" from more concentrated developments proposed by developers. Such low-density development clearly would inflict greater damage on the desert environment than compact development, but citizen opponents of the development appeared more interested in preserving what they regarded as a desirable way of life than in desert conservation.

Concentrating Rural Development. Another means of conserving rural lands, whether for agriculture, environmental protection, or simply open space, is by taking steps to concentrate future development in and around existing settlements. Crossroads communities, villages, even small towns can coexist within conservation areas if properly planned and developed. Some local governments have adopted plans and zoning that encourage any development in rural areas to locate in areas adjoining already built-up areas. This policy has the double effect of reducing development impacts on conservation areas and improving the critical mass of development in some areas to make some urban services, such as transit, feasible. Adherents of neotraditional development are very supportive of this type of development, as it closely corresponds to their concept of compact urban development.

Loudoun County, Virginia, for example, adopted a comprehensive plan in 1991 that called for retention of rural qualities in much of the county.[23] Plan policies discourage extension of water and sewer lines to rural areas and promote clustered residential development in rural villages and hamlets. These policies are to be implemented through application of rural design guidelines, rural subdivision options that encourage clustering, acquisition of open space easements, density transfers, and use-value assessments for farmland. Rural villages with a minimum area of 300 acres, for example, can be developed for 100 to 300 dwelling units, plus some community-oriented retail and office space, on 20 percent of the area, leaving the remainder in an open space conservancy. The county subsequently adopted new zoning provisions permitting neotraditional development districts, use of performance standards, and overlay districts to protect natural resources. Although some use has been made of these policies and provisions, most development continues to follow conventional designs and densities.

The principal problem confronted by public officials in promoting concentrations of development in rural areas is that it restricts potential development of most properties in rural areas while rewarding owners of property in and adjoining existing settlements. Compensatory techniques, discussed below, can help to overcome that obstacle.

Transfer of Development Rights. Programs that promote the transfer of development rights (TDRs) from one area or building to another have been employed in a number of communities. By allowing sale and transfer to other properties of valuable development rights, the concept provides a means of compensating owners for regulatory restrictions that reduce property values. First used to preserve historic properties in central business districts, the concept allows developers to purchase development rights from a property owner and move them to another building or site. The famous U.S. Supreme Court case, *Penn Central Transportation Co. v. City of New York,* 438 U.S. 104, 124 (1978), for example, which upheld the City of New York's disapproval of construction of an office tower over Grand Central Terminal, hinged at least in part, on the city's permission for the developer to transfer unused air rights to other properties.

Applied to areas rather than buildings, the usual TDR approach requires identification of "sending" areas—those in which property owners may sell development rights—and "receiving areas"—areas to which development rights may be transferred. As a result of transferring rights, property owners in receiving areas can increase densities of development on their properties. Thus the sale and transfer of development rights becomes a market transaction promoted and supported by a regulatory program. The sale of rights is recorded in property deeds, and the transfer is recorded through a certification by the local jurisdiction.

TDR programs have been used to protect the purity of Lake Tahoe in California and Nevada, by transferring rights from hillside second-home lots to in-town commercial development, and to protect fragile ecosystems in the New Jersey Pine Barrens by transferring rights from conservation areas to in-town properties. (See Chapter 8 for discussions of these regional programs.) Some local governments in Florida and other places have also adopted TDR programs.

By far the most experience with TDR programs has occurred in Maryland. As of 1994, 10 Maryland counties and one city have adopted some form of TDR. Montgomery County, Maryland, whose agricultural preservation program was introduced in Chapter 2, probably has the best-known transferable development rights program in the United States. Initiated in 1980, it has protected over 32,000 acres of farmland in the northern third of the county. Development rights purchased by developers have been transferred to older areas such as Silver Spring in the southern part of the county and in developing areas such as Olney in the central part of the county. Calvert County, whose clustering requirements were referenced in a previous section, also has promoted transfer of development rights. Begun in 1978 before Montgomery County's program, it has protected 4000 acres of agricultural land and its use continues today.[24]

Although an enduring topic of interest among planners, TDR programs pose notoriously complex administrative problems, which accounts for their rather limited use. Robert H. Freilich, a noted land use attorney, phrased it nicely by his comment that "the TDR approach has commonly been viewed as a conceptual all-star but a practical loser. . . ."[25] As knowledge of existing programs has spread, however, growth managers have become more familiar with the concept. Also, because legal concerns for providing compensatory mechanisms related to regulatory restrictions have mounted over the years, TDRs are being considered seriously in many communities.

A variation on transfer of development rights calls for *transfer of conservation credits* from developing properties to conservation areas. A version of this approach is employed in Dade and Broward counties in Florida by the South Florida Management District. The District negotiates off-site mitigation of conservation requirements for development projects. The approach is not unlike provisions in many communities' subdivision regulations that require or allow payment of fees in lieu of reserving parklands within a subdivision site. The park fees are pooled by local governments to provide funds for acquisition of properties in more suitable park locations. In many respects, the concept also parallels the concept of mitigation banks, discussed in the next section.

Another variation on the TDR concept allows density transfers among adjoining properties to either provide more flexibility in planning devel-

Transferable Development Rights in the Long Island Pine Barrens

James Nicholas

Suffolk County, New York occupies the eastern half of Long Island east of New York City. For many years the county has been promoting the maintenance of active farming. County citizens approved a $24-million bond issue that provided funding for purchasing development rights from active farms. An average of $2000 per acre was paid for those rights over several years.

Recently, the county mounted a campaign to preserve the Pine Barrens, a large natural area running through the center of Long Island. Similar in many respects to New Jersey's Pine Barrens, this area constitutes the recharge area for a critical aquifer that is the sole source of potable water for over half a million residents. Preservation of the Pine Barrens would be much more costly than the farmland preservation program. Moreover, the conservative fiscal policies of recent years prohibited a further request to voters for issuance of bonded debt.

Suffolk County turned to transferable development rights (TDR) as a better solution. Of hundreds of TDR programs considered, perhaps four or five have prospered. The Suffolk County program, however, was designed to avoid the major obstacle of most TDR programs, the principle of use by right, by creating Pine Barrens Credits. The three municipalities participating in the program designated receiving areas in which the credits were established as uses by right, needing no extraordinary approval actions. The towns also provided an option for developers to propose use of credits in support of a rezoning petition.

Suffolk County Pine Barrens Credits were estimated to command prices of $12,000 to $24,000, depending on location. If realized, these prices will be some of the most valuable TDRs ever created. To assist in establishing a price level, a Pine Barrens Credit Clearing House was formed to purchase credits from property owners, although the prices offered will be below anticipated market prices to encourage operation of a private market in credits. If successful, this program will preserve the environmentally significant Pine Barrens at little public cost while respecting the financial and property interests of owners.

opment for specific sites or to promote concentrations of development in rural areas.

Mitigation Banks. When development adversely impacts environmentally sensitive land (particularly wetlands, but in some cases wildlife habitats), government agencies often require mitigation of those impacts either on the site or off it. "Mitigation," as defined by the Council of Environmental Quality, includes avoiding or minimizing development impacts, repairing impacts, reducing or eliminating adverse effects over time, or compensating for impacts by replacing them elsewhere. In the latter case, it quickly became clear that finding, financing, perhaps improving or restoring, and managing replaced resources was time-consuming and expensive for individual project developers, whether public or private. A common "bank" of land that could pool a number of project mitigation needs was a more efficient and even more environmentally effective way to satisfy such requirements.

Typically, mitigation banks are formed by public agencies and large corporations whose operations require occasional intrusions on environmentally sensitive lands. (State transportation agencies, for example, are common users.) They identify and acquire a large site with characteristics similar to those being threatened in other areas—an existing wetlands, for example, especially one already threatened and requiring protection and restoration. The wetland is restored and a management and maintenance program put in place. The values of the restored wetland are quantified as "credits" that can later be withdrawn, at a price, to compensate for unavoidable wetland losses elsewhere.

Two variations on this scenario include entrepreneurial banks established by private landowners or investors to sell market credits to whomever needs them, and joint projects formed by groups of developers who need to compensate for wetland or habitat losses on their project sites.[26]

The mitigation bank idea is one that could be applied, as in Miami and Dade counties, to regional open space and conservation needs. Developers would pay "in-lieu" fees to compensate for using open space in designated growth areas, which would then be used to acquire development rights in areas to be conserved. Such a process could be established by a county, regional agency, recreation district, or other entity with jurisdiction over a fairly large area in which both urbanization and conservation are desirable.

Conclusion

Defining "where not to grow" is an essential element of growth management. In addition to protecting valuable natural resources that might be adversely affected by development, conservation techniques prevent premature development in rural areas and reinforce policies for directing growth to desirable development areas that can be efficiently served by public facilities.

An important initial step in conservation efforts is identifying existing resources and evaluating their significance for sustaining community ecosystems, based on criteria on which there is general consensus. Some of these criteria are established by federal and state environmental laws; some reflect local attitudes and desires, as evidenced in the Scottsdale, Arizona program for hillside preservation. The value of understanding and carefully shaping conservation objectives is demonstrated in the experiences of Lincoln, Massachusetts; Maricopa County, Arizona; and the Chesapeake Bay Commission of Maryland.

At some point, conservation objectives must be considered in relation to economic and social objectives, which may require trade-offs and compromises. The planning process for determining development in keeping with protection of wildlife habitats in Carlsbad, California provides an example of multistakeholder consensus building that is being widely applied elsewhere as well. (Other processes for reaching agreement on multiple objectives are described in Chapter 9.)

Once the goals of conservation efforts have been defined, a battery of potential approaches to protecting resources can be employed. Some of the community and regional experiences recounted in this chapter show how a variety—and usually a combination—of acquisition and regulatory techniques has been effective in many areas.[27]

To close this chapter, a few words from Aldo Leopold, writing in 1934 on the subject of conservation as a matter of both public and individual interest:

> [C]onservation will ultimately boil down to rewarding the private landowner who conserves the public interest. It asserts the new premise that if he fails to do so, his neighbors must ultimately pay the bill. It pleads that our jurists and economists anticipate the need for workable vehicles to carry that reward. It challenges the efficacy of single-track land laws, and the economy of buying wrecks instead of preventing them. It advances all these things . . . out of a profound conviction that the public is at last ready to do something about the land problem. . . .[28]

5

Managing Development of Infrastructure

Into the 1960s, the county commissioners of Sarasota County, Florida paid little attention to growth issues and related infrastructure needs. Although rapid development was taking place along the coast, most of it was centered in the barrier islands and the two principal towns, Sarasota and Venice. The county government, dominated by rural interests, steadfastly refused to enter into the infrastructure business, hoping that the low level of public facilities would discourage development.

Development continued, however, spilling over town boundaries into unincorporated areas. The towns decided to forego annexation. By the early 1980s, indulging in piecemeal responses to growing pressures for supportive infrastructure, the county had granted franchises for 49 water supply systems and 115 separate wastewater treatment plants, issued permits for over 45,000 septic tanks, and approved establishment of drainage districts that constructed over 800 miles of drainage canals.

At that point, the county commissioners began to take a greater interest in the provision of public facilities, prompted by clear signals that the cities of Sarasota and Venice had no intentions of expanding their systems. During the remainder of the decade, the county took impressive steps to improve its management of infrastructure systems. The county

- determined to acquire all existing wastewater treatment systems over time and unite them into a workable regional system, to gradually phase out old treatment plants and build two regional plants;

- established five solid-waste service districts to finance waste collection and disposal, and acquired land for landfill sites;

- acquired another large tract to conserve potential water production sites and to extend a water supply system throughout the southern part of the county;

- received voter authorization in 1989 for a one-cent sales tax to overcome existing deficiencies on county roads and other facilities;

- prepared a stormwater management plan to reduce the amount of runoff and improve its quality, and established a stormwater utility to raise revenues to improve stormwater management; and

- absorbed existing Sarasota and Venice parks and recreation areas into a countywide park system and stepped up acquisition of new parks.

In addition to these forthright steps to grasp responsibility for infrastructure development, the county began in 1981 to prepare and follow five-year capital improvement programs that identified future needs, determined priorities and scheduling, and defined expected funding sources. Beginning in 1989, in response to the 1985 state growth management act, the capital improvement program became a vital part of the county's growth management program, keying public investments in infrastructure to requirements for adequate facilities to support expected growth. Along the way, the county government had become a key player in the local development process.

Sarasota County's experience is not unique. Citizens and public officials in many growing communities have refused to recognize the consequences of growth until it has overtaken them. Like Sarasota County, they hope to avoid responsibilities for planning and financing costly infrastructure systems. They play for time, believing that the issue might fade away. Only after a long period of temporizing with incremental "fixes" to tide them over until the next crisis do they accept responsibility for supporting growth with adequate, efficient systems of basic facilities.

Once officials in Sarasota County accepted that responsibility, they moved with admirable firmness to put their house in order. Led by county officials armed with firm plans, citizens voted one bond issue after another to retrofit existing development with new sewer, water, and road systems capable of extensions to serve new development. The commissioners reorganized county government to systematically plan and deliver public services. They made the capital facilities program, based on the comprehensive plan, the keystone of the county's budgeting for capital investments. Within a decade, they brought order to chaos and established a management process capable of supporting development well into the next century.

It is fair to say that infrastructure issues lie at the heart of most local governments' growth management programs. Concerns about efficient provision of costly public facilities provoke local officials to consider growth limits, growth boundaries, restrictions on rural development, and other management techniques. Community growth problems most often surface in the public consciousness as shortfalls in public facilities—congested streets and highways, overcrowded schools, deficient water supplies, and failing sewage treatment plants. These problems directly affect the daily lives of citizens, who clamor for instant solutions that frequently are impossible to deliver. Infrastructure issues loom large on the public agendas of most communities.

A Complexity of Responsibilities for Service Delivery

Over centuries, public officials invented a host of approaches to supplying public facilities. Based on the varied locational demands and physical character of the facilities themselves, and the funding and operational options for delivering their services, officials are offered many choices for determining specific responsibilities for planning, financing, and managing fundamental public services. Their decisions reflect several considerations:

- The significance of the facility for sustaining the health, safety, and welfare of community residents and workers; public education is usually viewed as a fundamental necessity, for example, while public golf courses may be considered an optional amenity.

- The efficiency of service delivery through large linked systems (e.g., sewer and water systems) common to all or through individual facilities (e.g., libraries, airports) more customized for individual needs.

- The ability to assign service costs incrementally to users, such as through metered water use, or as a common financial responsibility, such as a city hall building or a zoo.

- The size and complexity of the facility or system, which may require lengthy periods for design and construction (e.g., a sewage treatment plant) or be readily available (e.g., a police car).

The entities given responsibility for delivering specific services may be local public-works agencies (that build and maintain roads, for example), authorities functioning as arms of local governments (that manage water and sewer systems, for example), independent authorities or districts operating within one jurisdiction or across many (such as airport and transit authorities and commissions), and state agencies (such as transportation and health departments) that plan, fund, or regulate facility development.

Depending on the choices made, community residents may obtain water through individual wells, small community-scale treatment and distribution systems, or regional systems encompassing remote dams and reservoirs and lengthy pipelines. Citizens may drive on local roads built almost entirely by developers, higher-volume highways built by state and local governments, high-speed highways financed mostly by the federal government, or toll roads constructed and managed by public authorities or even private companies. Residents may send their children to nearby public schools or have them bussed long distances to consolidated schools, enroll them in private schools, or send them away to public or private institutions.

Each of these modes may involve different assignments for planning to meet future needs, securing financing, facility construction, and operational management. Responsibilities may be split among local, state, and federal governments, special authorities, and private companies; the relative sharing of responsibilities is constantly shifting.

The roles of public and private sectors in providing infrastructure, for example, have changed considerably over the years. At one time, it was not unusual for private companies to build toll roads and bridges or operate water-supply systems. Now major road systems are almost entirely a governmental responsibility. Before World War II, many local governments assumed responsibility for financing roads, sidewalks, and other facilities in new subdivisions. Since the war, developers are increasingly required to provide basic facilities in new subdivisions and often special amenities as well. Water and sewer authorities that once readily extended service to developing areas as an opportunity to broaden their markets now charge fees to pay for construction.

As these relationships evolve over time, every community acquires a distinctive approach to providing services that affects its ability to manage growth.

Managing Growth by Managing Infrastructure

For local governments to manage growth, they must possess substantial control over the delivery of public facilities and services to their residents. As the commissioners of Sarasota County learned, the location, quality, and timing of public facility construction is a major determinant in shaping the direction and character of community development. The popular view that new roads and sewers stimulate development is not entirely wrong. All too frequently communities open up new territories for development simply by extending key facilities. For homebuilders looking for desirable building sites or commercial developers selecting locations for shopping centers, available capacity in public facilities is a strong attraction.

The quality of facilities is also a factor. Sarasota County's officials understood that 115 sewage treatment plants and 45,000 septic tanks in a region known for a high water table could not sustain desirable development. Parents of school children know that a school system known for quality can boost home prices by a considerable amount. Developers planning large-scale residential projects can calculate in advance the price premiums that can be demanded for property near conservation areas, parks, and recreational amenities. The quantity and quality of water supply can be a major factor in attracting certain types of industries.

Local governments can control their future development, therefore, by directly managing the development of principal infrastructure systems or finding ways to influence the supply and quality of facilities. Typically they set standards for local roads, for example, and assert their interests in state and regional decisions on highway improvements. They operate water and sewer systems, often through special authorities controlled by local elected officials, or insist on approval of water and sewer development plans proposed by separate special districts. They require developers to abide by standards and plans for parks and open spaces. Communities that cannot influence the provision of basic facilities lack an essential tool for managing growth

In Tracy, California, the city manager and formerly its planning director, Michael Locke, saw the handwriting on the wall in the early 1980s. Tracy, a town of 15,000 residents in the farming region of the San Juaquin Valley, was feeling the first pressures of development emanating from the expanding San Francisco economy. Locke was determined to ensure that oncoming growth would not overwhelm the town's services.

As part of the updating of Tracy's general plan in 1982, city officials decided to manage the city's future expansion by using specific plans. California statutes allow preparation of detailed development plans and related zoning provisions for specific properties or groups of properties, which then are incorporated in the jurisdiction's general plan and zoning ordinance. The city targeted 27 parcels on the outskirts of town, 2140 acres in all, for future urban expansion and subsequently annexed the properties. Two specific plans were prepared, one for residential areas and one for industrial areas. A major concern of the specific plan process was to "provide a strategy for constructing essential public improvements," in the words of the residential plan (p. 1-1).

Each specific plan defines permitted uses and densities, provides design guidelines, and identifies needed public facility improvements and standards for their development. The residential plan meshed development of about 7500 new dwelling units with existing development and identified sites for schools and parks. The industrial plan proposed expansion of industrial, office, and warehousing uses. Financing programs were prepared to address all anticipated construction of public facilities to serve the new development. The programs outlined the financing mechanisms for funding each type of improvement and summarized funding by type of improvement for each year of the expected eight-year construction process. A more detailed financing plan listed specific improvements, their estimated costs, and their phasing.

Thus each parcel owner in the specific plan areas could determine the amount and type of development permitted on his or her property, associated needs and timing for public facility construction, and cost-sharing plans for funding construction. The plans allowed developers to advance the schedule by funding facilities and being repaid when capital funding became available as scheduled.

Although Tracy's program has been modified and stretched out in response to the abrupt decline in California building since the early 1990s, it continues to guide the development process and is being adapted for use in additional planned town expansion.

Tracy's determination to apply positive public management approaches in responding to rapid community expansion demonstrates how local officials can meet increasing needs for public facilities. In formulating comprehensive plans, they make decisions about future directions of development and standards for the amount and quality of desired facilities. More detailed functional plans may be drawn up for specific types of facilities, such as transportation and water and sewer systems, that define existing and future infrastructure capacities. Six-year capital-improvement programs draw on this information to lay out a schedule for timing and sequencing of facility construction, improved facilities, estimated costs, and expected sources of revenues to pay for improvements.

These aspects of conventional local planning programs provide a fundamental plan of action for infrastructure development and a process by which to track achievements. The programs may be supplemented by growth boundaries that establish limits for extensions of urban services and by other public policies that require clustering and compact development. In addition, two types of growth management techniques are becoming widely used to assist in supplying infrastructure systems to support new development: adequate public facilities requirements and special financing measures.

Linking Development to Infrastructure Capacity

One of the most commonly used growth management techniques today makes development approvals contingent on the availability of facilities adequate to serve the proposed development. Regulations for *adequate public facilities* (APF) require evidence that capacities of public facilities are adequate to serve prospective development before subdivision plats are approved or building permits issued.

Eminently sensible at first glance, such requirements are spreading throughout the United States. Responses to a 1991 survey by the League of California Cities indicated almost one-third of all California communities have APF provisions.[1] A 1995 survey of Maryland counties showed that 13 counties and four cities were administering APF regulations.[2] In many communities, such requirements act as the principal technique for managing growth.

Most APF requirements deal only with one or two types of facilities, such as roads or sewers, that have caused critical problems in the community. A substantial number of communities, however, apply APF regulations to the full range of public facilities, although certain "problem" facilities usually become the principal focus of attention.

APF requirements may be spelled out in a few sentences or in longer sections that incorporate standards and criteria. They may be adopted as separate ordinances or, more often, as provisions in subdivision regulations. Typically, the evaluation of facility adequacy is conducted during the subdivision approval process. The evaluation will determine whether facilities impacted by the proposed subdivision have sufficient capacity to support the development. If, for example, the amount of traffic generated from a proposed project will decrease the level of service of a nearby road intersection below the established standard, then the development must be postponed until (1) public programs are scheduled or funded to improve the intersection's capacity, (2) the developer promises to institute traffic management programs to reduce traffic generation to desired levels, or (3) the developer commits to funding or constructing capacity improvements to meet the standards. The de facto moratorium on further development exists until agreement is reached on one or more solutions to the congestion problem.

The concept of adequate facilities provisions was first suggested as early as 1955, when Henry Fagin, president of the Regional Plan Association of New York, described a system of regulating the timing of growth based on innovative regulations in several small New York towns. Writing in Duke University's *Law and Contemporary Problems* journal, he advocated tying development permits to a schedule of infrastructure improvements, thus guaranteeing that public facility capacities would be adequate to serve new development.[3]

This regulatory approach received legal support in 1971, when New York's highest court upheld the innovative zoning amendments adopted by the town of Ramapo, New York (described in Chapter 2). The ordinance was invalidated by the trial court but upheld on appeal by a split decision, in *Golden* v. *Planning Board of Town of Ramapo,* 324 N.Y.S. 2d 178 (N.Y. 1971). Although the decision was controversial, the case established the use of adequate facilities requirements as a proper exercise of the police power.

Ramapo adopted zoning amendments that set up a point system by which each project was required to demonstrate the adequacy of key components of public infrastructure. An 18-year schedule of public improvements linked to development phasing was also established. Unfortunately, the phasing system depended on construction of several types of public facilities (such as sewers and roads) by other jurisdictions and agencies over which the town had little control. In addition, the town never adhered to its schedule of improvements. Without improvements, further development virtually stopped; 15 years later, citing a long decline in the town's fortunes, town officials voted to dismantle the system in favor of a program to stimulate economic development.

Ramapo-type provisions are still the norm in many communities. However, some have broadened APF requirements by establishing "thresholds" of facility capacities, environmental qualities, and other elements of community development. The thresholds define performance standards that must be met before further development is allowed, such as level-of-service standards for public facilities and services or water and air quality standards for the community and region. A proposed project that fails to meet one or more of the thresholds can be rejected or required to mitigate its impacts to achieve approval.

The city of Chula Vista, California, south of San Diego, formulated threshold standards that were used in evaluating its general plan scenarios as well as in evaluating proposed development projects. Adopted in 1987, the standards addressed 11 topics, including air quality, fiscal impacts, and nine public services, all shown in Figure 5.1. Cumulative impacts are determined in annual evaluations of the city's development in relation to the standards.[4]

As described in Chapter 8, Florida and Washington have adopted state growth management laws that prohibit local governments from issuing development permits unless adequate infrastructure is available concurrently with development—the *concurrency* rule. All local governments in those states are bound by such provisions.

Procedures and Methods

Typically, adequate facilities provisions are keyed to annual capital improvements programs that define a schedule of public facility construction for a six-year period. Such programs presumably define the local government's fiscal capacity to meet infrastructure needs in a responsible manner. Any development proposed for areas not adequately served by present or programmed infrastructure, therefore, conflicts with the community's announced expectations and responsibilities for supporting growth.

Chula Vista's Threshold Standards	
Air Quality	Annual report required from Air Pollution Control District on impact of growth on air quality.
Fiscal	Annual report required to evaluate impacts of growth on city operations, capital improvements, and development impact fee revenues and expenditures.
Police	Respond to 84% of the Priority I emergency calls within 7 minutes and maintain average response time of 4.5 minutes. Respond to 62% of Priority II urgent calls within 7 minutes and maintain average response time of 7.0 minutes.
Fire/EMS	Respond to calls within 7 minutes in 85% of cases.
Schools	Annual report required to evaluate school district's ability to accommodate new growth.
Library	Provide 500 square feet of library space adequately equipped and staffed per 1,000 population.
Parks and Recreation	Maintain 3 acres of neighborhood and community parkland with appropriate facilities per 1,000 residents east of Interstate 805.
Water	Annual report from water service agencies on impact of growth and future water availability.
Sewer	Sewage flows and volumes shall not exceed City Engineering Standards. Annual report from Metropolitan Sewer Authority on impact of growth on sewer capacity.
Drainage	Storm flows and volume shall not exceed City Engineering Standards. Annual report reviewing performance of city's storm drain system.
Traffic	Maintain Level of Service (LOS) "C" or better as measured by observed average travel speed on all signalized arterial streets, except, that during peak hours, an LOS "D" can occur for no more than any 2 hours of the day. Those signalized intersections west of Interstate 805 that do not meet the above standard may continue to operate at their 1991 LOS, but shall not worsen.

Figure 5.1

Chula Vista's threshold standards. Chula Vista's threshold standards are used by the city in preparation of the city's general plan (as a means of evaluating the plan's potential effects on quality-of-life objectives), as well as a tool for analyzing and setting requirements for individual projects. (Table courtesy of the Chula Vista Planning Department.)

Communities usually will allow development if facility improvements scheduled in the capital improvements program will provide the necessary capacities, although some communities base the decision on the availability of improvements in the next two or three years of the program, which are considered more certain of achievement. Some communities allow approval of development only if funding for specific improvements has been authorized or appropriated in the annual budget. Most adequate facilities requirements include waiver clauses for selected types of development deemed to be highly desirable (such as affordable housing) and to allow developers to "advance" the official schedule of improvements by contributing funds or undertaking construction of facilities. Since many communities fail to schedule improvements and authorize sufficient funding to keep up with development needs, developers often use the waiver provision.

Some communities have been particularly successful in linking together their plans, facility programs, and APF requirements to manage growth. One is Carlsbad, California, up the coast from San Diego.[5] Caught by a surge of growth in the 1980s that quickly overwhelmed existing infrastructure systems, Carlsbad's city council passed one interim growth control measure after another—six in less than a year. In 1985, city officials began working on a growth management program that was enacted the next year and subsequently ratified by voters.

The program unequivocally required that development could take place only if adequate facilities were available concurrently with development. Of the eight purposes of the growth management program spelled out in the adopted ordinance, five referred to the need to link development to orderly provision of public facilities and services. The program specified the content of a citywide facilities plan and local zone plans, and outlined a three-tiered procedure for their preparation, review, and approval, shown in Table 5.1.

Table 5.1

Carlsbad's Three-Tiered Growth Management Program

	Citywide Facilities Improvement Plan	Zone Plans	Individual Development Applications
Performance Standards	Establishes standards	Shows how standards will be complied with as development occurs	Must demonstrate that standards will be maintained
Provisions of Facilities	Shows existing inventory and future buildout needs	Shows how and when new facilities will be funded and constructed to accommodate growth	All conditions of approval must be complied with, and specific facilities must be constructed concurrent with development
Funding of Facilities	Outlines various funding options	Proposes specific financing mechanisms for each facility	Funding must be provided prior to final map approval, grading permit, or building permit, whichever occurs first

The Citywide Facilities and Improvement Plan was adopted just two months after enactment of the growth management program. It defined the existing and future level of development in the city, specified 11 public facilities that would be evaluated for adequacy and spelled out performance standards for each one, and identified the existing supply of facilities and future needs to accommodate existing and buildout demands.

Buildout is projected to occur by 2015, based on estimated development of about 54,600 dwelling units, representing a 160-percent increase over the units existing in 1986 but a 35-percent decrease in units permitted by the general plan. Similar projections were made for commercial and industrial uses. These estimates are being revised downward as zone plans are completed, which take greater account of existing development, undevelopable acreage, and other constraints on development.

The plan specified performance standards for each type of facility, as shown in Table 5.2. The city also estimated thresholds of development at which facilities will require improvement to continue meeting performance standards. The combination of standards, thresholds, and detailed zone plans provides an overall management plan for assuring timely infrastructure improvements concurrent with development.

The city also delineated 25 zones for which more detailed plans for public facilities and financing approaches were to be completed before further development could take place within the zone. Six zone plans for mostly developed areas were prepared by the city, but other plans are prepared by property owners guided by city staff. As of 1995, 23 plans have been adopted by resolution of city council; the two remaining plans involve properties with long-standing development problems.

In addition to the citywide and zone plans, finer-grained analyses of facility requirements are conducted for projects under consideration for approval. The analysis allows consideration of potential facility impacts of specific types of proposed development and evaluation of any special features of the site or existing facility systems. It also provides an opportunity to attach conditions for implementing the zone plan.

A somewhat different approach was adopted by Montgomery County, Maryland. After enacting APF requirements in 1973, county officials and planning staff gradually elaborated the process of determining existing and future facility capacities and potential project impacts on those capacities. For years, the planning board has been using complex computer models to estimate traffic and fiscal impacts of proposed developments.

In 1986, the county began publishing an annual (not biennial) accounting of available facility capacities for new housing and employment in 18 policy areas. The "Growth Policy Report" defines the capacity of each policy area for further development, thus putting landowners and developers on notice about areas in which development may be ap-

Table 5.2
Carlsbad's Performance Standards

City Adminstrative Facilities	1500 square feet per 1000 population must be scheduled for construction within a five-year period.
Library	800 square feet per 1000 population must be scheduled for construction within a five-year period.
Wastewater Treatment Capacity	Wastewater treatment capacity is adequate for a least a five-year period.
Parks	Three acres of community park or special-use area per 1000 population within the park district must be scheduled for construction within a five-year period.
Drainage	Drainage facilities as required by the city must be provided concurrent with development.
Circulation	No road segment or intersection in the zone nor any segment or intersection out of the zone impacted by development in the zone shall be projected to exceed service level C during off-peak hours, nor service level D during peak hours. "Impacted" means when 20 percent or more of the traffic generated by the zone will use the road segment or intersection.
Fire	No more than 1500 dwelling units outside of a five-minute response time.
Open Space	Fifteen percent of the total land area in the zone, exclusive of environmentally constrained nondevelopable land, must be set aside for permanent open space and must be available concurrent with development.
Schools	School capacity to meet projected enrollment within the zone as determined by the appropriate school district must be provided prior to projected occupancy.
Sewer Collection System	Trunk line capacity to meet demand as determined by the appropriate sewer district must be provided concurrent with development.
Water Distribution System	(1) Line capacity to meet demand as determined by the appropriate water district must be provided concurrent with development.
	(2) A minimum 10-day average storage capacity must be provided prior to any development.

proved. For the most part, the key test of adequacy is road capacities, although in some cases school capacities are also critical. The capacity ratings are tied to the annual capital improvement program, so that as improvements are made capacities are revised. In addition, each proposed project is subject to a local-area transportation review.

The county's ability to project facility capacities has been complicated by the unpredictable delivery of improvements promised in the CIP (affected by the usual annual politically inspired decisions), by the difficulty of matching incremental demand increases to the timing of major facility construction, and by continuous changes in consumer demands and expectations for facilities. Also, the development boom of the late 1970s and 1980s was concurrent with reductions in state and federal funding for capital facilities.

The planning board responded to these problems by introducing more complex methods for projecting and meeting facility demands. With the slowdown in public funding, developers were forced to "contribute" more funding to counter capacity shortfalls, especially for roads. The county also instituted an aggressive traffic demand management program to reduce traffic by such measures as carpools, van pools, and transit subsidies. In the past decade, about 100 trip-mitigation programs have been approved by the planning board.

These experiences indicate that APF regulations can become centerpieces of local growth management programs. They also suggest some of the administrative and technical complexities introduced by this relatively simple concept, including issues of standards and public roles in supplying infrastructure.

The Issue of Standards

Adequate facilities provisions immediately raise issues about the technical procedures by which adequacy is determined. Two types of analyses are required: one to determine the adequacy of *existing* infrastructure capacity, and the second to determine the *potential* impacts of proposed projects on that capacity.

To determine the adequacy of existing infrastructure, measurements of the use of existing facilities are compared to established capacity standards. Chula Vista's threshold standards referenced earlier and shown in Figure 5.1 indicate some common capacity standards. One well-known measure is level-of-service (LOS) standards for road and highway capacities. Level-of-service standards promulgated by the Institute of Transportation Engineers rate traffic delays caused by congestion at intersections or on lengths of highways. Ratings range from "A" to "F" with level F defined as a delay greater than one minute. Many urban roads and highways operate at levels of C or D. Ratings are determined by traffic counts at selected hours, usually peak commuting hours.

Public officials and the general public have become quite knowledge-able about these service levels and often have strong views about ac-ceptable levels. For that reason, LOS levels frequently are used to deter-mine the adequacy of street capacity: Streets operating at congestion levels lower than C or D, for instance, may require that development ap-provals be postponed until improvements are made.

Other types of capital facilities demand different measures of ade-quacy, some more technically based than others. Standards of water supply, for example, must consider peak flows, fire fighting needs, water quality issues (from overused wells, for example), and availability of ad-equately sized pipes. Sewer systems demand measures of effluent qual-ity as well as collection systems. Fire protection measures usually adopt standards of fire insurance companies that define maximum distances from stations. Park and recreation standards can be based on a wide range of published standards relating acres of parkland to population. Air quality standards are set by federal rules and continuously moni-tored.

Capacity standards, however, frequently are rather subjective deter-minations based to some extent on scientific data and to a greater degree on local experience. Transportation engineers, for example, understand that LOS standards are only crude measures of actual congestion. An F level at one intersection may be a nuisance, for example, but not a cri-sis in traffic movement. A sprinkling of F-level intersections throughout a street network that affords many optional routes similarly may not pose grave congestion problems. In addition, LOS ratings usually are de-termined during peak commuting hours and thus do not reflect general traffic conditions. However, selection of an appropriate level to be used as the standard is basically a political decision based on citizen tolera-tion of congestion. Residents of Chicago are likely to have a different view of traffic congestion than those in Manchester, Vermont. "Rush hour" in small towns may be frustrating but last only five minutes. The worst traffic in many suburban communities may occur on Saturdays when shoppers clog the roads. "Adequacy" is a subjective term that ap-pears to work on a sliding scale related to the urban experience of local residents.

Furthermore, it is not uncommon for "acceptable" levels to be set above current levels, thus automatically putting a brake on future devel-opment until the condition is improved. In this way, APF requirements can be employed as a no-growth measure.

The next part of the adequacy test is measuring the potential impacts of proposed projects on capacities of existing facilities. Here again, pro-jections of infrastructure needs are based on community standards that may or may not be realistic and reasonable. Usually, local consultants and public administrators mutually agree on suitable projection measures for determining future facility needs. In specific instances, however, these may not be suitable. For example, the use of general acres-per-thousand population standards to determine appropriate park and recreation land may be inappropriate for certain types of residential development. Allocations of traffic from proposed projects to a surrounding street network also call for educated judgments rather than reliance on infallible science.

Unintended, Undesirable Consequences

The necessity of using these measures, standards, projections, and judgments in determinations of adequate capacity means that results are never foolproof. One early consequence of the Florida concurrency requirement, for example, was that the regulations appeared to encourage development in rural areas, where road and other infrastructure capacities were available or could be inexpensively expanded. At the same time, the requirements were hampering development in congested urban areas considered prime targets for future development. Also, APF regulations do not differentiate among sources of impacts. Should a community's development be curtailed because its roads are congested by traffic from other jurisdictions? How should regional air quality problems affect development decisions in an individual community?

These kinds of problems indicate that the premises and assumptions underlying the standards must be continuously examined for their reasonableness and appropriateness to the specific circumstances. Montgomery County, Maryland, for example, decided that its standards for highway levels of service should take lower priority than its planning goals for focusing concentrated development around Metrorail stations and promoting affordable housing, both of which were being derailed by APF requirements. In 1995, after 22 years of imposing adequate facilities requirements, the county waived them to allow development to continue in station areas.

Issues of Public Responsibility

Adequate facilities provisions, on the surface, are eminently reasonable: Who would argue that development ought to be allowed to overload public facilities? The formulation of regulatory requirements for adequate facilities, however, raises administrative issues that frequently create problems in application of adequate facilities requirements.

The assignment of basic responsibility for providing public facilities is one issue. Unlike Carlsbad's program, most adequate facilities provisions are silent on the matter of local governmental responsibilities for ensuring that facility capacities are maintained in reasonable equilibrium with needs. Although one of the primary functions of government is to plan, finance, and administer public services, some local governments appear to abdicate responsibility for maintaining adequate facilities. By implication or in practice, part or all of that responsibility is shifted to the private sector.

Local governments, however, should not attempt to escape their responsibilities for supporting development by simply enacting adequate facilities provisions and then sitting back to watch developers scramble to provide facilities. There are good reasons why local governments should remain active in planning, funding, and managing basic systems of public facilities. Leaving such functions totally to individual project developers creates physical and funding gaps in the systems. Fresno, California, for example, requires developers to fund and construct several basic types of public facility systems. Developers' plans are guided by city-prepared functional plans, and funding is derived from impact fees tailored to each area and type of facility. Although local builders credit the program with keeping costs down, the city has had to step in from time to time to make connections between developer-installed systems. Because these actions were not anticipated, planning and funding them was troublesome.

Another problem in passing responsibility to the private sector is that local governments relinquish a great deal of control over planning and timing of development, which is a vital part of most community development strategies. Even with the most elaborate standards and diligent public reviews, shifting planning and funding burdens to developers lets developers decide when, where, and how infrastructure will be constructed. It also means local officials risk losing touch with infrastructure needs and emerging problems in delivering basic services.

The second issue of public responsibility is that adequate facilities requirements frequently pertain to facilities not under control of the local government—a problem experienced in Ramapo. It is safe to say, for example, that most development stoppages due to adequate facilities requirements are created by capacity deficiencies of state and federal highways. Congestion on such roads can be cured only through regional or state action, yet local ordinances require maintenance of a certain level of service before development will be approved. Local governments and developers caught in such a squeeze have only a few options:

- Persuading the responsible agencies to act more quickly to correct deficiencies, or stepping in with innovative financing methods to move construction schedules ahead.

- Modifying standards or capacity measurements (after Florida adopted its concurrency requirement, local planners indulged in inventive ways to measure highway capacity to avoid development moratoriums).

- Waiving requirements for certain desirable types of development.

A third issue concerns public responsibilities for keeping up (or catching up, in most cases) with infrastructure needs. In many communities, on the day that an adequate facility ordinance takes effect, some facilities are already inadequate and others are becoming inadequate due to long-term public failures to invest in improvements. Often capital improvements programs suffer the first cuts in local budget deliberations; year after year, most programs fall short of meeting demands. Imposition of adequate facilities requirements in these circumstances means that future development is hampered by the inadequacies of past governmental efforts.

Henry Fagin's original proposal for adequate facilities requirements is instructive in this regard. He recommended that such requirements be placed within a framework of public programs for scheduling and financing infrastructure. He wrote: "A municipality exercising this system for regulating the timing of urban development should be obliged by statute to carry forward programs of municipal facility and service expansion reasonably related to development trends."[6] He called, in other words, for a quid pro quo: A government that requires adequacy should take reasonable steps to ensure adequacy. Governments that fail to take those steps raise the issue of whether they are intent on supporting development or seeking to stop it. Westminster, Colorado, for instance, adopted the Ramapo system many years ago, limiting annual growth to keep it in line with scheduled investments in infrastructure. Although, unlike Ramapo, the city has kept to its schedule of improvements, its reluctance to increase investments over time to meet rising demands suggests that maintaining adequate public facilities is not the major purpose of the growth limits.

APF regulations, while apparently simple in concept, require long-term legislative commitments to responsible programming of public facilities and a great deal of administrative effort in application. They are not automatic devices that, once installed in local regulations, operate without further concern. Their effects on community development goals and on the development process need to be carefully tracked and occasionally mitigated.

Using Exactions and Impact Fees to Finance Infrastructure

Traditionally, local governments have funded public improvements from general revenues, often based on property taxes; from issuance of municipal bonds repaid from local revenue sources; and from state and federal funding programs. Frequently, several sources are combined to fund improvements. Because many types of public facilities are expensive to construct but will have a lengthy useful life, they are usually funded by

bond issues that spread costs over 15, 20, or more years. General obligation bonds, backed by the full faith and credit of the municipality, are
repaid through general revenues, including property taxes, and have a
fairly low interest rate. Revenue bonds are repaid from specified sources
of revenue, usually fees and charges for services, and carry a somewhat
higher interest rate. In addition, the bond market has invented a large
number of variations on general obligation and revenue bonds to suit
various needs of local governments or conditions of the bond market.

Bonds are repaid from a variety of revenue sources. For many years,
the basic source was property taxes, but by the mid-1980s, property
taxes had dropped to less than half (47 percent) of all revenues from
local sources; their decline in significance continues today. Instead, sales
and income taxes and various types of excise taxes, fees, and charges
have increased in importance. Small increments of sales taxes are earmarked to improve roads and parks and preserve open space. Excise
taxes on specific goods and services can impose taxes on airport landings
and hotel rooms that help fund airport improvements and convention
centers. Communities have increased the variety of fees and charges
they levy, such as landfill charges, fees for use of recreation areas, automobile license fees, and public parking charges, because they are paid by
users of those services who benefit from the facilities they fund.

Public sentiment in recent years has favored wider use of such special
taxes, fees, and charges to relieve the tax burden on the general public.
It is not surprising, therefore, that funding for public facilities required
to support new development is increasingly drawn from developers and
their client consumers. "Development should pay for itself" is a phrase
heard across the nation. Use of alternative funding sources for infrastructure investments—particularly exactions, impact fees, and special
taxing districts—is an important element of many growth management
programs.

1. *Exactions*

This general term covers the variety of ways in which developers are required to contribute to provision of public facilities related to their developments. Variously termed "exactions," "extractions," and "proffers,"
these contributions may include dedication of land for facilities, actual
facility construction, or payment of fees to be used for facility construction. The importance of this facility-financing approach has increased as
more and more local governments turn to the private sector to fund infrastructure improvements.

Exactions generally are imposed during the subdivision review
process through subdivision provisions that require developers to fund,
build, and dedicate for public use the basic facilities required for residents and tenants of their developments. Typically, local streets, sewer

and water lines, drainage facilities, and parks and recreational facilities are funded in this manner. In addition, many jurisdictions also require developers to fund selected improvements to major streets within or on the borders of their projects, nearby intersections, and drainage improvements in the general area, and to reserve school sites. Subdivision provisions often specify the standards to be applied to determine the size and character of such improvements.

These kinds of exactions have become quite common and are broadly supported by law, as discussed later in the section. Most developers now expect to underwrite these infrastructure costs as part of the development process. In fact, most developers prefer to control the quality and timing of such improvements to coincide with their project objectives and construction schedule.

Communities also have become quite adept at demanding other types of exactions, such as special facilities and amenities that may benefit the larger public as much or more than project residents. Such exactions occur when developers request rezoning or use special procedures, such as PUDs, that require approval by a board or legislative body. Public officials (and neighborhood groups) often find this an opportune time to request additional contributions from developers.

Developers of office buildings in downtown San Francisco, for example, must contribute public art objects and child care facilities as public benefits. A developer in Arlington, Virginia received project approval only after promising to pay the full costs of a tunnel under a public street to the local Metrorail station. Other developers have had to offer scholarships for neighborhood youths and restoration of existing neighborhood parks. Developers in rural counties sometimes find it necessary to build fire stations badly needed for the whole area. Legally, developers are obligated only to offer facilities and improvements that benefit primarily their developments, but developers pressed to move forward with a project often agree to other contributions as well.

These kinds of extraordinary exactions are less likely to be forthcoming than they were in the heady development days of the 1980s. Lenders are more circumspect in determining appropriate financing for up-front development costs, and the long lull in development from the mid-1980s to the mid-1990s thinned out the ranks of developers capable of anteing up additional funds to meet community demands for amenities. Concerns for stimulating economic development and responding to recent Supreme Court decisions limiting public demands for land and facilities also have tempered innovation in exactions.

Impact Fees

Impact fees are a newer form of exaction increasingly imposed by communities across the nation. (Other terms are "systems development charges" and "development fees.") Impact fees are charged for each new dwelling or increment of nonresidential space to defray the costs of public facilities required to serve the development. For local governments, impact fees have several advantages over traditional property taxes in paying for facility expansions:

- Fees require new development to absorb at least some of the costs of new services and facilities, thus relieving the tax burden on current residents and businesses; in essence, they give public notice that developers must compensate communities for development impacts on community facilities.

- Fees are collected as development occurs (usually when building permits are issued) rather than a year or more later when residents receive tax bills.

- Fees provide a useful means of pooling funds from individual projects to pay for facilities in other locations, such as highway and interchange improvements, water trunk lines, sewage treatment plant improvements, and community parks.

Fees on new development have been widely used for many years to help pay for facility improvements outside development sites. For example, many water and sewer authorities require builders to pay "hook-up" or "tap-in" fees to connect into water and sewer systems; revenues from such fees are used to improve trunk lines, pumping stations, treatment plants, and the like outside the project site. Subdivision regulations in many communities also provide for developer payments "in lieu" of on-site parks and recreational lands; the funds collected are used to purchase parklands in the most desirable locations. Impact fees simply extend that concept to other types of facilities.

Impact fees are most often charged for sewer and water improvements, roads, and parks. Some local governments also charge fees for schools, drainage, police and fire, and other facilities impacted by development. Some communities, especially those in California, charge consolidated fees for a complete array of public facilities, including administrative buildings and libraries.

Ordinances imposing fees spell out methods for calculating them, so that developers can determine in advance their expected payments. Most communities allow developers to build facilities directly to offset required fees.[7]

Impact fees can range from a few hundred dollars to many thousands of dollars. A survey of 33 jurisdictions by the Center for Governmental Responsibility at the University of Florida found the full range of impact fees in 1990 to average $9425 for single-family houses, $4858 per 1000 square feet of industrial space, $5848 per 1000 square feet of general of-

Developing Defensible Impact Fees

Arthur C. Nelson

Development impact fees are one-time charges assessed on new development to pay for their proportionate share of facilities needed to serve it. To the surprise of many public officials who may view impact fees as a magical source of new revenue, impact fees should be conceived as part of a comprehensive growth management planning process. If viewed principally as a revenue-raising device their legal defensibility is often lost.

Five distinct steps are required in formulating defensible impact fees. First, community goals that support the need for impact fees must be established, such as minimizing taxpayer burdens, fairly apportioning facility costs based on demand, providing adequate facilities when and where needed, and facilitating economic development by generating new revenues earmarked for expansion of community facilities.

The second step is preparing projections of growth, land area, and required facilities to portray an overall picture of current and future community characteristics and demands for infrastructure. Included should be determinations of desired facility standards for all community facilities (e.g., acres of park land per 1000 people, peak-hour traffic per land mile).

Third, based on growth projections and facility standards, needs for future facilities should be determined. This involves a combination of spatial analyses, such as the location and densities of future development, and financial analyses focusing on the costs of providing facilities in various locations and with various characteristics. In addition, analyses of the extent to which existing facilities have capacity to meet future demands and the cost of building or expanding facilities must be determined. The result of this step is a fairly clear picture of where development will go, how it will be served, and how much facilities will cost.

The fourth step is determining the phasing and funding of needed capital facilities over time—a capital improvements program. Specific facility costs and revenue sources are identified. The gap between costs and revenues can be filled, at least in part, by impact fees. This step, in other words, defines the magnitude of fee revenues required to meet future infrastructure needs.

Finally, along with zoning, design review, and other implementation measures for growth management, impact fee programs are determined. There are many technical details in calculating and administering impact fees, for which a number of publications supply guidance. The point is that impact fees basically serve a regulatory function in ensuring provision of adequate public facilities when and where needed. As such, they are one component of a growth management program—the tail on the dog, so to speak (although in some controversial cases it seems to be the tail that wags the dog).

fice space, and $6990 per 1000 square feet of retail space. (Many communities, however, impose fees only on one or two types of infrastructure, which significantly reduces the above averages.) Not surprisingly, fees have increased substantially since a previous survey in 1988—up 39 percent for single-family houses, for example.[8]

A few communities have adopted special types of fees, often called "linkage fees," intended to assist in financing housing programs and special amenities. The best known and most stringent is San Francisco's Office Housing Production Program, which requires developers of downtown office buildings of over 50,000 square feet of floor space to pay fees for improvements to transit, housing, public art, child care, and public open space. Boston levies fees on nonresidential development, including institutions, to provide funds for housing improvements.

Issues in Imposing Exactions and Fees

Exactions and fees raise four major concerns that must be considered in establishing local policies for financing facilities: legal constraints, equity considerations, and administrative concerns.

a.) *Legal Constraints.* The extent to which local governments can demand contributions from developers, and for what purposes, has generated a considerable amount of litigation in state and federal courts. (See the summary of major court cases in Chapter 2 for some details.) Three constitutional guarantees—awarding property owners compensation for public taking of property, equal protection, and due process—limit local governments' powers to require exactions. Exactions must be clearly related to a public purpose, applied equally to all types of development to avoid an exclusionary effect, and not be arbitrary and capricious.

The general test applicable in virtually all states, is that exactions should bear a "rational nexus" to a development's impacts on local public facilities. A local government may, for example, require a developer to improve a certain road intersection if the developer's project will generate enough traffic to warrant the improvement. The local government cannot, however, legitimately require developers to pay for improvements to intersections many miles away that traffic from their projects will seldom use.[9]

The legal foundation for impact fees is more complicated than for other forms of exactions. First, it must be established that fees are allowable under the police powers granted by the state to the local government, rather than defined as a form of tax for which specific state authorization is usually required. In some states, local governments have proceeded to adopt impact fees under liberal home rule provisions. In other states, local governments have secured special state legislation allowing them to adopt fees. A number of states have adopted state enabling legislation allowing communities to adopt impact fees under certain conditions and restrictions.

Assuming that impact fees are allowable local acts, their calculation and administration must meet stiffer criteria than those used for other types of tax revenues. To avoid double taxation, the amounts of fees should take into account regular taxes that property owners will pay for public improvements and must not include funds needed to correct existing deficiencies (for which current residents are responsible). In administering impact fee programs, fees collected from specific developments must be expended within a reasonable time for facilities in areas that will benefit those developments.

Equity Considerations. Exactions and fees also raise some issues about who should pay for infrastructure improvements. At one time, it was assumed that the general community should be responsible for funding major infrastructure systems, the theory being that long-lasting facilities are enjoyed by generations of beneficiaries who gradually contribute to facility expansion through taxes. Then, in response to rapid postwar growth, local governments began shifting responsibilities to developers for funding facilities on their development sites. But that simple division of financial responsibility appears to be breaking down. Public officials, urged by taxpayers, are increasingly concerned that developers contribute to overcoming any impacts that new development may have on capacities of public facilities. One result, developers complain, is that many citizens besides those in their projects benefit from improvements they pay for, including future generations of users. The key is balancing direct impacts that can be mitigated through exactions and fees with long-term community benefits that call for public/private sharing of facility funding.

Another issue concerns governmental services that are financed on the basis of ability to pay: That is, people who earn more, pay more. Elementary and secondary education, for example, is normally considered important enough to society as a whole that it is financed largely by property tax revenues that reflect levels of personal income. To equalize school funding among jurisdictions, most states provide for state taxation that is redistributed to local school districts according to measures of need. Which capital facilities should be financed in this way and which should be targeted for payment by specific users is a continuing issue. Current trends appear to favor wider use of user fees, excise taxes, and sales taxes to fund community needs, thus reducing the availability of some facilities and services to lower-income people.

The question becomes more complex when one realizes that much infrastructure confers value on property it does not directly serve: A good park system, for example, improves property values throughout a community in addition to offering direct benefits to park users.

Another problem arises when exactions and fees provide high-quality facilities in developing neighborhoods without corresponding improvements taking place in existing developed areas. San Diego experienced severe community conflicts when its fee-based system for financing capital facilities failed to provide funds for upgrading facilities in older neighborhoods. The city first had waived impact fees to stimulate reinvestment in those areas, then found that development was too anemic to produce adequate funds for improvements.

Finally, a major equity issue concerns the effects of exactions and fees on market factors such as the price of housing. This issue is discussed in the section on effects of growth management in Chapter 9.

Administrative Concerns. Exactions and fees pose two major administrative concerns: (1) the general lack of administrative guidelines or rules for determining exactions and (2) the planning and management complexities inherent in the use of impact fees. As noted earlier, many exactions of land or improvements, especially those located off the development site, are negotiated during project approval procedures. Guidelines seldom exist to determine the appropriate types or amounts of exactions, to suggest how financial responsibilities should be shared among public and private interests, or to guide negotiations. As a result, developers often complain of extortionary exactions unrelated to the impacts of their projects, and public officials frequently believe that developers are not being required to do enough.

These problems supposedly are solved in large part by the use of impact fees that provide predictable measures of impact and resulting payments. It takes expert knowledge, time, and effort, however, to create legally sound and politically stable fee programs. Simply to calculate reasonable and legally defensible fees, for example, requires the following information:

- Definition of communitywide facility standards (similar to those required for adequate public facility regulations).

- Determinations of existing deficiencies in facilities in meeting those standards (which cannot be corrected by impact fees on new development).

- Determinations of existing facility costs and funding sources for those facilities.

- Allocations of costs to new development, accounting for the extent to which new development contributed to funding existing facilities and future capacities in existing facilities.

- Adjustments that should be made to reflect prices and costs over time.

Once enacted, impact fee programs require that correct fees are collected for each project, taking into account provision of facilities directly by developers, and that timely expenditures are made for construction of facilities that benefit the payers. Cities such as San Diego that use impact fees as a major mechanism of financing employ full-time staffs to administer their programs.

Exactions and impact fees should not be considered a panacea for solving facility funding problems. Negotiated exactions and fee revenues rarely cover all infrastructure associated with development (partly because fees are usually set arbitrarily low to avoid litigation). Both types of contributions to facility funding depend on market behavior: When development downturns occur, developers stop delivering exacted facilities and paying fees, as many communities discovered in the late 1980s. Although fees are paid when building occurs, it may take time for fee revenues to build up enough to fund specific improvements. Neither type of funding provides facility improvements for existing neighborhoods.

For these reasons, exactions and fees should be employed as one of several sources of revenue within an overall public program for financing capital facilities. In this context, they can provide essential funds to permit development to proceed.

Indeed, infrastructure improvements funded by exactions and fees often add market value to their projects. Public requirements for open space or drainage, for example, usually enhance building sites. Environmental features preserved from development often become valuable amenities for the site's residents and tenants.

For developers and builders, impact fees can deliver tangible benefits. Payment of fees entitles developers to expectations that they can proceed to develop and that facilities will be available when needed. Developers who construct facilities in lieu of fees are able to maintain a significant amount of control over the timing and quality of those facilities.

Conclusion. Many communities have enthusiastically embraced the concept of exactions and impact fees as a means of shifting facility costs for new development to the private sector. In some ways, these methods complicate the development process, since they introduce intricate accounting and administrative requirements. Also, exactions and fees cannot substitute completely for general public funding of some improvements. In other ways, they help to improve the predictability of the process, since they promise permission to develop once the exactions are made and the fees paid. Particularly when conceived as one element of a comprehensive program for funding and scheduling construction of facilities necessary to support development, they can play a significant role in community growth management.

3. Special Taxing Districts

Searching for new ways to finance infrastructure, many communities have borrowed and updated an old technique: special taxing districts. Special districts, which may be called authorities or commissions, provide services to residents within circumscribed areas. New facilities are funded by assessments on those who benefit directly from the services. Traditionally, districts were formed to target certain areas desiring or needing distinct services. Assessment districts, for example, might be established to provide sewer service to areas once dependent on septic tanks or to fund sidewalk construction or new libraries. Now, special districts are being established to fund planning, construction, and management of services required by new development, either within a large-scale development project or across a number of projects.

A wide variety of districts exists, since their use is dictated by state laws that differ greatly from state to state. Special taxing districts are allowed in all states, but they are particularly numerous in some states, including Illinois, Texas, California, Florida, and Pennsylvania. In every case, state legislation spells out requirements for initiating, financing, and operating specific types of districts. Some districts are given powers to function almost completely independently, like local governments; others are dependent on local governments (and sometimes regional agencies) for approval of their formation, annual budgets, and funding programs, and may have local legislative bodies as district governing boards. Most districts are single-purpose districts, for constructing roads, or building junior colleges, or promoting soil conservation; some states enable formation of multipurpose districts that can supply almost all the facilities and services required to serve new development.

Local governments often form assessment districts or public improvement districts to permit levying a special tax on property owners who wish improved facilities. Alternatively, property owners, including developers, may initiate formation of districts to provide financing for public facilities within their properties.

Forming Districts to Support New Development

Districts are usually formally initiated by petition from one or more landowners to a local government. Prior to circulating the petition, landowners work out a general plan for development of desired facilities and determine costs and construction phasing. The landowners/developers employ a variety of consultants to draw up detailed development plans, impact and cost analyses, and phasing and financing programs. Assuming that formation of the district is approved by the local government (and sometimes regional or state agencies), the district elects a governing board that organizes a bond issue based on estimated infra-

structure construction costs. Bond proceeds then are used to construct
facilities. Bonds are repaid through assessments on properties within the
district; as land is sold for development and values increase, revenues
will rise to meet costs.[10]

The developers of Pelican Bay, a resort development on 2100 acres
near Naples, Florida, formed an improvement district in 1974 with the
approval of the city and surrounding county. (The special state act to
allow the district was later the basis for a general state act enabling the
establishment of community development districts.) At the time, Naples'
water and sewer facilities were inadequate to support the proposed development. The new district allowed the sale of bond issues to fund new
wells and a water treatment and distribution system, wastewater collection and treatment, a drainage control system, and street lighting. Roads
and recreation facilities were funded by the developer and turned over
to the community association for maintenance. As development proceeded, additional bond issues were sold to pay for system expansions.
The bonded debt, as well as all maintenance and management costs,
were funded through annual assessments and specific service charges. In
1989, in accordance with the original agreement, the district was reorganized as a dependent district under the responsibility of the county.

District Advantages

Special taxing districts are especially useful as a means of funding facilities for new development. Forming a district avoids taxing the general
public or current residents for facilities required by new residents. Instead, districts spread the costs of improvements over a targeted group
of consumers, who directly benefit from the facilities they pay for. In addition, because most districts can issue bonds to finance improvements,
they extend the payment period over 15 to 20 years. They are also invaluable in developing areas where local governments have little incentive, administrative capacity, or financial resources to fund infrastructure. District bond issues are usually not subject to local governmental
bonding limits and thus add to, rather than detract from, local governmental bonding resources.

Some public finance analysts also claim that special districts, because
they function outside the local political process, can deliver services
more efficiently than general-purpose local governments.

Disadvantages of Special Districts

Political scientists have looked askance at special districts because districts substitute for, and may compete with, local governmental functions. The proliferation of districts, they believe, weakens the powers of
local governments and increases administrative inefficiencies and fiscal

inequalities. For this reason, municipal officials frequently oppose state laws enabling formation of special districts.

The existence of many special districts providing a variety of services also is believed to lead to confusion and complexity in the governance process. Citizens rarely know district board members and boards frequently act with little accountability to the public or in coordination with other governments. In almost all states, districts function with little oversight from the state or any other governmental entity. One of the most difficult tasks in many local and regional growth management programs is to win cooperation from special districts that provide key services to developing areas.

Most of these issues can be resolved by ensuring that local governments retain significant control over district activities and budgets, rather than allowing districts to act independently. In King County, Washington, in the Seattle area, for example, the county obtained legislation to require numerous water and sewer districts to expand service areas in conformance with local comprehensive plans. Similar measures to ensure coordination of facility improvements with planning policies, as well as careful attention to the financial basis for establishing districts, can allow districts to function as useful partners in financing infrastructure.

Alternative Special Districts

A type of special district popular in a number of states is a tax-increment financing (TIF) district. TIF districts depend on earmarked tax revenues raised only from new development to finance capital improvements. Assessments are based on net increases over the existing property tax base. For this reason, TIF districts are often used for redevelopment areas that need fresh infusions of capital for improvements.

Another specialized type of district is the transportation improvement district, organized to assist in funding roads and transit systems in certain corridors or areas. New Jersey's Transportation Development Act of 1989, for example, allows counties to apply for state approval of districts that then draw up transportation improvement plans, issue bonds, and construct improvements. The county manages the process and approves all expenditures.

For many communities throughout the nation, therefore, special taxing districts have offered a useful alternative to local governmental financing of infrastructure.

Privatization

In recent years, a number of local governments have experimented with the idea of having private companies build and operate public facilities.

It is not a new idea: Private water companies, private solid waste disposal facilities, and private transit companies are not uncommon. Semi-private authorities manage many toll roads and bridges. Special taxing districts that provide basic services are often managed by private companies under contract to the districts. And in many small- and large-scale developments, community associations own and manage recreational and other facilities.

Proponents of these types of ventures claim that private companies provide superior service at lower cost (partly due to more efficient management but also because of lower wage scales). Public officials, however, often worry that private companies may make unreasonable profits or fail to provide equal, adequate service to all residents. Private concerns also have had trouble raising the significant amounts of capital required to launch a new facility. Perhaps for these reasons, despite a great deal of interest in privatization and some highly publicized examples, no great rush has occurred to convert public facilities to private ones. Privatization appears to be the exception rather than the rule in financing infrastructure improvements.

Combining Funding Resources

Most communities realize that adequate funding of infrastructure to support development will require reaching out to a variety of financing sources to structure a program that balances public and private contributions. Sarasota County's experience in funding its ambitious capital improvements program described at the beginning of this chapter is instructive. The county has employed a number of financing mechanisms that draw from both public and private resources. In 1982, voters approved issuance of revenue bonds to acquire the large tract of land in the rural area needed as a water supply resource. In 1973 and 1986, general obligation bonds were approved for beach acquisition. Voters approved a one-cent gas tax increase in 1988 to pay for road improvements. In 1989, a one-cent local-option sales tax was approved to pay for a variety of road, park, school, and library improvements to correct existing deficiencies. In 1983, the county also instituted impact fees on new development for roads and parks.

These measures provided adequate funding for the county's infrastructure needs for many years. But managing facility funding is an ongoing process, and the county is facing new decisions. The local-option sales tax comes up for renewal in 1999, and as yet there is little enthusiasm for extending it. Until recently, impact fees and developer exactions were fairly effective in providing for new infrastructure needs, but recent cuts in residential fees (from about $2650 to $1650 per unit) and waivers for economic development have reduced fee collections. After a very wet 1995, county residents are demanding visible drainage improvements from the drainage utility, which for several years has expended assessment revenues on planning. In addition, the 1995 planning commission decision to forestall expansion of the growth boundary due to infrastructure funding constraints signals an emerging general concern about future funding.

As another example, Tracy's program of infrastructure financing illustrates the detailed thought given to the city's plan for expanding infrastructure systems. Even before the specific plan process began, the expansion of the sewer system had been funded through an assessment district established to cover the specific plan areas; landowners were paying from $5500 to $7500 per acre per year for 20 years to retire bonds for sewer improvements. A similar district was established for water system improvements. The $60-million price tag for educational facilities was financed through another type of assessment district, a "Mello-Roos" special taxing district created by a joint powers agreement between the city and the several school districts involved. A proposed community park was to be funded by general obligation bonds. Road construction was financed directly by developers within their sites and, for major arterials, impact fees were assessed.

Infrastructure required for industrial and commercial developments was to be funded through small assessment districts that would reimburse developers for their funding of initial construction of improvements. To spur industrial development, the city determined that industrial properties would not be subject to Mello-Roos assessments for educational facilities nor development fees for other types of improvements.

These financing arrangements required infrastructure construction to be phased gradually as funds built up. For example, all land acquisition for parks, schools, and rights-of-way was deferred to the latter years of the plan; developers were required to reserve sites for later purchase for market value plus interest. No road improvements were scheduled for the first year of the plan in order to allow revenues from builder fees to accumulate, but thereafter specific road improvements were funded each year.

These examples serve to illustrate the ways in which communities have mixed and matched funding opportunities to create workable programs of public facility expansion. Local governments attempting to manage growth have combined projections of needs, detailed schedules of improvements, and innovative financing mechanisms. Managing growth through supportive infrastructure programs is a powerful tool for accommodating and directing community development.

6

Preserving Community Character and Quality

The growth management approaches discussed in the previous chapters largely focus on the amount, rate, and location of growth and change, all important factors in the development process. This chapter deals with growth management concerns that, while less quantifiable, are arguably of prime significance for most people: maintaining and improving the *quality* of community development. The growth management movement, after all, emerged in part because of the growing understanding that traditional planning and zoning techniques may succeed in screening out the worst kinds of development but cannot be depended on to produce the most satisfactory qualities of development. An important component of growth management, then, are techniques to retain valued aspects of community character and ensure desired qualities in new development.

Surprisingly, quality-oriented techniques are seldom considered to be "growth management." Typical lists of growth management techniques, including one of 47-items formulated in the 1970s,[1] include no examples specifically addressing quality control, although one or two (e.g., zoning bonuses and incentives) might be employed for that purpose. The most vivid legal battles over growth management techniques have been fought over restrictive growth limits, boundaries, and infrastructure requirements. Recent publications on growth management give community quality short shrift. Somehow community character seems to be viewed as falling outside the principal aims of growth management.

For many people, however, that's what public control of development is all about. Jan Krasnowiecki, in his incisive critique of zoning as an effective tool for guiding development, pinned down the principal concerns about development for most residents and voters: what it looks like and how it changes community life.[2] Without doubt, most anti-growth movements around the nation have evolved from widespread perceptions that new development will adversely affect the character of existing communities. Almost without exception, statements of planning visions or goals highlight the importance of promoting development compatible with the community's unique character. Quality, not quantity, is often the first objective of growth management.

Urban Design: The Elusive Elixir of Growth Management
Richard E. Tustian

Quality of life is an often-cited but seldom defined concept. Usually it includes two ways of experiencing the public dimension of a place: how it "looks" and how it "works"—or its form and function. Many growth management programs focus only on functional and quantitatively measurable elements such as jobs, housing, transportation, and education. These programs miss the important contribution of the "form" dimension to the composite experience of quality of life. This dimension is important for the meaning and sense of identity it gives to individual inhabitants of the community.

It is in this dimension that urban design finds its central mission. Urban design has been called "the art of relating structures to one another and to the natural setting to serve contemporary society." Although the focus is on form, urban design must also consider the function for which form gives shelter. The goal of urban design is to find the best fit between the function to be served and the form to serve it. How to do this within the political setting of growth management decision making presents some real challenges.

The first challenge is the dichotomy created by the Constitution between private-sector rights and public-sector rights. The courts have given local and state governments only a guiding principle, not a definitive rule, for using the state's police power to regulate private use of land. To satisfy judicial review, a regulation must (1) declare the regulation's public purpose; (2) articulate a clear, close relationship (a nexus) between this public purpose and the regulation; and (3) show that the regulation does not constitute a disproportionate burden on the individual property owners involved. The public purpose of environmental regulations, for example, is focused on preservation of specific objects in the natural environment.

The purposes of urban design, however, are more difficult to define objectively. Spatial shapes and relationships are difficult to translate into functional terms or to quantify. Although great advances have been made in recent years

The importance of quality as a factor in growth management is reinforced by recent trends in community goals for development. The continued quest for more compact development, for example, emphasizes the significance of high-quality project and building design. Building relationships and the character of urban spaces become significant factors in making higher-density development livable and marketable—unlike low-density sprawl where the landscape often hides poor design. Other current interests in retrofitting older shopping and business centers to produce functional mixed-use centers, and promoting transit-supportive development, also demand close attention to design relationships and details. In addition, infilling neighborhoods with new development that

in environmental and behavioral science, the subtleties of form-and-function relationships is still not well understood. Partly this is due to changes over time in many human psychological constructs and attitudes that affect public attitudes as well.

The second major challenge facing urban design is to understand what people really want in terms of community form, to determine the possibility of obtaining that form, and, if so, at what cost. At present, it is only possible to speculate on the direction of public opinion. To this observer, public attitudes seem to be veering away from the perceived sterility of large-scale, sleek, and rationally derived forms of community development. People seem to be looking instead for comfort and pleasure in small scale, warm and fuzzy, and culturally derived forms. As the world emphasizes "high tech" people want "high touch," although with high tech convenience.

The most popular coalescence of these ideas applied to urban form is the New Urbanism movement, which, though small in size, seems to be attracting an expanding constituency interested in its challenges to the orthodoxies of contemporary society. The movement's main objectives seem to be (1) to shift society's attention from the products of our industrial economy to the places in the natural environment they affect, and (2) to shift the scale of concern from one appropriate to automobiles to one appropriate for pedestrians.

In the train of these two objectives follow a number of issues to be resolved, including the role of public transportation, the conversion of building industry prototypes, the marketability of such prototypes, the revision of building and public works codes to permit construction at the pedestrian scale, the articulation of public purpose rationales that can withstand judicial scrutiny, and the invention of market and regulatory tools that work at the finer grain of detail demanded by "small is beautiful" notions. Only time will tell whether a major paradigm shift will emerge broad enough to embrace this range of issues.

respects the existing historic and architectural character requires an ac-
knowledgment of existing community qualities.

Bitter experience tells us that the grand strategies of growth management such as growth boundaries, conservation of rural land, coordinated
provision of infrastructure, and promotion of infill and redevelopment
can succeed only if detailed attention is paid to maintaining and enhancing the quality of existing and emerging neighborhoods and community centers. In both San Diego and Portland, to name but two of
many examples, policies to curb urban sprawl by encouraging infill development in existing neighborhoods ran aground over resident's complaints about incompatible building designs and other impacts of infill
projects. In neither case had the city groomed zoning and building provisions to require types and styles of development compatible with existing neighborhood character.

It is only proper, therefore, that growth management programs incorporate ways and means of ensuring that appearance, design, community
amenities, and preservation of valued areas and buildings are taken into
account in the development process.

The "Quality" Dilemma

The apparent reticence of growth managers to acknowledge the importance of regulating development quality probably is due to two related
factors: the difficulty of defining desired qualities in written regulations
and the slow acceptance of the concept by the courts. Development regulations that specify quantifiable aims, such as 35-foot building setbacks,
45-foot building heights, and 10,000 square-foot lot sizes, carry a great
deal of weight in the law.[3] They are also easy to administer, since public
officials have little room for interpretation of the rules. Writing regulations pertaining to desired development qualities, however, is considerably more complicated. How to specify attractiveness, or well-designed
building relationships, or how new buildings can be compatible with historic ones? Regulators usually understand that many factors enter into
these qualities and wish to leave room for designers and developers to
creatively respond to specific site and building conditions.

Regulating Key Design Elements

Many communities have resolved this issue by singling out certain "appearance" aspects of development for special regulatory attention—typically the features most irritating to many citizens. Modern zoning ordinances, for example, usually contain extensive sections dealing with sign

controls, fence heights and locations, design of service areas for commercial buildings, landscaping in parking areas, landscaped buffers between commercial and residential areas, and the like. Entire books have been written about these types of aesthetic controls, and the regulations themselves are often extensive and complex.[4]

The latest wrinkle in these types of regulations are tree conservation requirements. Inserted in subdivision regulations or adopted as separate ordinances, these provisions are intended to retain existing trees, both individual and in woodlands, and require replacement of trees lost during construction. Trees are considered valuable for their aesthetic and environmental qualities as well as for health and economic benefits. The regulations normally require an inventory and conservation plan for all healthy trees exceeding a minimum size. A road being designed as a new entry for an existing neighborhood in Aspen, Colorado, for example, was sited to avoid all but two of a group of large cottonwood trees. In accordance with Aspen's tree protection regulations, they were replaced on an inch-for-inch basis with new cottonwood trees planted between the road and the bordering meadow.[5]

In the hands of competent designers and responsible developers, these cosmetic approaches to quality control can produce highly satisfactory results. In other hands all bets are off. Landscaping can hide some buildings some of the time, but rarely substitutes for good site and building design. Elaborate sign controls adopted in many communities often fail to mitigate the clutter and distraction of signage. Mark Hinshaw, an urban designer who participated in preparation of Seattle's downtown design controls, observes that typical aesthetic controls dwell on superficial aspects of the visual setting. He comments:

> Design review should be broadly oriented and encourage the creative application of design principles to a specific site. [Conventional] aesthetic controls seek to severely limit choices, while design review attempts to expand choices. Aesthetic control is concerned with product, while design review is concerned with performance. Aesthetic control is exclusionary; design review embraces different solutions to general criteria.[6]

In keeping with Hinshaw's outlook, some communities, as described in later sections of this chapter, have found ways to go beyond conventional zoning standards to specify particular design qualities for certain types of development. Often these provisions are contained in individual sections or separate ordinances that establish design guidelines and special review procedures for determining the appropriateness of proposed project or building designs.

Establishing Legal Acceptance

For many years, legal support for regulation of aesthetic qualities of land use was equivocal, at best. These approaches are now finding increasing support in the law. The U.S. Supreme Court first spoke out on the issue in *Berman* v. *Parker* (348 U.S. 33 [1954]), writing that

> the concept of the public welfare is broad and inclusive. . . . The values it represents are spiritual as well as physical, aesthetic as well as monetary. It is within the power of the legislature to determine that the community should be beautiful as well as healthy. . . .

Berman, however, was really an eminent domain case; the application of these statements to zoning was unclear. Then the U.S. Supreme Court's decision in the Grand Central Terminal case (*Penn Central Transportation Company* v. *New York City,* 438 U.S. 104 [1978]) signaled that local controls over landmarks—and by implication, other aesthetic concerns—were constitutional. Several court cases involving billboard controls in the early 1980s, especially *Metromedia, Inc.* v. *City of San Diego* (453 U.S. 490 [1981]) added strength to the aesthetic rationale by allowing local governments to phase out nonconforming billboards to improve community appearance.[7]

For many years after *Berman* v. *Parker,* state courts generally continued to regard aesthetics as an unsound rationale for development regulations. However, a number of state courts now reflect the views of the Florida Supreme Court: "Zoning for aesthetic purposes is an idea whose time has come; it is not outside the scope of the police power." (*City of Lake Wales* v. *Lamar Advertising Association of Lakeland,* 414 So. 2d 11030 [Fla. 1982].)

These and other cases have established local governments' powers in most states to regulate for the enhancement of community character and livability. Yet the subjectivity of many regulatory measures and an on-going concern in most communities for allowing considerable latitude for landowners' use of property continue to cause debate over these types of regulations.

Encouraging Good Design

Given widespread uncertainty over the language and legality of strict regulatory provisions, planners and public officials have tended to employ more subtle means to induce quality in development. They adopt guidelines rather than mandatory, prescriptive requirements. They offer incentives for developers to follow certain design principles or provide amenities. They provide performance standards that encourage alternative design solutions. They delineate historic and other zoning overlay districts that establish public objectives for special treatment of important community features. They create advisory groups and provide them with written standards and criteria by which to advise on project and building designs. In a few unusual circumstances, where developers will contribute almost anything to develop, public officials demand quality as the ticket for project approval.

Design Review Procedures

Most of the regulatory approaches to maintaining and improving community appearance and development quality depend, sooner or later, on design reviews by review boards and commissions. Similar in many ways to planning commissions or zoning boards, such review bodies are usually made up of five to seven members appointed by the local legislative body. Members generally are chosen from professional groups such as architects and landscape architects, although most boards include some lay citizens. Decisions of review boards may be advisory, with decisions left to planning commission or council action, or may be final subject to appeals. In some cities capable of employing specialized staff, design reviews are carried out as an administrative function by public staff.

Design reviews must be based on published guidelines and procedures, with public notice of hearings and decisions. Preapplication conferences are useful to establish understandings about required information and potential issues. Review boards also benefit from staff analyses of proposals. Approvals often are conditioned on design changes worked out in discussions among board members, staff, and developers—a process that urban designer Mark Hinshaw, in his primer on design review, calls "communication, cooperation, collaboration, and negotiation." An appeals procedure must be established and approvals enforced through monitoring of construction.

Clearly, design review takes time and effort, not just of review board members but of applicants and public staff as well. Procedural rules and design guidelines must be carefully formulated to provide a sound basis for board decisions. Even then, conflicts are likely to arise over design details, sometimes stirred by more basic concerns over the scale or density of proposed projects. For major projects, design reviews can become protracted and time intensive. Because design reviews are highly discretionary processes, however, it pays to formulate detailed guidelines and conduct serious evaluations to provide both a legal basis for decisions and broad community understanding of the desired goals of the process.

Design Guidelines

Many communities have encouraged good design by adopting guidelines that identify significant design concerns and define development characteristics that satisfy those concerns. One of the most influential efforts at formulating guidelines—Hinshaw calls it "the single most important document . . . in rethinking the value of design rules"[8]—was the Urban Design Plan for San Francisco published in 1971. An example of its detailed advice on design character is shown in Figure 6.1. Planners and designers have borrowed many of its ideas in preparing guidelines for today's development.

A comprehensive effort to address quality and appearance issues in growth management has occurred in the city of Scottsdale, a wealthy suburb of Phoenix. Its residents, although generally conservative in their regulatory outlook, have taken great pains to maintain the quality of development during a period of rapid growth. As the city almost doubled its population since 1980 to a level of 160,000 in 1995 (in part through large-scale annexation), the city council adopted a variety of design

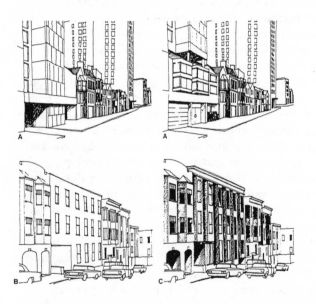

To conserve important design character in historic or distinctive older areas, some uniformity of detail, scale, proportion, texture, materials, color and building form is necessary.

A: Large buildings impair the character of older, small-scale areas if no transition is made between small-scale and large-scale elements.

B: New blank facades introduced into areas of older, more detailed buildings detract from neighborhood character.

C: New buildings using textured materials with human-scaled proportions are less intrusive in older areas characterized by fine details and scale.

Figure 6.1

San Francisco design sketch. The pathbreaking urban design guidelines adopted as part of the comprehensive plan of San Francisco in 1971 included many sketches of ways to conserve the character of existing neighborhoods while allowing new development. (From *The Urban Design Plan for the Comprehensive Plan of San Francisco,* prepared by the San Francisco Department of City Planning, 1971.)

guidelines for redevelopment of older areas and for new development. Its general plan includes an Environmental Design Element that spells out design guidelines for the general character of development, open spaces and streetscapes, historic and archeological sites, environmental resources, and public art.

The "Character Plan Guidelines" call, for example, for protecting the visual quality of special districts, important roadways, open space, and community landmarks (all depicted on maps); for promoting project designs that "are responsive to people's needs, site conditions, the natural environment, and indigenous architectural approaches"; and for building designs that "reflect the form, scale, materials, and design features of the district within which they are sited." The open space guidelines propose, in part, designations of scenic corridors along major streets and an interconnected open space system as shown on an open space plan. The "Streetscape Plan Guidelines" call for arcaded walkways, shade trees, decorative paving, and landscaping in downtown and urban areas, and for native and/or desert-adapted trees and plants throughout the town. The zoning ordinance contains additional requirements, including an entire page devoted to native plant species that must be left in place or relocated when development occurs. Other guidelines are provided for preserving historical resources and archeological sites, air quality, habitat sustainability, water supply and quality, and energy.

Guidelines also have been adopted for downtown and other areas, and for medians of major roads. More specific criteria and provisions are spelled out in several district and corridor plans, reports on "artscape" goals and objectives and historic architectural resources, and a citywide preservation plan.

The guidelines are generally applied during site plan reviews, when the city's design review board examines proposals for all development except individual single-family homes. The design review board can request changes in exterior finishes and colors, roof lines, and other site and building design factors. Applicants can appeal board decisions to the city council; however, the board is chaired on a revolving basis by council members, which means that relatively few council decisions reverse board decisions. A recent example involved a proposed McDonald's restaurant that intended to rim its distinctive roofline with neon lights. The board required that the lights be recessed to reduce glare.[9]

Another upscale suburban community, Plano, Texas, north of Dallas, also has adopted design guidelines for a variety of purposes. Growing from 3500 people to 167,000 in 35 years, Plano has absorbed tremendous growth, much of it for middle- to high-income housing, related high-end retail development, and business parks.

Plano's interest in design quality may spring from its location in a prairie landscape, a treeless plain with few notable features. In such an environment, new development cannot depend on trees, hills, and valleys to disguise or enhance its image. Also, Plano has grown as an upscale residential environment in which residents desire and even expect design amenities. Florence Shapiro, a former city council member and mayor, credited the highly educated community with demanding a standard of quality that could be easily implemented.

With developers already interested in high-quality development, the city made a firm commitment to supporting good design. Plano's planning office has adopted design guidelines for major transportation corridors, retail centers, and multifamily housing development and is preparing single-family residence guidelines. The comprehensive plan contains two sections on design, one spelling out basic elements of urban design and another recommending design guidelines and standards for development along major highway corridors in the city. Zoning overlays and special districts are also used to accomplish urban design objectives. In addition, the subdivision regulations incorporate a number of design requirements.

For example, guidelines for design of retail corners on major intersections were incorporated in the comprehensive plan in 1985, and provisions dealing with rear building facades were added in 1986. (See Figure 6.2.) The guidelines address the appropriateness of retail locations (e.g., at corners of major intersections rather than as linear strip centers), efficient site shape and size (generally 10 to 14 acres), and site accessibility (from major thoroughfares). They also recommend consideration of storefront visibility, limitations on separate "pad sites," potential reuse and adaptability of buildings, consistency of roof and facade treatments, and other design concerns. The guidelines require submission of facade design plans with site plans.

As a result, residential subdivisions generally are walled or bermed, turned away from major streets, and marked by landscaped edges and decorative entrances. Commercial areas are sleek in appearance and screened from residential areas. Offices and industrial buildings boast the newest brand of architectural design and are set among acres of landscaping.

In this development climate, strict design regulations, per se, appear unnecessary. Developers vie with one another to produce well-designed projects and buildings and to incorporate the newest types of amenities. (In some cases, city officials have suggested tempering the amenities, which can become a maintenance burden for homeowner associations.) Recommendations by city officials for design changes and special features almost always receive positive responses.

The city's design guidelines, which are continuously reviewed and refined, provide a framework for staff discussions with developers on design attributes of their proposals. A few years ago, for example, the city

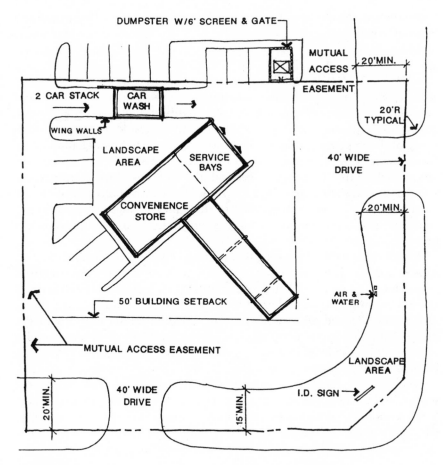

Figure 6.2

Plano design illustration. Plano's simple but effective design guidelines for
retail corners are illustrated in several alternative site plans with common features of landscaped edges, access points, and placement of buildings in relation
to streets. (From *Design Guidelines for Retail Corner and Service Station
Development,* prepared by the City of Plano Planning Department, 1991.)

and a number of developers cooperated in a program to bury power lines
along Preston Road, a major commercial thoroughfare. Although the project cost almost $200 per linear foot, developers and property owners
along the route perceived a major benefit in improved appearance and
were persuaded to foot the bill. The resulting attractiveness of the area
stimulated development and generated higher land values along the
road, and led to citizen approval of a $500,000 bond issue to landscape

and enhance the design of a proposed overpass at Park Boulevard and Preston Road.[10]

Appearance Ordinances

Two dozen or more Chicago-area suburban towns employ a somewhat different approach to guiding design quality. They use "appearance codes" or "anti-monotony codes" in reviewing development proposals. Many of the appearance codes are based on the initial model adopted by Glenview in 1969 that pertains to multifamily residential, commercial, and industrial development. In general, the codes establish performance standards rather than precise requirements. These standards allow developers and builders a great deal of flexibility in meeting code provisions but also allow the review body a considerable amount of leeway in interpreting the standards.

Rather than requiring a specific numbers of trees and shrubs based on a list of approved species, for example, the codes establish a criterion that landscape treatment will "enhance architectural features, strengthen vistas and important axes, and provide shade." Building materials must have "good architectural character" and "be selected for harmony with the building and adjoining buildings." Adjacent buildings of different architectural styles "shall be made compatible by such means as screens, sight breaks, and materials."[11]

Some recent versions of the appearance codes are more concerned with varying the styles of single-family homes in subdivisions—hence, "anti-monotony" codes. The provisions require variations in rooflines, windows, construction materials, and colors. The codes limit the number of similar-styled houses allowed in a row or on a block.

Comprehensive Guidelines

The *Grand Traverse Bay Region Development Guidebook* provides yet another approach to aesthetic regulations.[12] Produced through the leadership of the Traverse City (Michigan) Area Chamber of Commerce, the guidebook describes comparative "common" and "better" approaches for a broad array of design concerns, with the overall goal of retaining the region's natural beauty on which its economy is based. (See Figure 6.3.) It includes guidelines for maintaining natural landscapes and wetlands as well as providing lighting and curb cuts. On the subject of community appearance, for example, it contrasts the typical clashes of individual architectural styles along a commercial corridor with the better approach of limiting the range of building styles, shapes, roof angles, and other design features to be compatible with the character of neighborhood buildings.

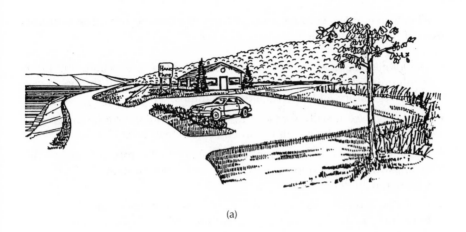

(a)

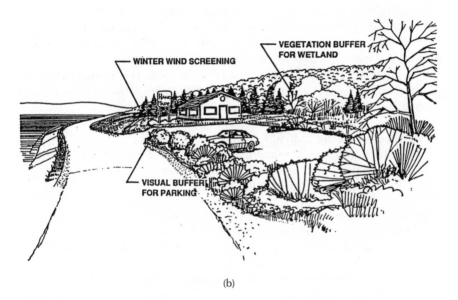

WINTER WIND SCREENING

VEGETATION BUFFER FOR WETLAND

VISUAL BUFFER FOR PARKING

(b)

Figure 6.3

Grand Traverse Bay guidelines. The guidelines, published to guide local regulatory efforts throughout the region, illustrate (a) common practice and (b) better practice, exemplified by these sketches of buffering development with plantings. (From the *Grand Traverse Bay Region Development Guide Book*, prepared by the Planning and Zoning Center, Inc., 1992.)

These examples suggest some common themes among community uses of design guidelines:

- Guidelines serve to announce public objectives and visions for future community character and appearance that can be applied through a variety of regulatory and nonregulatory mediums.
- Guidelines are usually advisory in nature, providing criteria and performance standards by which proposed projects can be evaluated.
- Guidelines frequently are employed within a regulatory framework that establishes ground rules and requirements that prompt negotiated responses to guidelines.
- Guidelines often offer a range of choices that allow developers and builders to tailor responses to specific site and market constraints.

In permitting flexibility in design responses, however, the examples of guidelines described above frequently resort to rather general language that allows many interpretations. Many communities' guidelines depend on broad statements that leave plenty of room for subjective decisions—the "I know what I like when I see it" approach. Terms such as "compatible" and "desirable" are sprinkled throughout the design criteria with little attempt to further define them. The burden of translating these general statements into regulatory determinations falls on the review process and the individual whims of reviewers.

Officials in Hartford, Connecticut learned that lesson in administering the 1984 incentive zoning ordinance for downtown. The review criteria stated in the ordinance were quite general:

> Where reviewing a project . . . the board will determine whether the applicant has demonstrated that the project:
> (a) creates an attractive environment that is in harmony with the . . . downtown district;
> (b) is compatible with and enhances the design concept of adjacent buildings; and
> (c) encourages an active and vital pedestrian environment.
> In making its determination, the board will consider criteria such as massing, height, materials, color, harmony and proportion of overall design, architectural style, siting, scale, and fenestration.

Developers and their architects submitting applications for bonuses under the new zoning provisions were concerned that these rules allowed too much leeway for decision makers. As a result, the review board issued more detailed guidelines in 1986, with more explicit evaluation standards for the nine bonus features. For retail development, for example, the rules require at least 15 percent of floorspace that fronts on or connects to the pedestrian circulation system must be used for retail trade, and that retail trade uses must front on the pedestrian system.[13]

It is impossible to lay down a hard-and-fast rule about the appropriate specificity of guidelines. They depend too much on the complexity of the guidelines subjects, the competence and attitudes of the review boards and their staffs, their statutory status, and the general development climate (rancorous or cooperative) of the community. It is clear from experience, however, that highly detailed guidelines cannot guarantee design excellence and highly flexible guidelines leave much to discretionary decision making. Somewhere between those extremes is the place to be.

Guiding Design Through Special-Area Plans and Zoning Districts

The quality of community character and appearance can be promoted through preparation of detailed plans and adoption of special zoning districts. Many communities use such methods to identify important area attributes and define future actions necessary to maintain and enhance them. These more detailed planning processes allow closer attention to the qualities that make up the special character of built environments.

Downtown Plans

An example of this approach is planning for downtown revitalization, which communities throughout the United States have been conducting for decades. In addition to promoting new development, most such programs are heavily oriented to improving the appearance of public streets and open spaces and promoting restoration and reuse of buildings with distinctive historic and architectural qualities. Baltimore's rejuvenated downtown waterfront and San Diego's Horton Plaza and Gaslight District, for example, exemplify the exciting transformations that have taken place in many major cities. These efforts have been guided by detailed planning and implementation programs, most involving extensive use of design guidelines. Perhaps the most far-reaching and influential planning and regulatory guidance of downtown development have taken place in San Francisco, beginning with the Urban Design Plan completed in 1971 and continuing through its downtown plan adopted in 1985 and its subsequent amendments. Portland, Oregon also employed design guidelines as part of its downtown rebuilding efforts over many years. Its "Special Design Guidelines" for the Lloyd District adjacent to downtown suggest the potential range and definitiveness of guidelines for special areas. (See Figure 6.4.)

SPECIAL DESIGN GUIDELINES CHECKLIST FOR THE LLOYD DISTRICT, PORTLAND, OREGON

──────────────── Findings Checklist ────────────────

Project: _____ Case File No.: _____ Date: _____

Location: _____

A. PORTLAND PERSONALITY		APPLICABLE	DOES COMPLY	DOES NOT COMPLY
A1-1	Connect public facilities to the river	☐	☐	☐
A3-1	Support a convenient pedestrian linkage through the superblocks between the convention center and Lloyd Center	☐	☐	☐
A3-2	Make superblock plaza inviting and easily accessible from Holladay Street	☐	☐	☐
A5-1	Develop identifying features	☐	☐	☐
A5-2	Accommodate or incorporate underground utility service	☐	☐	☐
A5-3	Incorporate works of art	☐	☐	☐
A5-4	Incorporate water features	☐	☐	☐
A5-6	Use public right-of-way design criteria established for the Lloyd District	☐	☐	☐
A5-7	Integrate the civic campus into the Lloyd District	☐	☐	☐
A5-8	Integrate the Lloyd Center Shopping Center into the Lloyd District	☐	☐	☐
A8-1	Incorporate active ground-level uses in parking structures	☐	☐	☐
A9-1	Provide a distinct sense of entry and exit	☐	☐	☐

B. PEDESTRIAN EMPHASIS		APPLICABLE	DOES COMPLY	DOES NOT COMPLY
B1-1	Protect pedestrian areas from mechanical exhaust	☐	☐	☐
B1-2	Incorporate additional lighting	☐	☐	☐
B1-3	Design projects to attract pedestrians to the Broadway/Weidler Corridor	☐	☐	☐
B3-1	Provide pedestrian crossings spaced at traditional one-block intervals	☐	☐	☐
B3-2	Improve pedestrian crossings on N.E. Broadway	☐	☐	☐
B6-1	Provide pedestrian rain protection	☐	☐	☐

C. PROJECT DESIGN		APPLICABLE	DOES COMPLY	DOES NOT COMPLY
C1-1	Integrate parking	☐	☐	☐
C1-2	Integrate signs	☐	☐	☐
C2-1	Maximize view opportunities	☐	☐	☐
C3-1	Design to enhance existing themes in the Broadway/Weidler Corridor	☐	☐	☐
C3-2	Orient development along the Lloyd District eastern edge toward adjacent neighborhoods	☐	☐	☐
C6-1	Step back upper building floors along Holladay Street	☐	☐	☐
C10-1	Use masonry materials	☐	☐	☐
C10-2	Design exterior building walls that are transparent in glazed areas and sculptural in surface	☐	☐	☐
C10-3	Use light colors	☐	☐	☐

Figure 6.4

Portland Design guidelines. Portland's checklist for evaluating design features of proposed development projects identifies the major design elements desired in the Lloyd District, a large mixed-use center near downtown Portland, Oregon. (From *Central City Developer's Handbook,* prepared by the Portland Bureau of Planning, July 1992.)

Such big-city guidance of development quality has been well publicized. However, throughout America many midsize and smaller cities and towns have succeeded in greatly improving the appearance and attractiveness of their downtown areas.

Scottsdale's enthusiasm for encouraging good design, for example, generated a number of special-area plans, including plans for several parts of the downtown area. Downtown Scottsdale has problems, common to many older business districts, of no longer being the city's geographic center or most convenient location for shopping and business. A downtown plan was launched in the early 1980s to counter the declines brought on by the establishment of competing business areas. Still important as a center of government, the arts, specialty retailing, and medical services, downtown needed a fresh input of business activity. The plan emphasized road improvements to provide better access and creation of an attractive, pedestrian-oriented environment.

The plan was backed by development regulations that provided a flexible, incentive-based approach to private development in the downtown area. Downtown design criteria in the zoning ordinance allowed developers who assemble land, provide improvements, or employ innovative designs in accordance with the plan to receive density bonuses, height adjustments, and other regulatory awards. Architectural plans for proposed downtown buildings, especially in designated redevelopment areas, were closely examined by staff, who can, and have, required changes in awning colors, signs, and other design details.

The plan succeeded in attracting about two million square feet of added space. Still, much remained to be done, so the city sponsored two redevelopment plans, one for the southeastern sector and one for the "waterfront" along the Central Arizona Project canal. The plans, adopted in 1993 and 1994, identify deficiencies and opportunities and recommend improvements and potential new construction. Unlike redevelopment plans in many cities, however, the plans simply provide frameworks for coordinating public improvements and guiding reviews of private proposals; development activities are left to private-sector initiatives. The real estate downturn of the late 1980s, unfortunately, dampened the pace of development in downtown until recently, when activity has been picking up.[14]

Corridor Plans

Another area for which special plans and zoning increasingly are employed are commercial corridors—major streets lined with older commercial uses. Such areas typically are unsightly, cluttered with poorly designed buildings and garish signs, and street traffic is congested by a multitude of turning movements into individual parking areas. Raleigh,

North Carolina is one city that has adopted overlay zones to improve traffic flow and the appearance of major commercial corridors.

As befits a city attempting to preserve established neighborhoods as well as to guide development in urbanizing areas, Raleigh has developed more than 20 small-area plans dealing with particular neighborhood or area development issues. The city also has adopted a number of overlay zones for such special areas as the airport, watersheds, and protection of a state park's surroundings. In 1995, the city adopted plans for six areas as amendments to the comprehensive plan.

Now the planning department is preparing plans for five entryway highway corridors, focusing principally on details of access and appearance. Most of the corridor plans have proposed pairs of collector streets parallel to the highways, which would improve access to bordering properties and permit reductions in access points from the main highways. The collector streets, if not existing, are constructed by developers of new projects along the routes. The city's 1995 budget included funds to assist in connecting segments of collectors. The corridor plans are implemented by adoption as zoning overlay districts that regulate landscaping, setbacks, and signage along the highways.

Raleigh has taken additional steps to improve the design and appearance of the city's neighborhoods and commercial areas. Virtually all nonresidential development requires site plan approval to control the details of site and building design more closely than typical zoning and subdivision controls. Sign and billboard ordinances adopted years ago included amortization provisions that are beginning to take effect, greatly reducing the number of billboards and sizes of signs.[15]

Plano, Texas adopted overlay zoning districts in 1993 for its Preston Road and the Dallas North Tollway corridors. Much development in these corridors was a hodgepodge of uses regulated by a variety of zoning districts. Developers were beginning to evince interest in further development along the corridors, which the city viewed as important future employment areas that should be attractively developed. The overlay districts imposed design standards for landscaping and signage, as well as requirements for underground utilities easements. Now the city is proposing to establish a new "Tollway Employment District" zone as a long-term solution for this area.

Special Zoning Districts

Another emerging phenomenon in development regulations is the tailored zoning district, created to meet the needs of an existing area. It is similar in nature to the "specific plan" concept popular in California. Zoning provisions are written to correspond to a specific plan for a proposed development, then inserted by amendment as a new district in the zoning ordinance. The difference is that tailored zoning districts apply to existing neighborhoods and business districts, and their provisions are written to satisfy special characteristics and circumstances of those areas. They may result from strenuous planning exercises or be crafted quickly to meet a particular need or threat.

Richard Babcock and Wendy Larsen's book on special districts details New York City's extensive experience in creating 37 such districts during the 1970s and 1980s, mostly in response to threats that cherished special areas would fall prey to office building developers.[16] So the "Special Midtown District" in Manhattan incorporates the Theater District, the Preservation Subdistrict, and the Fifth Avenue Subdistrict. Zoning provisions in the Theater District require a special permit for demolition of any theater not designated as a landmark, restrict uses and signage, and mandate certain urban design features such as retail continuity along the street and pedestrian circulation on the site.

Babcock and Larsen observed that these special zoning requirements arose in reaction to widespread perceptions that city officials, including planning commission members, were not doing enough to preserve valued areas. The special zoning districts provided an extra element of protection against developers' attempts to change the character of the areas.

San Francisco also uses special zoning districts, mostly to deal with commercial streets in residential neighborhoods. Although most residents wanted existing businesses to remain, they were leery of their expansion at the expense of upper-story affordable housing. They were also disturbed by increasing numbers of bars and take-out food shops and replacement of existing buildings of architectural significance. Sixteen special districts to address such issues were incorporated in the revised zoning ordinance in 1987. As another example, Chicago adopted a "Planned Manufacturing District" to protect older industrial areas from redevelopment for residential purposes. Once an area is designated as such a district, additional provisions and restrictions can be written to respond to specific local circumstances.

Bonuses and Incentives

Many communities have chosen to promote improved qualities of design and appearance through optional regulatory provisions that provide incentives for responding to specific public design objectives. Although this approach can be and is employed for a variety of uses and areas, the most dramatic examples pertain to downtown development. New York City's incentive-based zoning regulations for Manhattan, adopted in 1961, allowed developers to build higher buildings if they incorporated pedestrian plazas and arcades, housing, and theaters. A 1982 revision attempted to simplify the incentive awards to reduce lengthy case-by-case decision making and added urban parks and subway system improvements to the list of features that could generate density bonuses.

Seattle installed incentives in its downtown zoning provisions in the mid-1960s. The development of a 1.5 million square-foot, 76-story office tower that took full advantage of the incentives offered stimulated a complete revision of downtown zoning. The 1985 version restricted total densities and building heights, but allowed density awards for 25 "public benefit" features, from day care facilities and rooftop gardens to plazas and transit-station access. Hartford's 1984 Downtown Development District regulations offer 17 features whose provisions would allow greater density. Bellevue, Washington provided for more than 20 incentive features in its 1981 zoning regulations.[17]

Montgomery County, Maryland used density incentives to generate public benefits in the form of transit-related development, public art, and streetscape improvements in business districts around Metrorail stations. Working with developers and the Washington Metropolitan Area Transit Authority, for example, the county's planning office encouraged high-density development in transit station areas. The zoning density bonus procedures allow the planning board to condition approvals on design features and public benefit features.

In the Bethesda business center, a highly attractive regional location, the combination of the zoning density incentive with a ceiling on potential development imposed by the area plan generated intensive developer interest in projects around the Bethesda Metrorail station. County planners announced that projects offering a high quality of construction and significant public amenities would be first in line for approval. Eight major office complexes and a hotel were constructed through the optional zoning procedure that became known as the "beauty contest." In the competition, developers offered open spaces, public art, and other community-oriented facilities to satisfy the pedestrian-oriented design criteria of the Bethesda plan. In addition, the Bethesda Urban District raised funds to redesign and redevelop the downtown streetscape. In a matter of a few years, the Metrorail station area was transformed into a modern regional center with many attractive features.[18]

Unlike the experience in Bethesda, incentive programs in most communities have been accompanied by downzoning. Reductions in previous densities of development, permitted by right, increase the likelihood that developers would be willing to contribute publicly desired development features to gain permission for greater density.

The problem experienced with all incentive zoning programs is that they depend on real estate market activity and pricing levels to produce results. During the office-building heyday of the 1980s, developers eagerly used incentives to build as much space as quickly as possible. With potential rents soaring, project income could digest the costs of providing special features. In many cities, however, sharp reductions in market activity and profit levels in the late 1980s yielded far fewer public benefits through incentives, and many developers that promised the moon to gain project approvals fell victim to markets that refused to generate needed revenues to pay for luxuries.

Incentives also raise issues of "zoning for sale" and highly discretionary decision making. Developers believe that downzoning to stimulate contributions to public needs, for example, amounts to a form of extortion, since public officials clearly understand that market forces are pressing for higher densities. Negotiations for rezoning or to gain density bonuses open up many possibilities for playing politics rather than playing by the rules. Terry Lassar, in her book on public/private deal making on development projects, observes that "the public bodies that must wheel and deal to secure [public benefits] often resemble hard-driving entrepreneurs more than disengaged protectors of the public interest."[19] Public officials understand, however, that public objectives for high-quality development are well served by incentive techniques. The essential ingredients for achieving a fair result in such negotiations are well-conceived design objectives and detailed guidelines to guide decisions.

Appearance and View Mandates

New York City's 1916 zoning ordinance laid out setback requirements to retain sunlighted streets that resulted in the famous wedding cake shapes of Manhattan's tall buildings. The city's 1961 zoning revisions that allowed higher buildings in return for preservation of open space at ground level combined with the new international architectural style to spawn a new convention—the rectangular tower in a plaza. Zoning has been used in other ways to influence building forms. San Francisco's 1985 downtown plan called for a halt to designing blunt tops of tall buildings. It requires "more finely detailed buildings" and sculptured building tops and encourages tapered rather than slab-like buildings. As an example from a smaller city, the downtown zoning regulations in Burlington, Vermont call for shaping buildings "in relationship to their position in the skyline and sympathetic to surrounding 19th-century vernacular architecture," including alternatives to flat-roof design.[20]

Assessing these efforts at promoting better design in downtown areas, Terry Lassar concludes that "the general consensus seems to be that highly prescriptive regulatory schemes and comprehensive design review programs generally do no more than weed out the worst. They are not guarantees of architectural excellence." She also notes that "because building design is subject to the vagaries of fluctuating tastes and trends,

the recent entrant, or 'alien structure' may very well be
over time into a city's 'icon.'"[21] San Francisco's disti
TransAmerica building, for example, whose design was
on its completion, has been accepted as an identifying s
across the world.

Another approach to preserving community characte
views from key areas to prominent features. Washingto
line Management Act of 1971, for example, required pre
only public access but also views along certain streets to
Austin, Texas restricts development in five roadway corri
country west of the city to protect scenic views. Six capi
serve views of their capitol buildings with zoning height and ....
visions. Denver adopted a series of overlay zones with building height
limits to protect views of the Rockies from the capitol grounds. Burlington, Vermont requires special site plan reviews of buildings taller than 35
feet to consider preservation of views to Lake Champlain.

These regulatory requirements in various cities suggest that citizens
will support rather rigorous restrictions on development to preserve features of recognized value to the community.

Historic Preservation

A major element of many programs to maintain community character
and appearance is preservation of historic buildings. Planning for protection of historic resources has spread rapidly; surveys of communities
with historic preservation ordinances found 421 in 1975 and about 1000
in 1983; in 1993, 1863 communities had historic preservation commissions. Twelve states that require local governments to prepare comprehensive plans include a preservation plan as an optional element and two
more states mandate preparation of a preservation plan.[22] Even in communities lacking these state incentives, preservation of historic buildings
and areas increasingly is viewed as a vital part of retaining the unique
character of communities.

Local preservation plans usually define the goals of preservation and
the historic characteristics of buildings and areas to be preserved, identify the historic resources present in the community, and propose public responsibilities, actions, and incentives to achieve preservation.
Among other benefits, the plan provides a process for considering historic resources for official designation as landmarks.

Preservation plans may be implemented by state or local financial and
tax incentives, of which there is a wide assortment in use, and by adopting local preservation ordinances and/or zoning districts to protect historic resources. The ordinances typically provide a process for officially

designating historic buildings and areas, after which proposed building demolitions and renovations must be reviewed by a commission or board. Most such reviews are advisory in nature—they may recommend against demolition or for certain design changes.

These regulatory actions usually are founded on the designation of buildings and areas as historic landmarks by federal, state, and/or local governments. Section 106 of the National Historic Preservation Act requires that any federal undertakings—funding facilities and programs, for example—that might affect historic resources must be reviewed to consider the potential adverse effects of such undertakings and possible alternative actions. State and local laws may require similar reviews.

The "consideration of potential adverse effects" does not prohibit demolition or changes in historic resources, especially those in private ownership. Listing of areas and buildings as landmarks simply gives the governments and owner advance notice of that possibility. The review process, however, does cost time and money (meaning a delay in the proposed governmental action) and opens up possibilities for litigation and associated additional delays and costs.

Zoning offers possibilities for greater control over historic resources, frequently in the form of overlay districts that establish and may require adherence to design guidelines. Some states require that local historic districts be classified as official zoning districts. Many of the New York special districts described in a previous section, for example, prohibit demolitions or major changes to historic buildings. The districts also may establish procedures for transferring development rights from historic buildings and areas to other areas.

To be effective, a historic preservation plan must be coordinated with comprehensive plan policies and with zoning and other regulatory requirements. Zoning, for instance, that allows major density increases for new development in historic areas provides incentives for tearing down old buildings, not keeping them. Indiscriminate granting of zoning variances and special exceptions can erode the special character of a historic district. Planning policies that promote maintenance of older neighborhoods will support preservation of historic buildings. This is a way of saying that historic preservation efforts must be part of a community's overall growth management strategy, not a separate and unequal element.

The efforts of Kane County, Illinois officials to establish a preservation program and then incorporate it in comprehensive planning policies demonstrate a successful process. Although the eastern half of the county is growing rapidly (as described in Chapter 3), the county's rural areas retain many landscape and farm-building features evocative of an earlier time. The publication of a description of many of these resources in 1977 led to a partial inventory in 1980, which was expanded by the county's planning department several years later to a systematic survey of historic rural structures. In 1987 the county board appointed a preservation committee to oversee the survey, evaluate the identified resources, and explore potential protection actions, including the need for a preservation ordinance and commission. A year later the county board enacted a historic preservation ordinance that established a commission with powers to propose designation of landmarks or preservation districts by the county board and to review significant alteration, construction, or demolition of landmarks. The commission prepared a preservation plan that was incorporated in the county plan in 1990, making preservation of historic landmarks a significant element of county development policy.[23]

More and more communities are acting to preserve historic resources as an essential element of their community character. In the process, they have enriched our knowledge of design factors, renovation techniques, and financing opportunities required to successfully maintain historic resources. Their experiences also demonstrate the ways in which the economic and quality-of-life benefits of historic preservation can work hand-in-hand with growth management strategies.

Two Popular Design Concepts

Many people's thinking about the character and design of growing communities is being shaped by two major design concepts being discussed across the nation. One focuses on recreating small-town or village forms of development in both urban and rural circumstances. The other, related, concept promotes pedestrian-friendly development to support mass transit service.

In rejecting urban sprawl and focusing on small-scale design concerns, both concepts attempt to recapture traditional forms of cities and towns as a means of creating more livable, attractive, and functional communities. Both design approaches are directly responsive to many growth management goals and strategies, although they frequently run afoul of conventional development regulations. As described below, they combine many of the design concerns discussed in the previous sections of the chapter.

The "New" Traditionalism in Community Design

Variously called "neotraditional design," "the new urbanism," and "urban villages" in urban areas and "village" design in rural areas, this design concept promotes a return to the qualities of earlier forms of development: Where homes are closer together and closer to the street, walking is made easy by attractive pathways connecting homes to shopping and community services, street systems are interconnected to reduce traffic congestion, forms and scales of development are comfortable and compatible, and open spaces of many kinds are readily accessible. The classic New England town is often invoked as the model for this design approach.

Harkening back to forms of development popular until automobiles came into wide use in the 1920s responds to many contemporary concerns, perhaps best summed up by Peter Calthorpe in *The Next American Metropolis,* when he asserts that

> . . . our communities must be designed to reestablish and reinforce the public domain, that our districts must be humanscaled, and that our neighborhoods must be diverse in use and population. And finally, that the form and identity of the metropolis must integrate historic context, unique ecologies, and a comprehensive regional structure.[24]

These designs for communities intend to put people closer together, lead them to meet on the street and in the community, create vistas and green spaces for their pleasure, and induce a feeling of security, convenience, and comfort in their living environment. The design approaches also are meant to sharply reduce conversion of open land for urban purposes and needs for automobile travel. Thus they fit the aims of many growth management programs for curbing urban sprawl, making more efficient use of infrastructure, and preserving open space and natural resources.

To achieve these grand goals, the concepts tend to focus on small-scale design concerns appropriate for development in small towns, villages, and city neighborhoods: architectural compatibility between buildings; relations of residences to streets; facade treatments and building relationships in commercial areas; pedestrian walkway networks; design of civic buildings and spaces; landscaping and streetscapes; locations and designs of parking areas and garages.[25]

Although most of these ideas have been espoused by planners and urban designers for decades, their re-packaging in comprehensive conceptual form has proven widely and increasingly popular. Dozens of development projects, both small and large in scale, have incorporated the basic design ideas. Hundreds of communities are exploring ways to implement the approach. Some communities' comprehensive plans are centered on promoting developments with these qualities, and zoning ordinances are being revised to permit the lot and yard sizes and building designs called for in the concepts. Many people in the development professions and in the general public have gained a new appreciation of the potential benefits of more compact and pedestrian-friendly living environments.

Such design approaches continue to meet obstacles in implementation, however:

• Most zoning ordinances and subdivision regulations require densities, lot and yard sizes, road widths, and other development standards inimical to new traditionalists' design ideas.

• The design focuses on small-scale, well-designed relationships between buildings and uses flies in the face of current "big-box" and nonintegrated development trends.

• Although many of the developments to date have found an enthusiastic market reception, their densities and design styles are not universally appreciated by consumers accustomed to conventional suburban development.

• The design emphasis on encouraging small-town folksiness and daily trips to the store probably succeeds more in eliciting nostalgia for a glorified past than changing contemporary ways of living that depend on cars, refrigerators, and television.

• Some of the design ideas and regulatory approaches proposed by proponents of the new traditionalism appear frighteningly absolute and inflexible, considering the range of site conditions and consumer needs to be addressed.

Nevertheless, the idea that people can reside closer together in an attractive environment that allows more choices of ways to live and travel, provides compelling aims for development that meets many growth management objectives.

Transit-Oriented Design

Peter Calthorpe, in association with a number of other designers, has made "transit-oriented development" (TODs) and "pedestrian pockets" everyday terms in the world of city planning and development. The rising interest in and construction of rail transit lines in many cities over the past two decades pointed to the fact that most suburban patterns of development lend poor support for use of transit. Transit planners have understood for decades that both bus and rail transit depends to a great extent on drawing riders from concentrations of residents and workers within walking distance of transit stations. In addition, ridership is increased if pedestrian access is convenient, pleasant, and safe and if pedestrians can satisfy a variety of trip demands near the transit stations.

Calthorpe and others have enlarged on this knowledge by defini detail the patterns and mixes of land uses that would best support transit use and the designs of pedestrian spaces and pathways that would be most attractive to transit riders. These design principles, which echo many of those promulgated in the new traditionalist ideas, are packaged in the concepts of TODs and pedestrian pockets. In addition, they are published in many manuals of transit-oriented design guidelines prepared for various transit systems.[26] Calthorpe and Associates also has applied these concepts in a number of project plans for various cities. Ironically, two of the best-known new-traditionalist/TOD developments, Kentlands in Gaithersburg, Maryland and Laguna West, outside Sacramento, California, are almost unserved by transit of any kind. (Laguna West enjoys the service of one bus line; Kentlands, none.) In *Transit Villages in the 21st Century*, Michael Bernick and Robert Cervero describe methods for creating mixed-use communities oriented to rail stations. Examples, however, are still evolving.[27]

These popular design concepts serve to promote specific ways and means of improving community appearance and development quality.

Conclusion

This recitation of activities in the "soft" side of growth management— preserving community character and livability through close attention to design aspects of development—indicates the range and intensity of concerns being pursued by communities across the nation. Two implications should be drawn from the description of regulatory and other efforts being practiced today. One is that design and appearance initiatives should be closely interrelated with other growth management activities. They can play a significant role in supporting and reinforcing other elements of growth management programs, and in turn can benefit from operating in a broad policy context established by other growth management techniques.

The second important implication is the extent to which techniques and actions for preserving community character and promoting high-quality design must work in conjunction with the development marketplace. Fine points of project and building design are significant only if and when development takes place. Even historic preservation is dependent on attracting profitable uses for old buildings and neighborhoods.

7

Achieving Economic and Social Goals

Community character and quality of life depend as much or more on economic and social factors as on the design and appearance concerns described in Chapter 6. For many communities, in fact, economic growth and social well-being pose critical and sometimes seemingly intractable growth management questions. Depending on their circumstances, however, communities may have quite different perspectives on the nature of their problems:

- Rapid growth in "bedroom" communities on the outskirts of metropolitan areas may be generating commuter traffic congestion and fiscal shortages as housing development far outpaces expansion of employment.

- Communities perceived as desirable residential areas may find that rising housing prices are driving out families with moderate to middle incomes and workers needed by local business and industry.

- Older suburban communities may be experiencing declines in business and neighborhood conditions as firms and residents move to more attractive locations in newer suburbs.

- Residents of central cities, who make up a large share of poor minorities in metropolitan areas, face continuing reductions of job opportunities, increasing crime, and deteriorating housing conditions.

- Rural towns may be losing jobs and residents as economic shifts leave them behind.

• At the regional level, income and tax disparities between rich and poor jurisdictions are continuing to widen, isolating the poor from jobs, housing,
and educational opportunities, heightening racial and other social tensions, and undercutting attempts to reduce sprawl and promote concentrated development.

These conditions arise from cross-cutting economic and social forces affecting all parts of the nation. National and regional economic forces promote expansion of some types of industries while others wane in importance. Together with changing labor and locational needs, these forces
lead to employment shifts from region to region and within regions. In
turn, these movements cause population changes that often intensify social tensions and generate diverse settlement patterns.

The effects of such shifts are of fundamental import for growth management. As rural residents move from small towns and farms to find
work in metropolitan areas, rural towns wither on the vine. Aided by
new highway systems, expanding metropolitan populations spill into the
countryside, forming numerous suburban jurisdictions. In the last 20
years, while the large cities of the 39 most populous metropolitan areas
gained fewer than one million residents, the suburban population increased by 30 million. The tremendous territorial expansion of urban
areas stimulates the movement of businesses and industries out of congested central locations to sites closer to their customers and workers.
Over two-thirds of the employment growth that took place in the 60
largest metropolitan areas from 1976 to 1986 occurred in suburban
areas outside central cities.[1] Meanwhile, inner-city minority populations,
enlarged by in-migration, are dissuaded from moving out by racial discrimination and other limitations on access to jobs and affordable housing.[2]

This process of social and economic change, extended especially over
the past half-century, has resulted in major disparities in economic and
social conditions among jurisdictions concerned with managing growth
and change. As urban cores and some inner suburbs suffer declines in
economic power and social stability, outer jurisdictions find it difficult to
cope with the needs of newcomers and the spread of suburban development. Individual communities formed to ensure a desirable living environment are bombarded by largely external forces that hamper efforts to
practice balanced growth management. Small towns and rural settlements can easily fall prey to footloose industries, giant retail operations,
and fly-by-night developers who promise much, deliver little, and wreck
local economies.

These changes, besides altering the balance of jobs and housing so desirable for livable communities, have grave effects on fiscal conditions of

many local jurisdictions. Declines in business and neighborhood conditions are paralleled by decreasing investments in maintaining infrastructure systems. Tax bases erode even as social costs rise. Competition among jurisdictions for tax ratables generates friction and unforeseen impacts on fiscal conditions and community character.

Concerns are growing among many urban development experts that these problems may affect the nation's future position in the global economy. Michael A. Stegman and Margery Austin Turner, top officials at the U.S. Department of Housing and Urban Development, recently wrote:

> The vicious cycle of poverty concentration, social despair, and fiscal distress that plagues much of urban America today weakens our nation's economic health and undermines the ability of metropolitan regions to compete in the global economy. . . . The distress and decline of high-poverty areas do not remain confined to the central city but gradually spread out to affect suburban areas as well. Older suburbs—and even some "edge cities"—increasingly find themselves in competition with newer areas of development that can attract more affluent families, retail centers, and jobs. . . . Central city decline is also a problem for us all because it can paralyze metropolitan growth and development.[3]

Growth management programs can be framed to address these problems in fundamental ways. They can redirect economic and social forces by balancing the spread of new development with efforts to stabilize or revive existing neighborhoods, business centers, and industrial areas and by modifying tax and infrastructure investment policies that influence so many locational decisions. They can mitigate the adverse outcomes of economic and social forces by improving opportunities for economic and social advancement, including better access to jobs, decent housing, and good public facilities and services. They can avoid furthering inequities by conscientious public facility siting and investment decisions.

These efforts almost always must involve a wide spectrum of activities normally the province of disciplines outside the usual realm of growth managers. Maintaining stable neighborhoods, for example, most likely depends more on the quality of local schools than on keeping up with street repairs or achieving an open space ratio of three acres per 1000 residents. Addressing the influences of poverty and joblessness requires efforts of skilled health and social welfare staffs as much or more than housing improvements. Growth management programs in many communities may need to place greater emphasis on reaching out to these professional disciplines to fashion solutions to fundamental social and economic problems affecting community development.

In any case, managing growth and change must link physical development with human development. Four areas in which this concern typically has been expressed are

- affordable housing programs for low- and moderate-income residents;

- economic development programs to retain and attract jobs;

- redevelopment, infill, and renovation programs to maintain existing neighborhoods and employment centers; and

- regional development controls and tax-sharing programs.

Affordable Housing Programs

The ubiquitous form of development regulation, zoning, became popular primarily as a means of protecting neighborhood and residential values. Ironically, the escalation of zoning standards for lot sizes, setbacks, and required amenities over the years has not only maintained values but in many communities has helped to push them beyond the realm of affordability for average-income as well as lower-income homeowners. This factor, plus the lingering housing needs of low-income people, has driven many communities to foster rehabilitation and production of affordable housing as part of their growth management programs. In addition, state laws in some states require local governments to plan and grant approvals for a full range of housing to meet local needs.

Programs to increase the supply of affordable housing have a long history, beginning with the U.S. Housing Act of 1937, which created public housing, and continuing through the Housing Act of 1949 and its many amendments. In the decades following the 1949 legislation, federal housing subsidies enabled many communities to form housing authorities and conduct housing programs that produced millions of units priced or rented at levels affordable to low- and moderate-income residents.

Beginning in the mid-1970s and continuing through the present day, however, federal funds have been drastically cut and production of new and rehabilitated housing has dropped off accordingly. Table 7.1 indicates the rise and fall of federal housing programs since 1937. HUD-assisted housing starts for construction or substantial rehabilitation fell from an annual average of 135,298 units during the decade of the 1970s to 61,245 per year during the 1980s.[4] During the late 1980s, HUD-assisted housing starts declined to fewer than 20,000 per year. By 1993, although 5.7 million housing units received financial assistance from HUD or the Farmer's Home Administration, an estimated 9.3 million unsubsidized renter households paid over 50 percent of their income for rent or lived in deficient housing.[5]

Table 7.1
The Cycle of Major HUD Housing Assistance Programs

Program	Year Enacted	1993 Status	Years in Operation
Public Housing	1937	7726 units	56
Section 202 Elderly	1959	10,475 units	34
Section 221(d)(3)	1961	Terminated, 1968	7
Rent Supplements	1965	Terminated, 1974	9
Section 235 Home Ownership	1968	Terminated, 1989	21
Section 236 Rental Housing	1968	Terminated, 1974	6
Section 8 New Construction	1974	Terminated, 1983	9
Section 8 Existing Housing	1974	38,416 units	19
Housing Action Grants, HODAG	1983	Terminated, 1989	6
Home Program	1990	39,106 units	3

Source: Mary Nenno, *Ending the Stalemate* (Lanham, MD: University Press of America, 1995), 88. Based on *Housing and Community Development Acts: 1937–1990*, and *HUD Budget Summaries and Appropriations Acts: 1981–1993*.

Many communities receive federal funds applicable to housing programs through the Community Development Block Grants (CDBG) program initiated in 1974. The grants, allocated according to need, cover a wide variety of activities designed to revitalize city physical and economic structures and improve the circumstances of low- and moderate-income persons. CDBG funds have become increasingly important in supporting local housing programs but compete with a wide variety of other activities eligible for program funding.

Furthermore, Nenno comments, although CDBG funding is intended to be targeted to high-need areas, in practice, communities often spread funding over many areas with little attention to long-term housing or revitalization strategies. The Housing Assistance Plans (HAPs) and Comprehensive Housing Affordability Strategies (CHAS) required by the U.S. Department of Housing and Urban Development (HUD) for communities receiving federal housing assistance were supposed to provide an assessment of housing needs and a strategic framework for community housing programs. In many cases, however, the plans often fall short of providing real direction for housing programs.[6]

With federal programs on the wane and local efforts in difficulty, state housing programs have taken up some of the slack, as have ad hoc local governmental and public/private housing programs. Local public/private partnerships for housing development have proliferated, using a variety of funding sources including low-income housing tax credits. Nongovernmental organizations such as BRIDGE (the Bay Area Residential Investment and Development Group), especially active in California; Jubilee Housing, operating in the Washington/Baltimore area; and the Local Initiatives Support Corporation and Enterprise Foundation, active throughout the nation, have become major players in stimulating production of affordable housing. Many of these organizations are supported by local housing trust funds that create a pool of investment funds for affordable housing.

In most communities, however, affordable housing remains a precious commodity and a weak component in growth management. Often local governments that mount ambitious growth management programs realize after the fact that increased development restrictions affect the availability of affordable housing. They then attempt to retrofit their programs by adopting special programs to provide subsidized housing, as described in a later section—sometimes a matter of too little, too late. Nevertheless, many communities recognize needs for affordable housing and make strenuous attempts to meet those needs despite the obstacles in place.

Raleigh, North Carolina's experience illustrates the range of problems frequently encountered. Like most older cities, Raleigh has its share of rundown housing and also has actively participated in federal housing assistance programs. Since 1935, Raleigh's housing authority and other city agencies have constructed about 2200 public housing units and, more recently, rehabilitated over 500 housing units and provided rent assistance to 1000 low- and moderate-income families.

Despite these efforts, the city still has a substantial housing problem, exacerbated by housing price increases and continued declines in federal housing assistance. To address these problems, a series of task forces and committees worked over several years, beginning in 1983, to identify potential public and private approaches to providing affordable housing. A task force in 1985 recommended that the city adopt annual housing targets: construction or purchase of 100 low-income rental units; rehabilitation of 100 substandard units; and housing assistance loans and grants to 100 homebuyers. Following the report, the city planning staff prepared a housing element for the comprehensive plan that laid down a basic principle for city involvement in housing issues:

> The city recognizes that it must become an active provider of housing for low and moderate income households . . . with the understanding that [this] can only be accomplished within an effective intergovernmental framework and in partnership with the private sector.

To implement this policy, the city began a multifaceted housing program financed with federal, state, county, and city funds. The program acquired and prepared housing sites for private and nonprofit builders, rehabilitated substandard housing, provided emergency shelters and transitional housing, and financed construction of a variety of housing for low to moderate income homeowners and renters. In addition, funds were authorized to organize the Triangle Housing Partnership, a public/private housing group, and $20 million in general obligation bonds were authorized to assist potential homeowners and renters.

These efforts in the 1980s declined in the 1990s. Funds from the bond issue have been fully allocated and current city leadership is debating future priorities. The local housing authority fell into disfavor as maintenance standards declined at its projects. Activities of the Triangle Housing Partnership virtually ceased. A statewide equity pool was spun off, however, to provide a mechanism to channel private sector funds to local efforts for using tax credits for low- and moderate-income housing. Additional city support for housing apparently will be limited to using Community Development Block Grant funds to support the programs formerly funded by bond financing. This will mean a significantly less ambitious effort compared to previous years.

Raleigh's record is not unique in its early ambitions and more recent tribulations. Its program, nevertheless, suggests some approaches to community housing needs that make sense in a growth management context. First, Raleigh's citizens and public officials engaged in a number of studies to determine overall housing needs, particularly gaps where supply was not meeting demand. Based on these studies, city officials set specific targets for rehabilitation and production of various types of affordable housing.[7]

S. Mark White's study of affordable housing strategies suggests that these targets might well be formulated as communitywide level-of-service standards for affordable housing, similar in concept to standards used for other factors of community growth and change. Affordable housing standards would identify affordable housing needs as a proportion of total future housing needs, define available and potential housing assistance resources (federal assistance, property taxes, public/private ventures, municipal property, and so on), and allocate responsibilities for communitywide support and developer contributions. White cites Boulder, Colorado's housing plan, which identified the proportion of the city's housing stock that would require subsidy based on the regional comprehensive plan. The share of housing already subsidized determined the existing level of service that should be maintained as a citywide responsibility. An excise tax on new development was calculated to provide the remaining subsidy needs.[8]

Raleigh also forged a program that blended public, semi-public, and private actions, tapping a wide range of funding resources. Its citywide bond issue, combined with state and federal assistance programs, helped support private and semi-public actions to provide affordable housing.

Together with the city's establishment of housing targets, these efforts became an essential element of Raleigh's growth management program.

The problems that Raleigh recently experienced due to drastic declines in federal and state housing funds are shared by many communities. In part because of those declines, a number of communities instituted incentive or mandatory requirements for developer contributions to affordable housing. "Inclusionary" housing programs require developers to incorporate affordable housing units in proposed residential developments. "Linkage" programs are similar, but generally are targeted to developers of nonresidential buildings, especially in downtown areas. In addition, communities made efforts to reduce obstacles caused by regulatory requirements and procedures in order to reduce development costs of housing. (Requirements adopted in some states that mandate community responses to regional housing needs are described in a later section of this chapter.)

Inclusionary Housing Programs

A number of communities take advantage of their status as desirable locations for residential development by requiring developers and builders to include affordable housing in market-rate housing developments. Housing prices in these communities have tended to rise in recognition of their premier position in the regional marketplace. In some cases higher housing prices also reflect restrictions on development (such as growth limits, moratoriums, high development standards) or the relative isolation of the community (such as many resort communities).

The consequence of rising housing prices is that increasing numbers of people are unable to find decent, affordable housing in the communities in which they work. Communities dedicated to providing housing opportunities for current residents, their children, and future employees are pressed to balance market forces with public programs that reduce housing costs for selected groups of consumers. Communities whose economies depend on housing employees within or near their jobs, such as ski resorts in remote mountain locations, must find ways to provide housing at affordable prices and rents for those employees (not unlike the towns erected by mining and mill corporations in earlier days).

Given the decreasing availability of public funds to support such housing, local governments have turned to the private sector for "contributions" to the stock of lower-priced housing. They reason that housing developers and builders can support some proportion of lower-priced housing with the profits derived from market-rate housing. In fact, most communities' inclusionary housing programs permit density bonuses or other permitting favors to offset developer and builder losses (or lesser profits) on lower-priced housing.

Rockville, Maryland adopted an inclusionary ordinance in 1990 whose provisions typify those in other ordinances. It requires all subdivisions of 50 or more dwelling units to include moderately priced units. Provisions call for

- a specified proportion of proposed housing units—in the Rockville ordinance, at least 12.5 percent of units in a subdivision—to be moderately priced, with a sliding scale of optional density increases for a higher percentage of moderately-priced units;

- definition of unit prices or rents as determined by regulations adopted by the Mayor and Council [or more normally as a percentage of household incomes of households earning a stated proportion of the area's median income];

- agreements between the developer and city controlling temporary rentals, limiting resale prices, providing for the city's optional purchase of a proportion of the units and its right of first refusal for unit resales (to control price increases), and other matters;

- options for developer construction of such housing, including land transfers to public or semi-public housing agencies and contributions to a public housing trust fund.[9]

Some inclusionary housing programs also stipulate that the exterior and interior design of units must be similar to designs of market-rate units, although they may be smaller and equipped with fewer amenities.

Rockville's program was adopted just as the real estate market postponed further residential development in the area. However, housing requirements are being applied to two major projects now in the approval process, which is expected to generate several hundred affordable units over the next few years. As described in Chapter 2, Montgomery County, Maryland's program, on which the Rockville program was patterned, has produced more than 9200 units of moderately priced housing over a 25-year period.

A similar program in Anaheim, California, part of then booming Orange County, generated almost 1500 units in just two years. Anaheim grants a 25 percent density bonus for developers who set aside housing for residents whose income is 50 to 80 percent of the area's median income; for developers who designate 25 percent of their units for very-low income elderly residents, the city also allows reductions in parking, unit size, and building height. Anaheim also assists housing production with revenue bond proceeds and offers low-cost loans, mortgage credit certificates, and reductions in mortgage interest rates to spur home ownership for residents who earn 80 to 120 percent of median income.[10]

A somewhat different approach has been pursued by remote communities such as Aspen and Breckenridge, Colorado. In these resort communities, prices and rentals for market-rate housing soared well beyond the income ranges of many employees. Both communities adopted performance-based point systems for rating proposed developments. In Breckenridge's ordinance, employee housing is desirable although not mandatory in new projects. Developers can obtain points toward project approval by promising to produce housing units for employees—units defined as deed-restricted for either long-term leasing or sale to a person residing in and employed in the county. For residential projects, for example, developers can pledge 10 percent or more of the gross dwelling area of proposed projects for employee housing. Unit design must be compatible with other units in the development, although they may be located off-site within the town's growth boundary.[11]

A home-grown effort in Boise, Idaho was initiated by a task force appointed by the mayor in 1993 to seek ways to build affordable housing. The group, incorporated as the nonprofit Boise Housing Corporation, found and obtained a donation of a passed-over site in an established neighborhood, and completed a mixed market-rate/moderate-income housing project just three years later. The development included 200 rental units and 43 for-sale townhouses. Three quarters of the rental units and 36 of the townhouses were allocated to low-income families. Funds from the Idaho Housing and Finance Association, federal low-income tax credits from the Idaho Power Company, special short-term financing arrangements by local banks, and in-kind contributions by local contractors, architects, and property managers underwrote costs for reduced rental rates and low-income homebuyers.[12]

A somewhat different approach was taken in Arlington County, Virginia, where residents of an existing affordable housing complex successfully lobbied for special protection through zoning. The county board of supervisors adopted an affordable housing protection overlay district in 1990 that required developers to replace affordable housing in comparable locations, preferably within the existing neighborhood. The zoning allowed increases in densities to provide incentives for incorporating moderate-priced housing in redeveloped areas, either by preserving existing housing or replacing it with similar types of units. The first development within the initial district offered 56 rehabilitated units and 47 new ones. To assist the development, the county loaned the developer $1.5 million and the developer obtained federal low-income tax credits.[13]

Such programs have proven quite successful in producing moderately priced housing and have generally been supported by housing developers who find the compensatory density a reasonable trade-off. Because the units generally are occupied by working people such as teachers and policemen, other residents have had few complaints about neighborhood impacts.

Housing Linkage Programs

During the real estate boom of the late 1970s and early 1980s, a dozen or so communities enacted requirements for commercial developers to contribute to housing programs in the form of fees or housing production. Essentially a variation on the notion of inclusionary housing, so-called "linkage" regulations were based on the premise that commercial development often displaced existing housing stock, frequently units in the affordable category, and generated housing needs through its attraction of employees. San Francisco's planning department originated the concept of linkage when it instituted its Office Housing Production Program in 1980. The vigorous expansion of downtown office space in that city coincided with a contracting supply of housing affordable to moderate- and low-income residents.

Other cities experiencing robust downtown growth, such as Boston, Seattle, Miami, and Washington, D.C., soon followed suit with linkage programs somewhat different than San Francisco's. Some programs were mandatory; others were optional as incentives for increased density. Some applied only to office developers, others to all nonresidential uses (and some to multifamily residential developers as well). Some applied only to downtown development, others to all development within the jurisdiction. Some were intended to generate all types of housing while others focused on affordable housing. Almost all programs allowed developers to donate fees to housing trust funds or contract with housing developers as options to developing housing themselves.[14]

The linkage idea also spread to communities in several states that required "fair share" housing related to regional needs. California and New Jersey communities, in particular, adopted requirements for developers of all types of projects to contribute to housing programs, greatly expanding potential affordable housing production generated by inclusionary housing programs.

Linkage programs have been vigorously opposed by developers, who believe that housing requirements imposed on downtown development risk making projects too costly to be competitive with suburban office development. In addition, they claim that cities are taking advantage of developers to correct long-standing and communitywide housing problems. The shortage of affordable housing in San Francisco, for example, was due not only to rising housing prices brought on by a robust real estate market but also to downzonings of residential densities, passage of a rent control law that reduced production of rental housing, and cuts in federal housing subsidies. Tapping unpopular office developers, however, to help meet housing needs for lower-income residents was and is politically popular.

Legal questions were also raised about linkage programs, particularly about the nexus between the housing requirement and the effects of downtown or nonresidential development. In most cities this question was resolved by commissioning a study that demonstrated that growth in downtown office space or other nonresidential development drew new employees whose housing needs altered the housing market in ways that created problems for lower-income families. White, in his analysis of linkage law, suggests four ways in which local governments can support linkage programs:

- Obtain state enabling legislation that establishes local powers to levy fees and/or provide a fair share of regional housing needs.

- Provide evidence that development affected by linkage requirements will contribute to or add to the need for housing or "will consume resources otherwise available for housing opportunities."

- Demonstrate that the jurisdiction is making good faith attempts to remedy existing housing deficiencies through other funding sources—in other words, that the linkage requirement is part of an overall housing strategy.

- Show that the extent of the housing contribution is based on a reasonable apportionment of overall housing needs based on a specific developer's prorated responsibility.[15]

In most cities, the real estate downturn in the late 1980s, especially in downtown office construction, cut linkage housing contributions severely. In the mid-1990s, continuing regulatory limits on the amount of downtown development in San Francisco and Seattle undercut generation of linkage-related housing, although in Boston institutional developments are yielding substantial housing contributions. Until commercial development rebounds nationwide, it appears that linkage programs are questionable as significant sources of affordable housing. Even then, many communities are likely to view linkage programs as disincentives to attracting desirable revenue-generating commercial development.

Streamlining Regulations

In years past, subdivision development and building construction required only simple one-time permits issued with a minimum of fuss. In most communities today, developers and builders face a bewildering array of zoning and re-zoning procedures, subdivision plan and plat approvals, conditional and special-use zoning permits, specific permits for site grading, foundations, sewer and water hookups, construction and environmental clearances at several levels of government, and design and other special reviews by various boards and commissions. In some places, the permitting process seems less like a system than an obstacle course.

Most regulations are beneficial but they also have costs, among them the amount of preparation to win approval, delays in the approval process, and the risks attendant to these investments of effort and time. In addition, complex regulatory processes are often manipulated by opponents of development to further delay approvals and increase costs of development. The upshot is that regulations can substantially affect housing costs, especially in the more affordable ranges. As discussed in the section on growth management effects on housing prices in Chapter 9, a $5000 impact fee, for example, may be a relatively insignificant addition to the cost of a house priced at $300,000 but a major problem for one priced at $90,000.

Federal and state agencies, as well as local governments in many areas, have promoted regulatory reform for many years as a means of achieving more affordable housing. One of the latest efforts was the 1991 report of the Advisory Commission on Regulatory Barriers to Affordable Housing.[16] The Commission found that NIMBY-driven exclusionary zoning, reluctance to zone for multifamily housing, "gold-plated" subdivision standards, large impact fees, and overburdensome permitting procedures were affecting builders' abilities to deliver affordable housing. Like the dozen federal commissions and task forces before it, the Commission recommended a variety of reforms centered on improving planning, policy, and infrastructure support for affordable housing in local growth management programs; promoting affordable types of housing such as manufactured housing and accessory units; and encouraging overhauls of local regulations to reduce requirements and complexities.

Dozens of publications produced by federal, state, and local agencies over several decades suggest specific ways of streamlining regulations to reduce costs of developing affordable housing.[17] Techniques for streamlining or reforming regulations include:

- Clarifying the organization and language of ordinances and coordinating provisions and procedures specified by different ordinances.

- Periodically updating provisions, weeding out unnecessary provisions, and evaluating standards and requirements.

- Simplifying and clarifying procedures to make the permitting process more understandable, including establishing procedures for interpreting questions, specifying conditions for routine approval of frequent minor applications, and spelling out standards and criteria for discretionary approvals.

- Publishing guidebooks and checklists for applicants and holding preapplication conferences for complex projects.

- Providing a central information center to provide basic information and route requests and questions to appropriate departments.

- Improving review procedures, including combined or simultaneous reviews by several departments, fast-tracking or expedited processes for noncontroversial and/or high-priority projects, and management information systems to track the flow of applications.

- Training board and commission members who deal with development permits and providing fair and consistent rules for hearing procedures and decision making.

These ideas have been put into practice in many communities but need periodic reexamination to compensate for the upward creep of new ordinances and provisions and to apply new technology in communication and construction.

Despite the availability of these approaches to improving housing affordability, however, experience in New Jersey and elsewhere demonstrates that many communities continue to manage growth in ways that defy regional housing needs. Other communities have been unsuccessful in shaping and funding well-conceived housing programs. On the plus side, where communities have seriously assessed overall housing needs, created incentives to produce affordable housing, and tapped a variety of organizational and funding sources to assist the process, they have managed to make substantial contributions to the stock of affordable housing.

Economic Development Programs

Communities have employed various tactics to stimulate local economic development since colonial days. During the twentieth century, in particular, local governments played significant roles in strengthening local economies, aided by federal and state assistance programs. Their growth management programs contributed to community economic vitality by producing infrastructure systems adequate to support economic growth and by making communities desirable places to live and work. At the same time, local public officials hoped to retain and/or expand employment opportunities for residents and the tax base for the jurisdiction by adopting programs to attract new industries, stimulate growth of existing industries, and revitalize declining business districts. Public officials understand that economic vitality is a key to maintaining the fiscal stability so important to providing needed services and facilities and enhancing residents' quality of life. This vital connection between economic opportunity and the other aims of growth management must be reflected in local programs to manage community development, especially as federal assistance programs wane in significance.

Federal and State Assistance for Economic Development

The first major federal efforts to aid local economic development were initiated during the great depression of the 1930s. Various public works and housing programs poured money into efforts to stimulate economic activity. Post World War II efforts continued to expand federal programs in such areas as small business assistance, manpower training, and attracting investments in declining areas. Often such programs worked at cross purposes, especially in connection with other federal activities, in promoting suburban expansion and rural development. In the past few years, however, federal program activity in support of local economic development has waned as federal budgets have been drastically curtailed.

Although small business assistance and manpower training continue to receive federal support, the chief federal efforts in recent years have focused on enterprise zones and, most recently, on empowerment zones. Enterprise zones were initially proposed in the early 1980s but, ironically, the legislation authorizing enterprise zones signed by President Reagan contained none of the tax credits, tax deductions, or financing devices needed to make it work. Instead, most states picked up the ball, authorizing over 1500 zones in a variety of forms that provide incentives for business and industrial development. Some states designated hundreds of zones, others one or a few. States allow local governments to offer existing or potential firms tax and other incentives for locating or expanding business within the zones, hiring disadvantaged workers, establishing employer-funded child care programs, and other actions calculated to improve employment opportunities. A few states dropped their zones, but several have placed greater emphasis on enterprise zone activities in recent years.

The Clinton Administration instituted the empowerment zone program in 1994 (authorized by the 1993 Omnibus Budget Reconciliation Act) to stimulate economically distressed communities to plan unique strategies for addressing local development problems. Nine zones were authorized to receive large block grants ($100 million for urban areas, $40 million for rural ones), and businesses in the zones will be eligible for tax credits and deductions. Another six cities were designated for grants but not tax benefits, and 91 other communities were designated as community enterprise communities and awarded grants of $3 million. A $30-billion fund was set up for additional assistance to all cities.[18]

The interest of communities in greater federal assistance was signaled by the flood of applications for the program from 519 jurisdictions. A sobering reminder, however: 90 percent of urban jurisdictions are not participants in the empowerment zone program.

The empowerment zone/enterprise community program encourages cities and towns to target efforts in particularly needy neighborhoods and to use a variety of tax benefits and regulatory waivers to promote program activities, especially job development. Awards were based in large part on the thoroughness of local planning efforts to determine proposed activities. Local planning for economic development, in fact, is the key to effective action.

Three years after the empowerment zone program was initiated, there is no clear movement by either the federal or state governments to coordinate or consolidate state enterprise zones with federal empowerment zones. A few states with both types of zones have merged them, but in other states political considerations weigh in favor of maintaining separate identities between the programs. Many states with enterprise zones are not affected by the empowerment zone program.

The temptation in economic development programs is to focus on big tax breaks and other subsidies to buy business interest in the community. Most local governments have relatively limited room to maneuver in financial offerings, but states do and have been making news for years with major deals for major companies. Alabama's inducements in 1993 to secure the nation's only Mercedes plant will cost the state almost $300 million—$78 million in sewer, water, and other utility improvements; $92 million in site acquisition and plant development; and $5 million annually for job training programs. The state also agreed to waive corporate income taxes and most employee income taxes. Offers to provide a visitors center and buy 2500 vehicles for state use were later dropped. Two years after the deal was made, however, the state is having trouble making good on its promises and is learning that projections of business benefits now appear overstated.[19]

Other states have made similar deals, although without such large promises. Tennessee, Kentucky, and South Carolina paid plenty for automobile plants. New York City gave more than $30 million each to Morgan Stanley and Kidder, Peabody & Company. California and Anaheim promised $800 million in road and other improvements to the Walt Disney Company to assist in expanding Disneyland. Utah gave $200 million to Micron Technology, Inc. to locate a plant in Lehi.[20]

Economists decry such public payments to industries that have already determined to locate within the United States and often within a particular region. Instead, they argue, states and local governments should invest in schools and improving community amenities that would provide attractive, long-lasting lures to new business. These are precisely the areas in which communities, through their growth management programs, can make the broadest impact on potential economic development. Marketing, site improvements, and financial incentives are best supported by community efforts to create an attractive, livable, functional quality of life.

Local Economic Development Techniques

Economic development programs throughout the nation rely on well-known approaches to attracting and keeping businesses. Many towns, cities, and counties are quite skilled at structuring significant economic development programs. Their approach usually consists of

- Formulating an economic development strategy that targets businesses and employment opportunities most compatible with other community objectives and most feasible given existing and potential community resources.

- Developing a marketing program that emphasizes community assets, including labor availability, transportation facilities, tax structure, accessibility to natural resources or existing related businesses, and attractive sites.

- Arranging financing tools to aid development, including tax abatements and waivers, establishment of community development corporations as conduits for public grants and low-cost loans to promising firms, and targeted financing mechanisms such as special taxing districts.

- Assembling and improving potential sites for business development, including obtaining appropriate zoning, addressing hazardous waste and other environmental site problems, and providing basic infrastructure.

- Making available public land or facilities as potential sites, offering public lease commitments in proposed developments, and providing supportive facilities such as parking, port facilities, and child care centers, and supporting services such as job training programs.

- Expediting the development approval process and reducing the complexities of existing zoning and building codes (especially important in existing industrial and business areas).

Long Beach, California offers an example of a city that pushed economic development with a strategic program conceived on a broad scale and implemented over many years. A mature city whose economy fell on hard times when defense industries closed down in the 1960s, Long Beach turned to economic development efforts to recoup its losses. Like many other older cities with decaying downtowns, waterfronts, and inner neighborhoods, Long Beach relied on intensive, long-term involvement of business and civic leaders to gradually improve its lot.

Beginning in the early 1980s, massive public efforts to expand port activities and redevelop downtown and inner neighborhoods paid off, aided by the general economic boom in southern California. Many residents, however, were upset with the changes being wrought in their heretofore comfortable environment. Unlike the typical suburb seeking to guide growth at its urban fringe, Long Beach's challenge was to manage redevelopment and improvements taking place throughout an existing community.

To meet residents' concerns, the city sponsored a two-year effort to craft a strategic plan.[21] In 1984, seven citizen task forces were organized to draft suggestions for improvements in access, economic development, housing and neighborhood development, infrastructure, quality of life, education, and human services. Working almost two years, the task forces identified current problems and issues in each area of concern, framed appropriate policies addressing those issues, and recommended specific city actions to implement the policies. All in all, the plan contained 98 recommendations.

Fifteen general policy statements encompassing all aspects of city development were adopted by the city council to launch the implementation of the plan. The policies signaled the city's intent to pursue important economic and social objectives such as the pursuit of international trade, development of housing for first-time homebuyers, reinvestment in existing residential neighborhoods, and improved public services.

The actions recommended in the strategic plan ranged from affirmative support for some projects already underway to reorganizations of several city departments, refocusing of some existing programs, calls for new development plans and programs, creation of new organizations for housing and neighborhood improvements, and increasing expenditures for public facility construction. Tables accompanying the strategic plan classified the actions as short or long range, indicated responsibilities for specific departments, defined first steps, and provided estimated capital costs.

The city reports periodically on specific actions taken to implement the plan. The first reports from 1986 to 1990 cited progress toward completion of a number of major projects previously initiated and other achievements that were primarily administrative in nature—reorganization of some departments and creation of a nonprofit housing organization, for example—or that amount to first steps toward implementation, including commissioning of studies and plans for various projects. Examples of specific advances by 1990 in high-priority areas included:

- Completion of the first phase of the World Trade Center and initiation of the next phase.

- Approval of a $132-million investment in port access improvements and substantial completion of a new pier.

- Ratification of a cooperative marketing program with the Chamber of Commerce, Port, and Convention and Visitors Council to attract new industries and keep existing ones.

- Initiation of private downtown development involving high-quality restaurants, entertainment, and specialized retail uses, as well as new market-rate housing nearby.

- First steps toward redevelopment of a blighted commercial strip.

The comprehensive nature of the city's efforts was borne out in other actions taken by the city. They included initiation of planning for transportation and parking improvements, reorganization of the Health Department, employment of a consultant to advise on child care programs, employment of a historic preservation officer to track preservation efforts, and appointment of a Drug Abuse Task Force. In addition, major efforts were made to improve conditions in existing neighborhoods, including zoning revisions to restrict nonresidential activities and reduce densities, deployment of more police foot patrols and expansion of the Neighborhood Watch program, and preparation of a street tree-canopy plan.

The most recent report by the city of Long Beach, on activities from 1986 to 1992, demonstrated substantial additional progress on "big-ticket" items:

- Completion of the second phase of the World Trade Center and initiation of planning for a third phase.

- Port facilities expanded by the completion of six new terminals and additions to four more.

- Downtown activities enhanced with the construction of a $95-million expansion of the convention center, enactment of a state enterprise zone and sales-tax rebate program, and adoption of new commercial zoning districts.

- Neighborhood preservation bolstered with zoning amendments to reduce multifamily densities and building heights, rezoning of 50 neighborhoods, formation of a nonprofit housing corporation to aid in developing affordable housing, and construction or rehabilitation of about 700 housing units.

- Revenues from the park and transportation impact fees funded four park improvements, initiated a downtown shuttle system, began a number of road improvements, and completed a light-rail connection to Los Angeles.

The 1993 report on progress on the strategic plan found that 93 of the 98 recommendations in the original plan had been substantially completed. With that, the plan was declared a success that would set the stage for the next phase of strategic planning for the city. The closing of the Navy base and hospital and large job cutbacks at the McDonnell Douglas plants demanded fresh attempts to keep Long Beach's economy moving. A base reuse planning committee was formed to pursue development opportunities for the base, capitalizing on plans long in preparation. The Queensway Bay Plan is expected to revitalize the entire harbor area by expanding the waterfront park system and waterfront esplanade, enlarging boating facilities, and creating a new commercial center with a museum and entertainment complex.

James C. Hankla, longtime city manager for Long Beach, observed that the strategic plan provided a "score card" by which to judge council actions on the annual budget and the efforts of individual city departments. The preparation of the plan "did a good job of moving the community back from the brink of a development moratorium," he said, and "managed to avoid a complete shutdown."

The price tag for accomplishing the strategic plan was estimated at $860 million, clearly out of reach for Long Beach for the immediate future. Nevertheless, the city's economic development strategy, intended to raise potential revenues through tax base expansion, has begun to deliver on its promises of greater funding for capital improvements. The city's approach to economic planning, embracing a broad range of activities and involvement of many citizens, has leveraged to the maximum its opportunities for economic and civic development and successfully encouraged substantial private investments.[22]

Improving Job Opportunities for Inner-City Workers

One of the most difficult and yet most important components of economic development programs is generating employment opportunities for inner-city residents. Analysts of urban social ills ranging from low educational attainment to crime and dysfunctional families increasingly are pointing to employment as the essential foundation for improving social conditions. For decades, federal- and state-sponsored job training programs have struggled to provide unemployed and under-employed workers with marketable skills. The transformation of welfare programs underway in the late 1990s will increase the significance of such programs and test their capabilities for producing lasting results.

Yet, job training is only one part of the picture. Access to jobs is another. Ever since World War II, industries and businesses have streamed out of central cities to locate in the suburbs. Inner-city workers find it difficult to take advantage of the unskilled and semi-skilled jobs available in communities 10 or more miles away from their homes, especially since many are dependent on public transportation. Programs to improve transportation access to suburban jobs have been moderately successful in some areas. Another tack is Chicago's Gautreaux program, which provides vouchers and intensive counseling support to some public housing residents in the inner city that allows them to find housing near suburban jobs. The program has received a great deal of nationwide attention if not emulation.[23]

Many central-city employment programs have focused on retaining and expanding employment in existing industries and businesses in core locations. The boom in downtown development and redevelopment during the 1970s and 1980s played a significant role in improving service employment opportunities for inner-city workers, although it did not stem the continuing loss of manufacturing jobs. In many older cities, however, commercial development and residential gentrification in inner-city areas conflicted with efforts to retain and attract industries. Demands for renovated office and residential space in close-in areas threatened to absorb industrial space, displacing existing industries and preventing potential industrial uses from locating in inner-city areas. Industries typically pay higher wages than retail and office jobs and yet require fewer skills, a boon for inner-city populations.

Indeed, Michael Porter (no relation), the current guru of economic competitiveness, asserts that, nurtured properly, mainstream businesses can be attracted to inner-city locations where they can reinvigorate the economy. Porter observes that inner-city residents are eager to work and have a low turnover rate, and that many minority-owned businesses thrive in inner cities by serving existing buying power in central areas.[24]

Chicago was experiencing a turnover of once-industrial properties to other uses, aided by old-fashioned zoning that permitted almost any use in industrial zones. In an effort to protect industrial districts from the spread of other uses, Chicago enacted new zoning provisions in 1988 that require industrial areas and buildings to remain available for industrial uses. Portland, Oregon began even earlier, in 1981, to establish "industrial sanctuaries" in a number of areas throughout the city, some to protect existing industries from impending gentrification and some to provide space for future industrial development. Blue-collar employment within the sanctuaries increased by 30 percent in the seven years following their designation, while overall industrial jobs in the city declined by 10 percent.[25]

Another problem for many inner-city sites is the lingering effects of past practices in toxic waste storage and disposal—the "brownfields" syndrome. Local public officials have grown to understand that environmental laws requiring cleanup of contaminated industrial and commercial sites constitute a serious challenge for city economic development. Some experts have projected possibilities that more than 500,000 sites may have questions significant enough to spark regulatory concerns.[26] The possibility of site contamination in properties formerly used for a

wide variety of industrial and commercial purposes raises significant obstacles for productive reuse of properties. Problems may range from large
quantities of buried waste of unknown toxicity to leaking gasoline tanks
at automobile service stations. The former usually are identified in the
1200 sites listed by EPA as national priorities; the latter types, called
brownfields, usually are easier to clean up.

However, total cleanup may be prohibitively expensive, and much
confusion surrounds the identification and appropriate treatment of
toxic substances. Federal, state, and local agencies often disagree about
remediation standards and procedures. With these issues, lenders are reluctant to finance development on such sites. They fear loss of collateral
value and potential liability if contamination is found.

For these reasons, local or regional agencies often must take the lead
in organizing and financing cleanup efforts to make sites and buildings
available for reuse. Even then, cleanup may prove too costly. The city of
Eau Claire, Wisconsin, for example, proposed to purchase a service station site to improve highway access for a nearby manufacturer. City officials expected contamination problems but were shocked to discover
that buried batteries had spread high levels of lead, with a potential
cleanup cost of $750,000. The city had no choice but to abandon the
project and the improvements, leaving the problem unsolved.[27]

City officials in Davenport, Iowa, aided by local business leaders,
proved more persistent in a similar situation. As part of an ambitious
downtown revitalization program called Rejuvenate Davenport, an underused factory building on the edge of downtown was proposed as the
new location of the *Quad City Times* newspaper, which was seeking
larger quarters. The city agreed to contribute toward its purchase, extend the existing tax-increment financing district to incorporate the site,
and build public improvements. Environmental consultants identified
minor contamination problems but, halfway into site clearance, extensive coal-tar deposits were found, requiring cleanup costs estimated at
$2 to $3 million. After lengthy negotiations, Rejuvenate Davenport and
the city agreed to split cleanup costs, with city funding coming from several sources, including the tax-increment district. The $4 million site
preparation cost made it possible for the newspaper to build a $24 mil-
lion plant in a location highly beneficial to Davenport's economic climate.[28]

Attracting Jobs to Growing Suburbs

Many suburban communities suffer from a surfeit of housing and a
dearth of employment. Not only does that pose a significant fiscal problem, since residential properties frequently generate revenues lower

than the costs of providing them with public facilities and services, but the lack of local jobs requires residents to commute, sometimes great distances, to other places for employment. Seeking a better balance between jobs and housing, suburban communities frequently make great efforts to attract industries and commerce.

The city of San Jose, California formulated an economic development strategy to stimulate employment growth as part of its Horizon 2000 General Plan adopted in 1984. The key objectives of the strategy were to

• capture 51 percent of countywide employment growth between 1980 and 2000 (compared to its 37 percent share in 1980) to provide employment opportunities for San Jose's residents;

• move toward a balance of citywide jobs and housing by providing more jobs than housing to overcome the city's historic role as a bedroom community; and

• increase the city's tax base to generate revenues for providing necessary facilities and services to residents and businesses.[29]

San Jose zoned major sectors of the city for industrial activity and protected them against conversion to other uses, a possibility the city considered and rejected in the mid-1970s. It offered up to 6000 acres of zoned, vacant land for industrial and business development. The city also carried out an aggressive redevelopment program, established an enterprise zone, and pursued downtown revitalization for many years. However, employment growth in the early 1980s lagged behind projections, and business development peaked in 1984.

Nevertheless, overall industrial growth continued, benefitting from the economic strength of Silicon Valley industries. Between 1980 and 1991, over 33.5 million square feet of industrial space received building permits. By 1993 a new study of industrial land supply and demand found up to 4600 acres still available for a projected demand of 2200 acres by 2010.[30] Although the study warned against significantly reducing the amount of zoned industrial land, it recommended that isolated parcels be rezoned for housing, because in the period after 1980 residential development had absorbed much of the land available for housing.

In fact, the city's 1992 land use inventory found that much of the land within the city limits was generally urbanized. Over 42,000 housing units had been developed from 1980 to 1990, absorbing 59 percent of the vacant land within the city, and residential land supplies were tightening.[31] In response, the city's planning department recommended intensification of housing development, both as infill within existing urbanized areas and in selected sites in developing areas. Not only would this policy provide a greater choice and supply of housing but it would support ridership on the city's light-rail transit lines. In addition, the city adopted a strategy calling for conversion of older, underused industrial lands to high-density residential and commercial use.

Thus San Jose's economic development strategy, based on retaining a supply of industrial land attractive to new business, was tempered by concerns for stimulating residential development of a nature that would widen housing choices and support transit service.

Another strategy for improving suburban economies (as well as reducing long-distance commuting) is encouragement of telecommuting. One estimate puts the number of telecommuters working at least part time at home or in satellite offices at nine million in 1994, twice the number counted in 1990, and projections indicate growth in telecommuters at 12 percent a year through the 1990s.[32] Suburban jurisdictions are beginning to realize the importance of this trend as industries move back-office support employees out to low-cost office space and establish satellite work centers where employees can work two or three days a week linked electronically to central offices.

The growth of home-office occupations has drawn much media attention to possibilities for "lone eagle" living in remote locations connected to the rest of the world by computers, express mail, and air travel. Most analysts believe, however, that the major impact of telecommuting will be felt in business reorganizations that establish work outposts but retain significant opportunities for face-to-face contact in workplaces. Thus suburban telecommuting centers will benefit from locations in business centers that provide a variety of services and accessible to and from major transportation links, including transit. Suburban communities that wish to attract economic growth can support telecommuting by zoning for such mixed-use centers and for home occupations related to them.

Small-Town Economic Revitalization

Small towns are especially vulnerable to economic change. Often they are one-industry places whose fortunes depend on survival of a single business or economic activity (such as food production). Regional, national, and even international forces can doom local firms and economic activities. Because few towns have resources to mount research and marketing campaigns to attract new businesses, they are at the mercy of such forces.

At the same time, small towns can be intensely impacted by economic growth that changes their character and livability forever. Eager to welcome new employment and tax base opportunities, local officials may literally "give up the store" to obtain developments that may wipe out local businesses and may prove short lived. Small towns are often targets of footloose industries and businesses seeking inexpensive sites, low-cost labor forces, and hands-off regulation. Such firms frequently make demands on local resources, then leave for greener pastures after a few years.

Small towns have taken advantage of growth opportunities by managing development rather than letting development manage them. To accomplish this, they have taken the following steps:

• Identified community assets (1) that they wish to retain in any future development and (2) that can be used to attract and keep new firms.

• Established relations with state and regional economic development groups that can provide advice and steer potential industries their way.

• Adopted plans and regulations that provide assurances of reasonable standards and qualities of development.

Community assets often go unrecognized by local residents. Blocks of architecturally interesting old commercial buildings, a town square, an adjoining historic place such as a Revolutionary or Civil War battlefield, or simply streets of well-kept houses can prove attractive to new residents and businesses. Many a small town has capitalized on tourism and recreational development by taking small steps to enhance its picturesque qualities and setting.

The key to managing small-town growth is to entice development without allowing it to destroy the very qualities that stimulated it. A quaint downtown can be revitalized as a specialty shopping center, for example, while steering large-scale new commercial developments to locations that benefit the entire community. Or developments on the edge of town can be designed to connect to and reflect the existing pattern and qualities of development. Most of all, towns can respond positively to growth opportunities without buckling under development pressures.[33]

Bethel, a town of 2400 people in the western mountains of Maine, had been declining for years as its traditional wood-products manufacturing plants lost ground in the marketplace. In the mid-1980s, however, the opening of a ski resort and increasing tourist trade began changing the economic climate. Applications for three condominium subdivisions submitted to the town in 1986 energized the town to revise its comprehensive plan and adopt new regulations to guide condominium development. In particular, the town increased site plan and subdivision fees to pay for increased staff to handle project applications and inspect construction, required developers to enter into agreements to pay for professional review of major projects, and required a "municipal facilities impact analysis" that could establish the need for impact fees or developer contributions to facility improvements. Forthright action by the town averted potential development impacts on the livability and fiscal stability of the community.[34]

In summary, communities of all sizes must shape economic development programs to respond to their specific needs. Given the interactions of economic activities with other facets of community growth and change, economic development programs will be most effective if integrated into broader growth management strategies and programs.

Redevelopment and Revitalization Programs

Efforts to redevelop or revitalize key business areas and neighborhoods are part and parcel of many of the affordable housing and economic development programs discussed above. Public officials and planners in many communities have established a considerable amount of experience in such ventures, beginning with federally sponsored urban renewal and redevelopment programs in the 1950s and continuing through neighborhood renewal, Model Cities, and Urban Development Action Programs in subsequent decades. Today, except for designation of empowerment zones in some cities, federal assistance is limited primarily to CDBG funding, and communities are hatching new ideas every day to accomplish needed revival and restoration of existing urbanized areas.

Communities have learned that reinvestment programs must be targeted, must attract a great deal of public/private collaboration, and must tap a wide variety of funding sources to underwrite costs: targeted, because resources are limited and turning downward slides into upward momentum usually requires arduous efforts over a lengthy period of time; public/private collaboration, because private-market economic forces must be harnessed to achieve long-term public objectives; a wide variety of funding sources, because private investment is risky and public sources are scarce. For these reasons, communities must plan carefully to identify areas susceptible to improvement and to formulate reinvestment strategies tailored to specific needs and resources of those areas.

Downtown Revitalization

During the 1970s and 1980s a tremendous amount of public and private investment stimulated highly visible and often exciting redevelopment of downtown properties across the United States. Downtown skylines changed radically as new office and apartment towers sprouted practically overnight; cities poured billions of dollars into new government buildings, stadiums, convention centers, museums, aquariums, and performance centers; historic districts were transformed into entertainment centers; waterfronts, ports, and transit facilities were overhauled and upgraded.

In many cases, these efforts were led by business groups organized to assist public redevelopment and improvement programs. The Cincinnati Business Committee, for example, focused the attention of 25 chief executive officers of major businesses on assisting the city to meet evolving needs. The Greater Baltimore Committee was instrumental in promoting planning and redevelopment of downtown Baltimore.

Although the development lull in the 1990s caused by overbuilding during the 1980s in many regions temporarily put downtown development on the back burner, the experience gained by both public and private sectors in spurring downtown growth established techniques and procedures still useful today.

The range of public/private efforts frequently undertaken to revitalize downtown areas is exemplified by San Diego's efforts over many years. Although a variety of streetscape and fix-up activities had been carried out in the 1960s, the real rebirth of downtown San Diego began in the 1970s with the city's adoption of a growth management program that favored infill and redevelopment (see Figure 7.1a and Chapter 3) and the city council's approval of the long-debated Horton Plaza Redevelopment Project. The Horton Plaza project, promoted by a business organization called San Diegans, Inc., focused the efforts of the city's redevelopment agency and a private developer on building a major shopping center in a formerly rundown part of downtown. The redevelopment agency assembled the land; the Hahn Company was selected as developer after a nationwide request for proposals; and, after many design changes and some financial tribulations, the center opened in 1985. It brought to downtown a multitiered, uniquely configured shopping complex, shown in Figure 7.1b, incorporating four department stores, 140 specialty shops, restaurants, a seven-screen cinema, and two performing arts theaters.

Horton Plaza was a key ingredient in the Centre City Community Plan adopted in 1976. A new public, nonprofit corporation, the Centre City Development Corporation (CCDC), was given responsibilities for strategic planning, urban design, developer negotiations, property acquisition, tenant relocation, public improvements, and public financing of redevelopment. The Corporation's program was to be funded primarily through tax increment financing, which uses the gain in tax revenues from new development to pay for redevelopment costs.

In addition to completion of Horton Plaza, the plan called for redevelopment in three areas: (1) extension of the traditional downtown to the bay where a new convention facility would be built, (2) reclamation of the historic Gaslamp Quarter adjoining Horton Plaza, and (3) a series of residential projects in the Marina area. After voters rejected construction of the convention center in 1981, the San Diego Unified Port Dis-

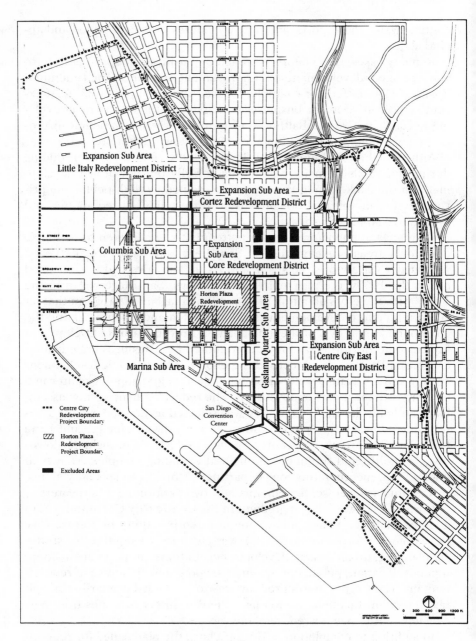

Figure 7.1(a)

San Diego's downtown planning map. The comprehensive nature of the Centre City Development Corporation's plans for downtown San Diego are depicted in this map of redevelopment districts. (Courtesy of the Centre City Development Corporation.)

202

Figure 7.1(b)

Horton Plaza. The Horton Plaza shopping center introduced an imaginative and highly active element to downtown San Diego that has invigorated other redevelopment efforts. (Photo courtesy of the Centre City Development Corporation.)

trict took over the project on port-controlled land, with conspicuous success in boosting the downtown economy. Meanwhile, an office boom fueled by private investments in the Columbia area, and traditional office core produced a new generation of office towers and doubled the amount of office space in downtown. Two of the towers were developed through public/private joint development projects related to the city's new transit lines.

Redevelopment of the Gaslamp Quarter, designated as a national historic district, followed a different path. Property owners fought redevelopment and maintained that city streetscape improvements would stimulate private rehabilitation of the Victorian warehouses and storefronts, then occupied by a tawdry collection of bars and down-at-the-heels businesses. With streetscape improvements incorporated in a redevelopment plan adopted in 1982, the CCDC negotiated with property owners to restore structures and attract new businesses. Significant upgrading occurred through private investments; only two properties were purchased by the redevelopment agency and resold for private rehabilitation. These efforts and the opening of Horton Plaza attracted business interest in the Gaslamp Quarter, making it the entertainment center of San Diego. More than 70 restaurants occupy restored buildings, upper floors are being converted to living/working lofts, and old single-room-occupancy hotels have been rehabilitated for continued occupancy by low-income tenants.

Development of downtown housing proved the biggest challenge. The plan called for adaptive reuse of warehouses for middle-income housing, new construction to expand housing options at all income levels, and rehabilitation of existing single-room-occupancy hotels for low-income housing. Nonprofit groups developed two low-cost apartment towers for seniors in the early 1980s, which corresponded with CCDC's assembly of land for two condominium projects that opened in the mid-1980s. The CCDC then negotiated with the railroads and the Metropolitan Transit Development Board to consolidate rail rights-of-way and create a two-mile linear park as the setting for new housing near the waterfront. The park is being developed as housing is built, with developers contributing to park improvements and maintenance. Two residential projects were completed in the early 1990s, and others are on the drawing boards. In addition, the trolley line extended along the park provides three stations as entrances to the Gaslamp Quarter, the hotel/convention center complex, and the Seaport Village shopping and restaurant center. Altogether, since 1985 more than 5000 residential units have been completed in downtown.

By 1992, the redevelopment agency had invested $150 million in downtown activities that had leveraged $1.7 billion in private investments. Now the CCDC has formulated a new plan, the Centre City Redevelopment Project, to expand activities into adjacent neighborhoods.

Recognizing the need to address homelessness and other social issues in these areas, the CCDC developed a social-issues strategy to create partnerships between social service providers, public agencies, and the community for housing and social services.[35]

San Diego's combination of strong public and private leadership, imaginative planning and action by a redevelopment organization, and major private investments demonstrates the cooperative and coordinated approaches used successfully in many cities. Older cities such as Cincinnati, Baltimore, and Hartford, whose downtown areas had been ravaged by the loss of retailing to suburban shopping centers, the drift of business to outer business parks and centers, and deterioration of downtown housing areas, found their downtown economies transformed. Other cities such as Seattle and Dallas, whose central business districts were faltering in the face of suburban growth, captured substantial new private investment and greatly expanded their civic infrastructure of governmental and cultural development.

Even in small towns and mid-sized cities, intensive public/private efforts over many years have channeled public and private investments into face-lifts and significant new projects. The "Main Street" project of the National Trust for Historic Preservation, which has helped many small communities to gear up for downtown revitalization, advocates four key steps: (1) forming an organization to hatch ideas and lead revitalization efforts; (2) developing a dynamic promotion campaign; (3) building on downtown assets through attention to design; and (4) expanding business through economic restructuring.[36]

Although downtown areas still face major problems, public and private investments in previous decades—including massive federal funding assistance in the 1960s and 1970s—have reestablished central business districts as regionwide business, governmental, civic, and entertainment centers. Downtown retailing will emphasize specialty merchandise and business services rather than performing as centers of regional shopping. In many cities, office development will continue, based on the agglomeration of fundamental public and private services clustered in downtowns. Civic, governmental, educational, and cultural activities will continue to draw people downtown. But with the absence of federal funding for redevelopment, cities will be pressed to find other means of stimulating and steering investments. In most cases, that means even greater reliance than in the past on collaboration between public and private interests to achieve success.[37]

Business District Improvements

The historical hopscotching of retailing and business services from downtown locations, to outer business strips and districts on major roads, to ever-larger shopping centers has created leftover business areas

in many communities. We know them by their forlorn facades, marginal
uses, vacancies, and bedraggled appearance. Some provide valuable merchandise and services for surrounding neighborhoods. Some have
evolved into specialty shopping or entertainment areas, perhaps inele-
gant but active. Some are simply catchalls for firms seeking cheap space.

Efforts to bolster the economic health of such business districts and
older shopping centers generally face major obstacles. Typically, neither
owners nor tenants can afford costly renovations, which often are complicated by building code requirements and lengthy review procedures.
Property and building values may be too high to allow private redevelopment unless development intensities are increased substantially, a solution often opposed by NIMBY-minded neighbors and city planning departments. Site assembly for new development can be difficult, as well,
given diverse ownerships and small parcels. In addition, investing in improvements to ailing business districts in declining neighborhoods can
be risky for both tenants and developers.

The key, of course, is tailoring an improvement program to the realities of the area—its market opportunities, the kinds of public improvements necessary to spur business development and private investment,
the interest and cooperation of business and property owners. Frequently, the "demographics" of surrounding neighborhoods offer unrecognized opportunities for improved shopping and business services. Or
the special architectural or historical character of the district suggests
possibilities for specialty markets.

To encourage wholesale improvement in the business environment,
public agencies can undertake major rebuilding of streets and sidewalks,
creation of public parking, replacement of signage, and even land assembly and redevelopment. Rundown districts do not necessarily require expensive renovations, however, especially if existing businesses
are worth keeping to serve local needs. As Figure 7.2 shows, simple public improvements such as new sidewalks and curbside plantings can
spruce up an area enough to spur private fix-up efforts. Public agencies
can arrange low-interest loans to stimulate business development and
allow tenant improvements. Business owners can formulate a unified
marketing program to attract more business.

Business district improvements benefit from organization of support
groups that can provide leadership and continuous business promotion.
The substantial redevelopment taking place in the Ballston area of Arlington County, Virginia, for example, is encouraged by the Ballston Partnership, made up of business, real estate, county government, and neighborhood representatives. The Partnership, aided by $200,000 in start-up
money and annual contributions from the county's economic development department, helps to coordinate public and private development
activities, provides a marketing center for the area, and develops public

Figure 7.2

Elk Rapids. Even small towns like Elk Rapids, Michigan can revitalize their downtown areas by such simple additions as a landscaped entrance from back-area parking lots to main-street stores. (Photo by Douglas R. Porter.)

signage and streetscape standards. A tremendous amount of office and housing development has taken place in Ballston over the past decade, in part due to Arlington County's emphasis on development around Metrorail stations.

As in downtown areas, many business districts have created organizations to manage essential common services and promote business activity. The Bethesda Urban Partnership, Inc. was formed to introduce more local control over enhanced services in the booming Bethesda, Maryland suburban business district. The Partnership oversees street and sidewalk cleaning, trash pickups, and landscaping in public rights-of-way, and is responsible for promoting community events and producing promotional information for the district. It is supported by an urban district special tax, parking fees, and maintenance charges for large-scale projects.

Old suburban shopping centers can be revamped as well, with or without public assistance. The Ballston area development in Arlington County described above, for example, included a project in which a developer turned a somewhat decrepit open-air shopping center into a three-level mall carefully designed to relate to adjoining development. In Manchester, New Hampshire the South Willow Shopping Center was rundown and poorly managed; a developer saw an opportunity to capitalize on an inexpensive property to generate a profitable project. Although the basic structures needed no upgrading, a new facade was added to provide a more inviting appearance. An unused parcel was developed as parking for an adjoining retailer. A major tenant paying low rents was replaced by a high-traffic retailer paying much higher rents.

More ambitious efforts may need help from public agencies. An aging regional shopping center in Boca Raton, Florida was purchased, cleared, and new infrastructure constructed by the city's redevelopment agency, which then leased 12 acres to a developer who built a new town center, complete with a traditional design and community park.

All of these efforts require thoughtful collaboration between business and property owners, nearby residents, and city agencies. As in the Gaslamp district in San Diego, a great deal of attention to needs and capacities of individual owners and tenants may be necessary to generate improvements.

Industrial Upgrades

Like efforts to revitalize other types of areas, improving industrial districts usually requires long-term approaches and substantial public support to overcome decades of decay and the blight of unsuitable facilities built on contaminated sites. Pittsburgh's experience in rejuvenating its economic base through perseverance and a long-term redevelopment strategy is one that many communities might profitably emulate. Its efforts were spearheaded by the Allegheny Conference on Community Development, a 50-year-old community action organization formed by civic and business leaders. The Conference framed and pursued the fundamental regional development strategy for attracting a broad range of new industries to replace declining steel and manufacturing plants. Regional leaders then formed the nonprofit Regional Industrial Development Corporation to actively promote and financially assist industrial development. The city's urban redevelopment authority—armed with powers to plan, acquire land and buildings, and improve sites for development—pursued successful projects that transformed downtown, many neighborhoods, and a number of industrial sites.

The Pittsburgh Technology Center rising on the banks of the Monongahela River just two miles from downtown reflects the dedicated work of all these agencies as well as state agencies. (See Figure 7.3.) The abandoned plant of the Jones & Laughlin Hot Strip Mill was purchased by the redevelopment authority in 1983 with the proviso that its owner clear the 49-acre site. The authority viewed the location as ideal for advanced technology firms, given its highly visible site near downtown and two

Figure 7.3

Pittsburgh Technology Center. The Carnegie Mellon Research Institute was one of the first buildings constructed in the Pittsburgh Technology Center on a former steel mill site near downtown. (Photo courtesy of the Urban Redevelopment Authority of Pittsburgh.)

major universities, Carnegie-Mellon University and the University of Pittsburgh.

The authority spent several years in preparing the site, including draining and filling subsurface pits and tunnels, raising the level by 8 feet to prevent future flooding, constructing roads and utilities, and providing entry landscaping, signage, pedestrian amenities along the river, and parking. Perhaps the most daunting challenge was the discovery of cyanide contamination in the 15 to 60 feet of industrial fill under the thick concrete slab that covered two-thirds of the site. After much study, the toxic materials were determined to be in a nonreactive form that would not require treatment or evacuation, particularly given the future industrial use of the property. That decision, however, held up development for a lengthy period.

The site is being developed through a cooperative agreement between the two universities, the redevelopment authority, the Regional Industrial Development Corporation (RIDC), and a local community development corporation. Construction of the University of Pittsburgh's Center for Biotechnology and Bioengineering was completed in 1992 and the

Carnegie-Mellon Research Institute building was opened in 1994, along with a building housing the research and technical facilities of the Union Switch and Signal Corporation. The $25 million in redevelopment funding came from the state departments of commerce and community affairs, the city and the city's redevelopment and water and sewer authorities, and private foundations. The state invested another $31 million for university research facilities.

The Technology Center's success rests on combined actions of state, regional, and city agencies, universities, and business-supported organizations, and on funding from all those sources.[38]

Neighborhood Rejuvenation

The wholesale clearance of buildings and displacement of residents generated by urban redevelopment programs of the 1960s and 1970s are a relic of the past, doomed by the political turmoil they created and the consequent demise of federal funding for such efforts. Yet, in most communities, some neighborhoods continue to need attention to prevent their slide into slums. Local governments and nonprofit organizations have responded to these needs with a broad array of revitalization approaches that have been tried and found workable.

Neighborhood revitalization applies all the tools employed to produce affordable housing—public/private partnerships, federal and state housing subsidies, local public and private funding, and tax abatement—but takes a broader approach to also deal with public facility improvements, crime, beautification, traffic, tenant–landlord relationships, and other issues. The city of Champaign, Illinois, for example, adopted a "Neighborhood Wellness Action Plan" in 1992 to coordinate service delivery to 15 neighborhoods as a means of improving their physical condition. Elements of the plan included stepping up code enforcement to improve property maintenance, targeting street and other improvements, and creating neighborhood centers to coordinate residents' voluntary cleanup, housing maintenance, and neighborhood watch programs. The plan designated "healthy," "conservation," "preservation," and "restoration" neighborhoods to establish priorities for city attention. To implement the plan, the city created a neighborhood services department with an annual budget of $2.8 million, funded mostly through utility taxes and federal CDBG grants.[39]

At a larger scale, Cleveland launched a series of programs to produce major improvements in neighborhood housing, service, and employment conditions throughout the city. Activities of community-based organizations and development of specific projects are supported by Neighborhood Progress, Inc. (formed by local foundations, civic and corporate groups, and the Ford Foundation), a city housing trust fund financed by federal CDBG and other funds, city-issued neighborhood bonds to fund site acquisition and improvements, and a $40-million revolving loan program. Thousands of housing units and a half-dozen neighborhood shopping centers were produced through these efforts, and studies indicate increasing demands for in-city housing.

One of the first outcomes of the program was development of a 49-unit, single-family, market-rate residential project in the Glenville neighborhood. First-phase units were priced at $81,000 to $100,000. Buyers were attracted by 30-year, low-interest mortgages provided by a public/private partnership and no-interest, deferred second mortgages offered through a special HUD grant. In addition, costs were lowered by a housing trust fund loan, city-funded infrastructure improvements, and donated street trees. In the Mount Pleasant neighborhood, 50 single-family homes on scattered sites were developed by a partnership between the neighborhood development corporation, a church-backed housing corporation, and a development firm. A lease/purchase arrangement allows low-income families to eventually own their homes. An 110,000 square-foot shopping center with a supermarket and 22 other tenants was developed in an inner-city neighborhood by a private developer associated with a neighborhood housing group and financed by a consortium of seven banks, city loans, and local foundations.

The momentum of Cleveland's program will be propelled by its designation as an empowerment zone in 1995, which will infuse $177 million in new federal funds into neighborhood revitalization efforts. The designation came in large part because of the city's focus on public/private partnerships to stimulate housing and job production, as well as infrastructure and social-service improvements.[40]

Other illustrations of neighborhood revitalization efforts include the following.

- The nonprofit Savannah (Georgia) Landmark Rehabilitation Project, formed by civic and business leaders, has renovated hundreds of derelict buildings in the historic Victorian District for low- and moderate-income renters, using a variety of private, state, local, and foundation funds; the goal is to create enough decent housing to stabilize the neighborhood.[41]

- In Boston, a development firm chosen through a public competition converted a 1950s garden-apartment complex into 392 triplex townhouse units. For attractive living conditions and security, the project provided private front entrances and backyards, children's play areas, a community building and day care center, and a reorganized street system. Current residents were guaranteed space in the rehabilitated units.[42]

- Property owners in the Avon–Dakota–Eton area in Anaheim, California instigated neighborhood and city actions to reclaim the neighborhood for its Hispanic residents. In an area previously ruled by drug dealers and gangs, a neighborhood organization of tenants and property owners developed a landscape plan, obtained trees and plants from the city's parkway maintenance department, and painted over graffiti. The city resurfaced streets, repaired sidewalks, upgraded street lights, trimmed street trees, assigned a team of patrol officers to walk the streets, and increased inspections for code violations. Then the city designated the area a target neighborhood for CDBG grant funds to improve housing conditions.[43]

The common threads in these examples are a close-knit collaboration between cities, neighborhood residents, and property owners or developers—true public/private partnerships; a holistic approach to improving neighborhood physical, social, and economic conditions; and a targeted approach to use of a broad range of resources. In addition, and significant for purposes of growth management, all the efforts took place within a framework of policies and regulations that stimulated and reinforced actions by specific neighborhoods.

Seeking Interjurisdictional Parity

Social and economic problems are exacerbated by their concentration in certain jurisdictions within urban regions. "Have-not" communities struggle to stem the flow of jobs and decent housing to outlying communities, while suburban jurisdictions reap the economic and fiscal rewards of business growth and upscale housing development. Communities harboring clusters of poor people lack resources for needed programs and facilities while other communities enjoy high-quality services and amenities. Concentrations of poverty separate people from jobs, reinforce dependency on welfare programs, raise crime rates, and reduce opportunities for effective education.[44]

Some people see these conditions as inevitable in a competitive world. Others see them as inequitable consequences of shortsighted governance and development policies that fail to recognize the social and economic interconnections between communities. Municipalities that have garnered major shares of regional business growth depend on other communities to supply affordable housing for many employees of those businesses. Residents of suburban communities may shop in one jurisdiction and work in another, and their quality of life is supported by teachers, police, maintenance and repair workers, and gardeners who live elsewhere, often long commuting distances away.

Residents of the Minneapolis/St. Paul region have been pondering these issues for several years, prompted by an activist state legislator, Myron Orfield. Although the Twin Cities Metropolitan Council had established a reputation over several decades as an effective regional organization, the results of the 1990 census showed significant and widening economic and social disparities among jurisdictions in the metropolitan area. Businesses, public investments, and affluent taxpayers were flowing to outer suburbs, leaving the central cities and inner suburbs with a rising crime rate and sharp increases in concentrations of poverty. Orfield, in an extensive analysis of growth trends backed by highly descriptive maps, pointed out that these shifts in growth patterns were promoted by suburban communities' adoption of exclusionary housing policies and by public spending practices that invested heavily in suburban infrastructure—not unlike circumstances in many, if not most, metropolitan areas.

Orfield's solution was in the form of two bills that (1) barred state aid to jurisdictions that restricted construction of multifamily and low-income housing, and (2) required that road improvements be planned to relieve long-term congestion and promote access of poor people to job opportunities. Although the legislature approved the bills, the governor vetoed them as punitive and premature.[45]

In 1995, however, the state enacted the Metropolitan Livable Communities Act that provides incentives for communities to meet regional goals for affordable housing. The act calls for local jurisdictions to submit community action plans showing how they expect to meet regional housing goals. Communities that refuse to participate in the program will be ineligible to receive state funds for pollution cleanup and may find their transportation funding affected, as well. State, regional, and local funding is being pooled to assist in affordable housing production. Although a voluntary program, this approach may yield positive results in some communities.

From a fiscal standpoint, many federal and state programs have been structured to "equalize" differences in wealth and status of local jurisdictions. Federal housing, education, and other programs are geared to channel more funds to cities and towns needing them most. At the state level, "equalization" formulas distribute tax revenues to local jurisdictions in ways that are supposed to give more assistance to those that need more. In most regions, however, those methods of balancing resources with demands still leave some jurisdictions distinctly less advantaged than others, and in recent years the concentrations of good jobs and decent housing appear to be gravitating to a few jurisdictions at the expense of the rest. Regional disparities, in other words, are widening.

Federal efforts to reduce disparities have foundered on the rocks of budget deficits and widespread antagonism toward social welfare programs. However, some states and regions have been promoting programs to reduce these disparities. Two types of initiatives are being pursued. "Fair-share" housing legislation and growth management housing policies in several states are requiring local jurisdictions to account for regional housing needs in planning and zoning for future development. A much-discussed housing program in Chicago is moving poor people to suburbs to gain access to economic and other opportunities. Also, the concept of sharing revenues among jurisdictions within a region is being given more scrutiny.

Fair-Share Housing Requirements

Several states, through special legislation or state growth management programs, require or encourage local governments to provide a range of housing for all income groups. New Jersey's Fair Housing Act of 1985 was passed in response to the famous Mount Laurel court decision in 1983 that required local governments to provide a "fair share" of regional housing needs. Aimed at overcoming communities' reluctance to zone for higher-density and multifamily housing, the act provides builders legal standing to force communities to allow development of affordable housing. A 1993 summary of the act's results found that the continuing resistance of many communities to the requirements has limited housing production under the program to about 13,500 units completed, rehabilitated, or under construction as of 1995—just 13 percent of documented needs. About 45 percent of the units were generated by inclusionary housing requirements and another 3300 from HUD funding. As of 1993, only a quarter of New Jersey communities had received state certification of housing plans required by the court.[46]

Affordable housing programs in Massachusetts were boosted by passage in 1969 of legislation familiarly known as the "anti-snob zoning act." Reinforced by subsequent administrative regulations, the act's goal is to ensure that at least 10 percent of a community's housing stock is available to low-income households. The act provides for local governments to issue a "comprehensive permit" for publicly subsidized housing projects that replaces all other required local permits. Permit applications are reviewed by local zoning boards of appeal, which may approve projects not otherwise complying with existing zoning. Applicants denied approval may appeal to a state appeals committee. Under these provisions, over 20,000 housing units in more than 400 projects were approved.

In addition, the state's program encourages local government involvement in the production of low- and moderate-income housing. Communities that formulate housing plans and demonstrate substantial progress toward meeting plan objectives have more leeway in determining approvals for additional projects. A state-sponsored mediation program also provides ways to negotiate settlements in disputed cases.[47]

Lincoln, Massachusetts' affordable housing efforts open a window into the effects of the state law. The town's traditional social diversity was threatened by median housing prices that increased from $106,000 in 1977 to $470,000 in 1990 (down from the peak of $550,000 in 1988). House lots sell for $200,000 to $300,000. In addition, upgrading of existing homes reduced the stock of moderately priced housing.

As they worked with property owners to balance open space conservation with development (described in Chapter 4), town officials pursued objectives for affordable housing, chiefly by setting aside a certain percentage of new units for lower-income families. With 8 percent of its housing stock moderately priced, Lincoln, in accordance with the Massachusetts anti-snob program, entered into a five-year agreement with the state to meet the 10-percent state target for affordable housing. To meet that target, for example, Lincoln approved development in the late 1980s of a 30,000 square-foot office building (one of the few commercial ventures allowed in the town) along with 120 units of affordable housing. Taxes on the office building helped pay for town services to the housing. In 1994, agreement was reached on a workable mix of affordable and market-rate housing for Phase III of the Battle Road Farm development. In addition, a bylaw to permit accessory apartments in cluster developments was formulated and adopted in 1994.[48]

Other examples of state efforts are California's requirement that local governments include housing elements in their general plans that respond to overall housing needs and requirements in both Oregon's and Florida's state growth management laws that require local governments to formulate comprehensive housing programs. Oregon's state growth management program adopted in 1973 incorporated a housing goal that called for each community to provide for a broad range of housing needs, including affordable units.

In 1981, Portland's Metro regional agency adopted a Metropolitan Housing Rule in furtherance of the state housing goal. The rule requires the region's 27 jurisdictions to meet "fair-share" housing needs by revising local comprehensive plans to allow for development of at least 50 percent of new housing as multifamily or townhouse units. In addition, plans must allow development to meet target densities established for each community, ranging from 4 to 10 units per acre. This "minimum density" threshold is unique among American metropolitan regions.

According to a 1991 study by 1000 Friends of Oregon, these policies have been very effective. Multifamily and townhouse development accounted for over half of all residential development from 1985 to 1989, a major increase from the previous average of 30 percent. The average minimum lot size allowed by local zoning dropped from 13,000 square feet in 1978 to 8300 square feet in 1982. The density of new residential development increased by 13 to 22 percent (depending on the housing type involved) over prehousing rule levels.

During this period, housing prices relative to per capita income remained well below levels in many comparable cities in the United States.[49] Meanwhile, Portland's inner neighborhoods have thrived and housing has been developed in and around downtown.

Florida's growth management act has not stimulated such dramatic action in that state's communities, but the 1992 Affordable Housing Act provided new sources of funding that are expected to stimulate more production of affordable housing. Other states, as well, have stipulated funding sources that are widening opportunities for producing affordable housing.

Tax-Sharing Programs

For many years, the concept of regionwide sharing of tax revenues related to development has tantalized planners and others concerned with reducing fiscal disparities among jurisdictions. Interestingly, the region most known for its tax-sharing program is the Minneapolis/St. Paul area now experiencing political unrest over its changing social and economic circumstances. The Twin Cities' program was adopted in 1971 as a means to reduce competition among local governments for tax-producing commercial and industrial development and to prevent severe tax-base disparities among jurisdictions. The Metropolitan Revenue Distribution Act provides that 40 percent of new local tax revenues derived from industrial and commercial development must be deposited in a general fund, which is then shared regionally through a formula that takes into account population and other factors. This program is supposed to allow local governments to make more rational decisions on development policies and spread revenues to communities that might be affected by new development outside their borders.

By 1991, the program had resulted in over 30 percent of the region's commercial and industrial tax revenues being shared among 188 communities, of which 31 contributed more than they received. The disparity between community tax bases (measured per capita) was 4:1, compared to a ratio of 22:1 without tax sharing.[50]

Clearly, this concept has merit for reducing fiscal disparities among jurisdictions. After many years of consideration, however, tax-base sharing has been adopted only in the Twin Cities and Charlottesville, Virginia (where the county returns revenues from tax base increases to the city in return for a nonannexation agreement). One planner in the Twin Cities offered the observation that if the tax sharing program were proposed today, it probably would be voted down. Thus, regional tax base sharing remains an intriguing but largely unused concept.

The feebleness of regional governance institutions in the United States, which are analyzed in Chapter 8, makes forthright attempts to address regional disparities highly unlikely unless states, as in Oregon, or federal agencies provide more direction.

Conclusion

In his study of the Baltimore region's growing pains, *Baltimore Unbound*, David Rusk (former mayor of Albuquerque) concludes that sprawling patterns of suburban growth in the Baltimore area are leading to abandonment of older neighborhoods and blue-collar suburbs and to the "hyper-concentration" of poor African-Americans in high-poverty neighborhoods in the city. To counter these trends, he urges establishment of a Portland-like regional government that could oversee regional programs for fair-share housing and tax-base sharing, as part of regional growth management.[51]

These regional initiatives could play a significant role in redirecting the development process in any metropolitan area. Among other benefits, the measures could stimulate redevelopment and revitalization of older neighborhoods, business centers, and industrial areas, which in turn would expand housing and job opportunities for many regional residents. As a strategy for retaining the vitality of existing urban areas while guiding new development, this regional policy framework could prove invaluable for managing growth in local communities as well as in metropolitan areas.

Lacking that regional framework, the job of inducing economic development and affordable housing production in declining areas is much more difficult, although not without hope. Greater public effort and investment is required to compensate for market forces that currently are encouraged by public policy to seek "greenfield" sites. The programs and projects described in this chapter demonstrate the extraordinary efforts that cities and towns must mount to revive older areas, improve employment and housing opportunities, and stimulate neighborhood conservation. Imagine the power and effect of such efforts linked to a regionwide growth policy that encouraged the full use of existing urban areas and discouraged unthinking sprawl into the countryside!

8

Regional and State Growth Management

Ever since local governments began to plan and regulate development, the limitations of their jurisdictional focus have been all too evident. Most of us understand that many aspects of development reach beyond the concerns of individual local governments. Our communities function within regional, state, national, and even global contexts of economic, social, and environmental forces. These contexts have grown in importance as metropolitan areas increased in size and complexity and as concerns about global economic competition and sustainable development burgeoned. Communities attempting to manage growth and change, therefore, should account for and deal with many external forces that demand coordination and cooperation with other jurisdictions.

To reach those objectives, regional planning agencies and state growth management programs were established in many areas. They define intergovernmental relationships to promote regional and state interests in local development policies and practices. Many varieties of regional agencies were formed to define regionwide development concerns, prescribe regional strategies, and coordinate local actions. States encouraged regional activities and enacted laws to instill state and regional concerns in local planning and regulation of development.

Dominance of Local Interests

All such efforts have been and continue to be stoutly resisted by local governments and their constituents. Americans traditionally value public decision making at the lowest possible rung on the ladder of governmental entities. They decry the "meddling" of state and regional agencies in local development matters and oppose requirements that local jurisdictions should recognize regional and state interests in their development policies. Their wariness over any diminution of their authority over development is defended as necessary to maintain their unique community character and interests, particularly their competitive position in the region's economy and tax structure.

The reluctance of local governments to allow regional and state entities to assume some authority in managing growth is illustrated by events in Palm Beach County, Florida, and San Francisco. In 1986, voters in Palm Beach County approved amendment of the county charter to create the Palm Beach Countywide Planning Council. The main mission given to the planning council was to establish a cooperative planning process to resolve or prevent incompatibilities and conflicts among plans of local governments, which were adopting and revising comprehensive plans in response to Florida's Growth Management Act of 1985. Opponents of the regional effort succeeded in attaching to the amendment a five-year sunset clause that could be invoked by action of a majority of local governments in the county.

Although the prime task of the council was widely viewed as determining incompatibilities among local plans, the charter language gave it broad authority to require local plans and regulatory actions to be consistent with the countywide land use plan to be prepared by the council. Local officials' suspicions that the county's planning powers could supplant local decision making led to a turbulent beginning for the council. Valuable time was lost and two executive directors replaced while council members argued over procedures and bylaws, committee structures, and elements of the work program. Meanwhile, local governments proceeded with completing their plans.

As the council moved into its work program, conflicts with local governments sharpened:

- A fast-track policy-writing process produced policy statements that stimulated disagreements about the breadth of the council's mission—simply documenting and resolving incompatibilities or formulating a countywide plan.

- Although the compatibility analysis proceeded with general agreement about the process and its outcomes, the council's determination to review local policies for potential multijurisdictional impacts raised local political hackles.

- The council's proposal to require 25-percent set-asides of "natural resources of multijurisdictional significance" drew complaints that the council was overstepping its authority.

• The charter provision requiring the county land use plan to meet state requirements and to be adopted as part of the countywide comprehensive
plan appeared to give the county commissioners final say on all local plan
amendments as well, a concept highly alarming to local officials.

With those apprehensions and disagreements, the Municipal League of
Palm Beach County readily obtained resolutions calling for dissolution
of the planning council. The county commissioner's response, putting
the issue before the voters in 1992, proved insufficient to save the council. With the demise of the countywide planning program, municipal officials established an interjurisdictional working group to provide a
forum for resolving issues and conflicts.[1]

In 1989, business, civic, and political leaders in the San Francisco region formed the Bay Vision 2020 Commission to chart a new course for
regional governance in the Bay Area. The region includes 98 municipal
jurisdictions within nine counties. Their voluntary cooperative efforts at
managing growth through the Association of Bay Area Governments
(ABAG) were viewed as insufficient to cope with regionwide problems. A
more strategic and effective approach was sought.

After a year evaluating potential models for regional governance, the
commission agreed on three principles that summed up its view of an appropriate approach:

• Achieving a prosperous economy, a livable environment, and a harmo-
nious society requires better management of growth and change, not a reliance on chance.

• Although diverse communities should be retained, concentrations of development dense enough to support mass transit are necessary to decrease
traffic congestion and attain air quality standards.

• The region needs not more but better government, including state growth
management policies, new infrastructure financing methods, and a new
regional growth management agency that would combine the regional
transportation and air quality agencies with ABAG.

The commission's report in 1991 laid out the elements of a regional
governance framework to promote cooperative, creative agreements on
growth issues. It recommended creation of a nine-county regional commission by merging the Metropolitan Transportation Commission, the
Bay Area Air Quality Management District, and ABAG. Other agencies
such as the Bay Conservation and Development Commission might later
be consolidated with the commission as well. The commission would
continue to administer programs already managed by the three agencies,
but would take on the additional major mission of adopting and implementing a regional plan. The plan was defined as a compendium of stan-

dards for meeting regional needs rather than land use determinations, and would make maximum use of county and city adopted plans. It would be submitted to the governor and state legislature to obtain authority for its implementation. The commission would also recommend measures for implementing the plan, including procedures for obtaining local plan conformance with the regional plan, state legislation for tax-base sharing, proposed additional mergers, and the continuance of the commission.

Sharp disagreements arose immediately over whether regional growth should be limited, whether the regional commission should be able to override local development decisions, whether growth should be redirected to already urbanized areas, and whether the new agency would become a supergovernment of development regulators. Underlying these concerns were suspicions of progrowth forces that antigrowth groups would use the regional governance structure to stifle or complicate the development process, and fears of antigrowth advocates that regional governance would erode their grassroots support.

The regional governance proposal in San Francisco paralleled in many respects a state-level movement to establish regional commissions that would merge existing agencies. However, proposed legislation to that end for the state and for the San Francisco region in particular received little support from Governor Pete Wilson and failed to make it through the state legislature. The movement for improving regional governance in the Bay Area sank without a trace.[2]

A survey of local planning directors' attitudes toward regional governance in California concludes that "resistance at the local level is to be expected when extending the role of regional government to growth management."[3] Although generally a majority of planning directors thought regional organizations would be helpful in carrying out some functions, most especially in managing transit, sewer and water, and road systems, planners' support for regionalism was less than overwhelming. Add to that the equivocal attitudes of citizens, as documented in several studies, and the experiences related in the paragraphs above appear to represent a dispiriting reality.

The Intergovernmental Dilemma

Despite resistance by local officials and many voters, extra-local interests continue to demand attention. Transportation systems require coordination at regional and state levels to function efficiently. Sewer and water systems spread throughout watersheds and across local jurisdictional boundaries. Ecosystems needing protection often are regional in scope. Social and economic disparities among jurisdictions threaten to disrupt regional economies unless addressed on an intergovernmental basis.

Examples of local growth management dysfunctions due to insufficient intergovernmental cooperation were pointed out in previous chapters:

- Montgomery County, Maryland found that traffic from neighboring jurisdictions triggered its adequate-facilities regulations to halt development in high-priority development areas.

- Boulder, Colorado's growth limits deflected development of affordable family housing to other towns in the region.

- Portland, Oregon's growth boundary cannot control development shifting across the state line to Vancouver, Washington.

- Although Lexington/Fayette County's growth boundary protected Bluegrass horse farms, unguided growth is taking place in neighboring counties and towns.

These kinds of problems have prodded public officials and their constituents to find ways to overcome interjurisdictional obstacles to coordinated and cooperative growth management. In so doing, they are challenged to translate state and regional interests into specific policies and actions while retaining a large measure of local government control over growth and development. The variety of approaches in use today is described in the remainder of this chapter.

Regional Growth Management

During the "good government" movement in the early years of this century, political reformers paid a great deal of attention to the concept of regional governance. Their enthusiasm bore fruit in a number of regional planning organizations, state planning commissions, and multistate river basin commissions established during the 1920s and especially during the New Deal years of the 1930s. The concept of region-based planning gained currency among geographers, planners, and political scientists as urban growth spread past city boundaries, new suburban jurisdictions proliferated, and threats to natural and rural environments became more perceptible. Lewis Mumford, in *The Culture of Cities,* characterized the emerging regional outlook in 1938: "The re-animation and re-building of regions as deliberate works of collective art, is the grand task of politics for the coming generation."[4]

During the period of rapid growth following World War II, the federal government gave a big boost to the concept of regional management of the development process. It encouraged formation of regional planning councils and/or substate districts to coordinate a multitude of federal grant programs flowing to local governments. Federal funds were available for regional planning and for a variety of regionally managed programs. Federal encouragement proved so successful that by the end of the 1970s local governments in almost all parts of the nation were participating in regional organizations. Every state included regional agencies of some kind, and many had formed regional groups to cover the entire state.

The first two years of the 1980s, however, saw a drastic curtailing of federal support for regional agencies. Programs were terminated and funding cut or dropped altogether. Only the metropolitan transportation planning organizations required by law continued to receive support, although their funding dwindled as well. With the loss of most federal funding, the regional councils that had been engaged in regionwide planning had to regroup. To attract local support, they turned to performing services useful to their constituent local governments, including data collection and projections, special studies, and certain services perceived by local governments as regional in nature.

The regional planning function suffered as well. Many local governments took a dim view of the regional planning efforts of the 1960s and 1970s, seeing them as rather abstract exercises of little practical value. Those views were critical, since regional agencies largely lacked regulatory powers and depended on local governments to implement plans. Once regional agencies became dependent on local governments for survival, many regional agencies gave up any semblance of strategic regionwide planning except for stitching together local plans or formulating airy and mostly toothless statements of regional goals.

Yet regional agencies persist in most metropolitan areas and provide significant services in aid of growth management. The regional transportation planning function, especially, has been given new life; in states that enacted state growth management programs, regional organizations have been given serious coordinating duties. A few agencies have gained credibility and power to substantially influence the development process.

Regional Agencies Today

Regional organizations that participate in growth management take a number of forms:

- Regional planning councils or districts.
- Metropolitan transportation planning organizations.
- Federal/state-chartered commissions or authorities charged with protection of environmentally sensitive areas.

- Regional public service authorities, such as airport or transit authorities or water districts.
- Regional business and civic leadership groups promoting planning.
- Ad hoc groups established by interjurisdictional agreements for selected purposes.
- Consolidated city/county governments and, in some states, county planning organizations.

Many large metropolitan areas harbor a number of these organizations, often with overlapping interests and powers. In general, the most effective regional organizations have consolidated several functions that permit strategic regional planning and some control over implementation activities.

Regional Planning Councils. Planning councils (or associations of governments or councils of governments) are the most widespread type of regional agency. They exist in some form in every state, and some states have designated council areas across the entire state. Typically they are made up of local governments whose elected representatives form the governing body. They may also organize standing subgroups of local administrative staffs, such as planners or finance officers. Although varying widely, their responsibilities often include:

- Assembling statistical information on regional population and economic development and projecting regional trends—important guides for local government planning but often subject to negotiated results and sometimes unilaterally modified by local officials.
- Providing a forum for sounding and exploring intergovernmental development issues, although consensus-building frequently devolves into elaborate games of mutual backscratching rather than significant resolutions of issues.
- Providing clearinghouse functions in planning, coordinating, or managing some federal and state programs such as programs for the elderly and job training.
- Carrying out research and educational activities on special issues of interest to members.
- Preparing regional development plans or strategic plans.
- Planning for selected regionwide infrastructure systems.
- Monitoring and promoting coordination of local planning activities.

The Portland, Oregon Metro Organization, indisputably the most successful metropolitan planning organization in the nation, possesses all these responsibilities and more. Thirty years ago, Portland was experiencing many of the ills of cities everywhere in America: a downtown in decline amid signs of inner-city neglect, development spreading outward into farmlands and forests, constant headaches over traffic and schools, annexation and incorporation wars, and proliferation of special service districts complicating public policies. Yet today Portland is viewed as one of the most desirable places to live in the nation, a metropolitan area that works in ways that other urban regions only hope to attain.

Many reasons are given for this transformation: Oregonians' passionate environmental interests, the Willamette Valley's world-class agricultural fertility that begged for preservation, Portlanders' intense concern with their living environment that stimulated them to tear down an expressway to build a park, and the slow economic growth that allowed Portland's public officials to prepare and enact policies whose effects might have been outpaced by impacts of more rapid growth.

Two major political decisions, however, wrapped all these factors together to provide a uniquely effective governance framework for the region. Oregon's growth management law adopted in 1973, one of the first in the nation, provides strong state guidance of local development policies. And within that state policy context, Portland's regional governance structure organized in 1970 and strengthened in 1979 has interwoven state and local development policies to form a cohesive strategic approach to development of the entire metropolitan area.

The road to regional governance was a rough one. Legislation to consolidate Portland and Multnomah County in 1926 to address sprawling suburban development failed to win approval. Postwar concerns over unguided development, however, resulted in the organization of a metropolitan planning commission in 1957, supplanted by the Columbia Region Association of Governments in 1966. The association encountered the usual problems in obtaining consensus on a regional plan and securing a stable funding base, and through the early 1970s its efforts continued to flounder.

However, the state legislature approved a proposal in 1970, later ratified by voters, to establish a three-county Metropolitan Service District. Conceived as a multipurpose agency, the District began feebly by managing solid waste planning for the region and, in 1976, by assuming responsibility for operating the Portland zoo.

The region's search for a viable regionwide agency came to a head in the late 1970s, when a Tri-County Local Government Commission decided to strengthen regional government by combining the planning functions of the association of governments with the District's service functions, and by directly electing the regional agency's governing body and executive rather than depending on appointed officials. The proposal was adopted by the state legislature in 1977 and, to the surprise of many, by the voters in 1978.[5]

Metro made its share of mistakes in the early days but it managed to build credibility with successful ventures. Its drawing of the state-mandated urban growth boundary for the Portland area was readily accepted by the Oregon Land Conservation and Development Commission. Metro has employed periodic reviews of the boundary as a means of coordinating local plans and widening citizen participation in planning. Solid waste management operations were expanded. Metro took the lead in planning and siting the state convention center, and then formed a commission to build and operate the center and to manage the Civic Stadium, the Portland Center for the Performing Arts, and the Expo Center. To carry out the federal transportation planning mandate, Metro established and staffed a joint advisory committee (as an ad hoc council of governments) to make key decisions on regional transportation policies. An affordable housing policy worked out with the state required half of all residential zoning to allow multifamily use and established minimum housing density targets for each jurisdiction in the region. Metro also launched Metropolitan Greenspaces to inventory and protect open spaces and natural areas.

Metro came of age with voter approval in 1990 of a state constitutional amendment to give Metro a home rule charter. The charter adopted by voters in 1992 provided for a seven-member council elected from districts and an executive officer elected regionwide. It also called for Metro to take steps toward adoption of a regionwide framework plan, including formation of a Future Vision commission to prepare a statement describing how the region would accommodate growth while respecting the region's quality of life, sustainability, and carrying capacity. Metro then formulated a strategic plan for the year 2040, recognizing that major development patterns evolve over a lengthy period of time. After evaluating four alternative regional patterns of development (see Figure 8.1), Metro adopted a plan that calls for minimum expansion of the urban growth boundary and substantial development and redevelopment in compact centers, all tied together by a regional rail and bus transit system.[6]

The regional framework plan for 2020 now being prepared is supposed to address in detail regional transportation systems, the urban growth boundary, and a variety of other planning issues, including coordination with planning policies of Clark County, Washington and standards and procedures to guide local land use decision making. The plan is due for adoption by the Metro Council by the end of 1997.

The immense amount of planning and coordination activity required by these responsibilities, and extensive consensus-building procedures followed by all the agencies, has drawn public officials and citizens into the planning process for over a quarter-century.

Metro, therefore, acting within the framework of the Oregon state growth management law, has established regional strategies and put in place effective plans and interjurisdictional programs that guide devel-

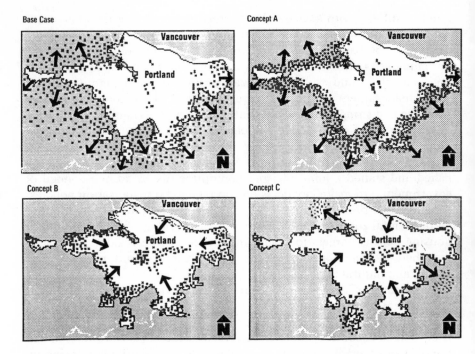

Base Case

Concept A

Concept B

Concept C

Figure 8.1
Portland plan alternatives. In its 2040 Plan evaluation process, Portland's
Metro council considered four alternative scenarios for the region's growth. The
plan finally selected incorporated elements of all three alternatives to adopt the
base case. (From *Concepts for Growth,* prepared by Metro, June 1994.)

opment throughout the region. These major program elements stand
head and shoulders above efforts to guide development in any other region in the United States.

Elsewhere, regional planning councils adopt strategies and policies
only by consensus of their local government members. In theory, this
might stimulate local governments to define regionwide development
strategies for guiding local actions. In practice, a single government can
exercise virtual veto power over policy positions, resulting in regional
statements that are so broad as to be almost meaningless. Furthermore,
local governments have made certain that regional agencies are unable
to implement strategies and policies without their individual acquies-
cence. As a result, most regional planning falls prey to three limitations:

• Most regional planning is only advisory in nature, leaving local governments to accept or reject regional policies.

- Even where regional agencies possess powers to require conformance of local plans to regional goals, they are reluctant to make the hard decisions for managing growth due to their administrative and financial control by member governments.

- Jurisdictions of regional agencies seldom coincide with actual metropolitan growth areas, either by encompassing vast rural areas that diffuse development issues or by leaving out urbanizing fringe areas; the planning orientation of most regional organizations is a decade behind the metropolitan development process.

Regional plans, therefore, seldom provide incisive direction for development and may be—and often are—ignored almost at will by member local governments.

The challenges to strong regional leadership in growth management have been overcome in some instances by state action to lend support to regional agencies and by the technical prowess and political acumen of regional administrators, as illustrated by Portland's Metro described earlier. Two other regional councils also offer examples of these qualities in quite different ways: the San Diego Association of Governments, and the Minneapolis/St. Paul Metropolitan Council.

The San Diego Association of Governments (SANDAG) was created as a typical association of 18 city governments and the county government in San Diego County. Through skillful administration over many years, SANDAG established solid credentials throughout the region for providing useful data and projections, functioning as the metropolitan transportation planning organization, and overseeing planning and management of a number of regional programs, such as wildlife habitat preservation, solid waste recycling, airport siting, and open space planning.

In 1988, after several years of controversy over regional growth management issues, the county's voters resoundingly approved a proposal to establish a "Regional Planning and Growth Management Review Board" to manage a regional growth management program. A Blue Ribbon Committee, made up of elected officials of each of the local jurisdictions and staffed by SANDAG, deliberated over a number of organizational options:

- Using the 13 existing general and special-purpose regional agencies, including SANDAG, to manage regional growth management through interagency agreements, local ordinances, and local and regional plans.

- Designating SANDAG as the Review Board, either by amending the existing joint powers agreement among local governments that established SANDAG or by new state legislation.

- Enacting state legislation to create a new regional agency as the Review Board and establish its membership, operating rules, and responsibilities.

After considerable public discussion and hearings, the Blue Ribbon Committee chose to confer regional growth management responsibilities on SANDAG, which then began the process of securing unanimous agreement among local jurisdictions for amending its joint powers agreement with them. By February 1990, all jurisdictions had approved the amendment and SANDAG became the Regional Review Board, with responsibilities for developing a regional growth management strategy for issues such as growth rate policies, phasing and distribution of growth, open space preservation, siting and financing regional facilities, and quality of life objectives.

According to the joint powers amendment, the Regional Board has persuasive rather than regulatory powers to ensure implementation of its plans. The amendment called for local agencies to "self certify" the consistency of the pertinent elements of their general plans with regional plans developed by the Regional Board. On request by a member agency, the Regional Board can review these self-certifications and make findings regarding their consistency. Enforcing consistency of local plans with regional plans (1) requires that a local jurisdiction question the actions of another local jurisdiction, always a politically charged move; (2) suggests that the Regional Board's findings will encourage local actions to reach consistency; and (3) establishes the possibility of third-party actions (e.g., litigation) to ensure consistency.

In a progress report on the regional growth management strategy in late 1993, SANDAG announced that the initial phase of the strategy program had been approved. It defined measurable quality-of-life standards and a description of the actions being taken by the regional agency and its constituent local governments to respond to federal and state mandates pertaining to water supply and quality, traffic congestion, air quality, sewage treatment, solid and hazardous waste management, and housing needs. (Examples of such mandates include state water quality standards, federal wetlands protection requirements, state requirements for congestion management programs, and state requirements for region-based fair-share housing programs.)

According to the regional strategy, local governments were to certify that their policies and plans were consistent with actions necessary to achieve these mandates. A conflict-resolution procedure was developed to resolve disputes. The initial phase of the self-certification process—filling out a consistency checklist—was completed, and then local officials determined actions necessary to reach total consistency between local policies and plans and necessary actions to achieve state and federal mandates.

The second phase of the strategy deals with five regional concerns: a growth forecast, economic prosperity plan, a land use element, an open space element, and a public facilities financing plan. Individual local jurisdictions are to present their plans and proposals for developing these elements to the Regional Board for comment and approval.

These procedures envision that the regional growth strategy will contain guiding principles and policies both *generated from* and *directed to* local jurisdictions—a type of cross-acceptance policy process.[7]

SANDAG's unique blend of regional and local policy making and implementation through persuasion has yet to prove conclusively effective. As a means of establishing tangible regionwide policies while overcoming local aversions to regional control over development, however, it provides a promising alternative to typical regional programs.

The Metropolitan Council of Minneapolis/St. Paul was established in 1967 to coordinate development in a seven-county, 140-jurisdiction region of 3000 square miles and 2.5 million people. The Metropolitan Council was created by the Minnesota legislature in response to a severe water pollution problem that required immediate planning for a coordinated and expanded regional sewer system. Once established, the council accrued responsibilities for other regionwide problems such as solid waste disposal, park and open space acquisition, airport siting, and transportation systems.

The council is not a super government but rather, in the words of a recent chairman, "a hybrid organization designed to increase centralized efficiency while still protecting a maximum level of local autonomy." While the council possesses more powers than most regional organizations, it influences metropolitan development through its planning and consensus-building functions rather than by regulatory means.

The council maintains a regional perspective through its appointment by the governor of council members from 16 multimunicipal districts. It is given some freedom of action by the financial support provided by a mill levy on all property in the region, which generates a substantial part of its budget requirements. It is responsible for preparing a regional plan and functions unofficially as the metropolitan transportation planning agency as well.

The Metropolitan Council influences the location and quality of development primarily through its planning for basic infrastructure systems and services. For example, it defines a metropolitan urban service area for sewer service that amounts to an urban growth boundary. Development outside the urban service area is supposed to be limited by communities to densities that can be served by septic systems—quite low densities given the generally poor soils in much of the urbanizing area. The Council considers extensions of the service area every five years or when a city's developable land within the service area falls below a 15-year supply. In practice, the limits of the urban service area are negotiated with individual municipalities, with those nearest the edge constantly contesting when and how the area should be expanded.

Sewer service is actually provided by the Metropolitan Waste Control Commission, but the Metropolitan Council has a good deal of influence over its policies. Eight of the nine commission members are appointed by the Metropolitan Council, and the council must approve the commission's implementation program, including its financial program, as consistent with the council's sewer policies. However, the commission also acts fairly independently in delivering what amounts to "wholesale" services to municipalities, who are responsible for managing local sewer systems.

The urban service area constitutes less than a third of the total metropolitan area. The urban service line has functioned relatively successfully to achieve contiguous urban development but has not promoted higher-density development. By and large, development patterns in the Twin Cities area have maintained the same low-density characteristics common to fringe areas of most American cities.

Transportation planning and management is directed by the council in much the same manner as the sewer system. The Regional Transit Board carries out metropolitan transit planning, operates the metropolitan bus company, and contracts with other bus companies and specialized vendors. The board's chairman is appointed by the governor; its members are appointed by the Metropolitan Council. As with sewer service, the council develops a transit policy plan as part of its metropolitan transportation plan, and the board carries out the plan with an implementation program approved by the council. Despite the close relationship between the council and the board, they have had sharp disagreements, among them the council's prevention of the board's intention to develop a heavy-rail system in the 1970s.

The highway part of the council's transportation plan is implemented by the Minnesota Department of Transportation. Although not required to follow the plan, the department usually does because the council has veto power over department plans for controlled-access highways and also manages relationships between the department and local governments and groups. A Transportation Advisory Board, made up largely of local officials, advises the council in choosing highway priorities and allocating federal funds. In practice, the council almost always follows the board's recommendations.[8]

Despite this plethora of interlocking planning, the Twin Cities' transportation problems look much like those in other metropolitan areas. The number of miles of severely congested freeways tripled in the 1980s and is projected to triple again in the next 15 years. Recent council efforts to gain legislative support to build a light-rail system have been unsuccessful, in large part because low-density development patterns make rail transit a marginal investment at best. A 1984 council study identified six corridors in which light-rail would be an investment competitive with other alternatives. However, the advisory task force that planned the system proposed 14 corridors (more miles than the Paris rail system) and a $2-billion investment to provide service to all the task force member's jurisdictions. The plan never received approval.

In the early 1970s the council carried out several studies that concluded that the cost of public services to uncontrolled development would be higher (by $2.2 billion over 20 years) than the cost for serving compact development. One result of that finding was the enactment of the Metropolitan Land Planning Act in 1976 by the state legislature. The act required all cities in the metropolitan area to formulate comprehensive plans, which were then subject to approval by the council for consistency with its functional plans. If the council can demonstrate that a local plan will adversely impact regional systems (e.g., highways), then the council can demand plan changes.

The act also gave the council the power to delay individual development projects for up to a year if it finds that the project will have an adverse impact of "metropolitan significance" on the region. During this delay period, presumably, steps can be taken to mitigate the impacts or even halt the project. The council has undertaken some 15 reviews but never delayed a project—compromises were reached.

The Metropolitan Council is one of the few regional agencies that actually prepares a regional plan. It began in the early 1970s with an elaborate process that led to adoption of the Metropolitan Development Framework in 1975, which included both a policy plan and an implementation program.

The council's famous tax-base sharing program was intended to provide some compensating mechanism for regional land use and facility-siting actions that might favor one jurisdiction over another. Most notably, the program was meant to reduce competition over high-value commercial and industrial development and prevent tax-base disparities. Since 1971, 40 percent of property tax revenues from new commercial and industrial development have been pooled in a regional fund and redistributed based on population and other factors. In effect, tax-base sharing compensates jurisdictions that receive less high-value development than other jurisdictions. Although tax-sharing remains a significant part of the council's program, its importance has declined as property tax proportions of total revenues have dropped.

The vaunted interjurisdictional consensus that supported the Council for so many decades fell on hard times in the 1990s, as minorities migrated into the central cities and fiscal and other disparities between suburban jurisdictions and Minneapolis and St. Paul began to surface, especially in the findings of the 1990 census. The Council was criticized for its slowness to respond to new regional imperatives to attend to social and economic development. Governor Arne Carlson, who earlier had indicated only lukewarm support for the regional agency, called for the Council to become either "relevant or extinct."

In 1994, the governor signed new legislation merging the regional waste control and transit agencies with the Council, broadening the Council's mission to incorporate operating as well as planning functions. In September 1994, the Council issued its "Regional Blueprint," a compilation of new policy directions that emphasize actions to build a stronger region. The new plan was intended to address widening central city problems such as poverty, crime, and unemployment, and to stress redevelopment and reinvestment in older urban cities and greater control over sprawl development in newer communities.[9]

The Council's new role, which could de-emphasize regional planning and the extent of its influence in regional development, is not yet fully discernible. Although still warmly supported by many area citizens, the agency continues to lack strong gubernatorial support. But local observers are hoping to see the Council revitalized and newly effective.

The stories of Portland, San Diego, and Minneapolis/St. Paul offer some useful lessons for other regional organizations. Both Portland's and the Twin Cities' agencies were established with state support, manage important regional services, are governed by boards with regional and/or state membership, and possess selected but significant powers to influence key elements of the development process such as transportation and sewers. Their regions have grown at only moderate rates. As the major urban areas in their respective states, they receive a great deal of attention from state legislators. The achievements of San Diego's SANDAG agency are due less to its inherent powers than its skillful administration and political acumen, as well as the sense of voters that the region's rapid growth required extraordinary measures.

Metropolitan Planning Organizations. These transportation planning agencies, known as MPOs, which the Federal Aid Highway Act of 1962 required in all metropolitan areas of over 50,000 population, are responsible for "continuing, comprehensive, and cooperative" planning for transportation. Most important, they are responsible for allocating federal and state transportation funding within their regions. Annually they adopt multiyear transportation improvement programs, similar in many ways to local capital improvement programs.

Because their establishment came during the period of founding regional land use planning agencies, the two types of functions frequently were combined in one agency framework. The combination suggests close working relationships between the two. But MPOs are different from regional planning councils in having some board members appointed by state governors and being closely affiliated with state transportation agencies rather than local elected leaders. Also, more and more MPOs have spun off from regional planning councils. MPOs have not proven to be as successful at coordinating and cooperating as hoped. As planning agencies they have no implementing powers; other state and local agencies carry out plans. States play a mercurial role, sometimes wielding power by changing priorities or dropping and adding projects at will. In fact, since 1982, states have been free to formulate and monitor their own programs to leave their hands untied by MPO programs. MPOs, like regional planning agencies, also have problems with regional boundaries. A transportation study recently completed for the U.S. 301 corridor in five Maryland counties east of Washington, D.C. contended with three MPOs, each with jurisdiction over part of the area.

The Intermodal Surface Transportation Efficiency Act (ISTEA) of 1991 was intended to improve matters. It calls for considering multimodal transportation options in planning for improvements, shaping transportation programs to reflect funding limits, recognizing relationships between land use and transportation, and involving community residents and interests in the planning process. The act prodded MPOs to plan more broadly and program improvements more realistically to meet metropolitan development needs. Some state transportation departments and MPOs have resisted the act's call for more comprehensive and inclusive planning. State transportation departments, in particular, have been powerful agencies well connected to state legislators, construction contractors, and others with stakes in doing business as usual. Other state transportation departments and MPOs have responded positively to ISTEA objectives in launching far-reaching planning studies and programs.

The U.S. 301 corridor transportation study offers an example of the "new wave" of transportation planning. The 50-mile highway corridor through five fast-growing Maryland counties east of Washington, D.C. was originally proposed as an eastern by pass for the Washington region. Environmentalists and others, alarmed by the highway's potential stimulation of regional sprawl development, successfully killed the proposal. Subsequently, the Maryland Department of Transportation (MDOT), working with environmental groups, formulated a different planning approach. A broadly representative task force was convened to work with MDOT in fashioning a transportation plan that would integrate multimodal travel options, supportive land use patterns, and conservation of environmental resources.

After three years of effort, over 200 meetings, and evaluation of more than a dozen alternative transportation/land use scenarios, the task force concluded that massive transportation investments would fail to resolve long-term highway congestion unless accompanied by effective transit and travel demand management programs and by land use policies that would concentrate growth and attract economic development to balance residential development. The 1996 report of the task force recommended a broad range of highway and transit improvements and travel demand management actions, to be supported by substantial changes in local land use policies to promote compact development in designated growth areas and limit rural sprawl.[10]

These kinds of land use recommendations had been made in other regional transportation studies to little effect, since neither MPOs nor regional planning councils controlled land use policies and regulations. So the U.S. 301 task force made two additional recommendations to put teeth in their plan. It recommended that major state investments in transportation improvements should be conditioned on the strengthening of local land use policies to provide positive support for transportation improvements. And it recommended formation of an intergovernmental working group to coordinate and monitor state and local actions in implementing the plan, essentially to bridge the jurisdictional gaps among the three MPOs in the area, MDOT and other state agencies, and the five counties and two municipalities involved.

Thus the U.S. 301 plan recognized the need for multijurisdictional coordination to achieve its objectives for transportation and land use in the corridor. With the governor's affirmation of the recommendations, and the working group in place, hopes are high that significant integration between transportation and land use will be achieved over the next 25 years.

Regional Environmental Conservation Agencies. Of all the regional agencies, regional environmental conservation agencies have proven the most effective at managing the development process. Many are well known—the Adirondack Park Commission, the Tahoe Regional Planning Agency, the Cape Cod Regional Commission, and the Chesapeake Bay Commission described in Chapter 5. Perhaps the best example of such agencies is the New Jersey Pinelands Commission because its major features echo many of those in other agencies: established after public clamor to protect a cherished resource; mandated by federal and/or state action; given narrow powers to override local development policies; administered with intensive efforts at intergovernmental cooperation; funded by sources not dependent on local governments.

The New Jersey pine barrens occupy about one-third of the state's land, generally located south and east of the New Jersey Turnpike. An ecosystem with a high water table, many marshes and bogs, stunted trees, and many species of plants and animals, the pine barrens was truly a backwater area. Scattered small settlements persisted from Colonial days, their economies dependent on small farms, bog-iron foundries, and cranberry bogs. In the 1960s, however, development threatened to spread east from Princeton and inland from the coast; proposals for new towns and major second-home projects were broached. Many local officials and property owners in the pine barrens were elated at the thought of coming development, but many were not; many environment-minded people outside the pine barrens were very concerned about potential development. Reaction grew over potential damage to the pine barrens ecosystem and particularly to the 17-trillion-gallon aquifer of exceptionally pure water underlying the area.

The federal government acted first, with passage of the National Parks and Recreation Act of 1978, which designated the pinelands as a national reserve. A year later, the state followed suit with the Pinelands Protection Act. The act created the New Jersey Pinelands Commission, a 15-member board (one appointed by the U.S. Secretary of Interior, seven by the governor, seven by local governments) to oversee conservation and development in a one-million-acre area with 52 municipalities and seven counties.

The act required the commission to adopt a comprehensive management plan. Commission members defined several goals for the plan:

- Protect the forested core of the area by directing development to the edges.

- Protect water quality and associated ecological features.

- Accommodate needs of projected population growth.

- Provide homes for people employed in the region, rather than second homes for residents of other areas.

- Adopt a process for mitigating economic impacts and recognizing vested rights.

The plan designated four types of areas. The preservation area, actually delineated in the state act, prohibits residential uses unless a landowner can demonstrate two-generation ownership. The protection area allows development of one dwelling unit for each 39 acres. Agricultural production areas are scattered throughout the other areas and provide for continued cranberry and blueberry production of great economic value. Regional growth centers were designated to accommodate future development. The plan was supplemented with a variety of environmental management programs and a transferable-development-rights program to compensate landowners for refraining from development.

Once the plan was adopted, local plans and regulations were required to conform to it through a certification by the commission. The process required many years and much coaching. The act authorized the commission to certify counties to conduct preliminary reviews of local plans, but no counties wished to participate in that politically heated process. The state helped the implementation process by establishing the Pinelands Development Credit Bank in 1985 to buy development credits in restricted areas and sell them to obtain higher densities in regional growth centers (similar in many ways to the transferable-development-rights program at Lake Tahoe). Also in 1985 New Jersey voters approved a $30-million Pinelands Infrastructure Trust Bond Act to fund sewer and other capital improvements in regional growth centers.

The Pinelands plan benefitted from federal and state mandates that established environmental values as prime objectives and from carefully crafted provisions to respond to economic as well as environmental needs. It also benefitted from an empathetic administrative staff that constantly worked to attain consensus with local officials and residents without wielding the state/federal hammer too visibly or often. Today the Pinelands management process is well established and functioning as smoothly as possible with 59 local governments.

The Pinelands' experience demonstrates several important factors in the relative success of environmentally-oriented regional organizations:

- The focus on a *clear objective*—preserving a significant environmental feature that provided a rationale for extraordinary action, whether the Alpine clarity of Lake Tahoe, the unique ecosystem and valuable aquifer of the Pinelands, or the fishing and recreational qualities of Chesapeake Bay.

- Federal and state actions that permitted *overrides of local decision making* on development matters by requiring conformity of local plans to agency goals and rules.

- Significant *financial support* to compensate affected landowners through transferable development rights or by outright acquisition of severely affected properties.

- *Funding* of planning and economic development programs to assist local governments in responding to regional objectives.

- Regional agency attempts to establish *cooperative relationships* with local governments and residents to build consensus instead of promoting conflict.

- Existence of an *organized constituency* of environmental interests that monitors and supports agency actions.

The experience of the Tahoe Regional Planning Agency is instructive on at least two of these points. The agency, established in 1969 as a bi-state organization, adopted a strong "command-and-control" stance toward regulating conformance with the agency's goals. Its plans and regulations promised to virtually wipe out values of 9000 platted lots around the lake; development approvals were made on a case-by-case basis, often with formidable conditions. Local governments retained little control over the development process. Political conflicts and litigation raised storms of controversy in both states, throughout several administrations. Not until the agency redrew requirements to provide more predictability and potential compensation for affected property owners did a conservation plan obtain approval. Even then, the bitter attitudes stirred by years of strife continue to affect implementation of the plan.

Other Regional Organizations. Regional coordination also is carried out in less official ways by a variety of other regional organizations. Some are business groups, such as the Greater Baltimore Committee that provided much of the leadership for revitalizing the Baltimore waterfront, the Allegheny Conference that for decades has promoted economic development in the Pittsburgh region, and the Bay Area Council that supports high-quality development in the San Francisco area.

In moderate- to mid-size cities, especially, such groups often provide the primary stimulus for regionwide planning and action. The "New Designs for Growth" project of the Traverse City Area Chamber of Commerce in Michigan, for example, is promoting better growth control practices in the five-county region of Grand Traverse Bay on Lake Michigan. Its initial efforts began in 1992 with publication of the *Grand Traverse Bay Region Development Guidebook.* The guidebook provides a compendium of model development practices, employing simple drawings to contrast inadequate and superior techniques for developing, building, designing, and protecting land. Now the Chamber is using the guidebook as a central tool for educating public officials and citizens and for instilling better standards of development in township and county plans and regulations. The Chamber program offers assistance in organizing public meetings and workshops to educate township leaders, residents, developers, and landowners about modern development practices that enhance economic returns while protecting the area's cultural and natural resources. The Chamber's efforts emphasize homegrown help to improve development practices.

Another type of regional initiative is illustrated by the efforts of public officials and business and civic leaders in the Boise, Idaho area to map out a strategy for dealing with short- and long-term infrastructure needs. Rapid growth in Boise and other cities and towns in Ada and Canyon counties has required establishment of new infrastructure systems and expansion of existing ones. In recent years, most response has occurred on a crisis-by-crisis basis. Regionwide, development is outpacing capacities and efficiencies of road networks, sewer and water systems, school districts, and other facility systems. Finding adequate funding for improvements is difficult with available financial resources.

The Boise Area Chamber of Commerce began addressing this issue as a major theme in its ongoing program. Its 1995 leadership conference focused on infrastructure needs and financing strategies. In 1996 it initiated a study, managed by the Future Foundation, to determine existing and future needs throughout the region, explore models of regional organization to better manage infrastructure development, and identify new funding sources. The Chamber will continue to encourage region-wide actions to provide an organizational framework for managing infrastructure development and financing.

On a somewhat larger scale, the New York Regional Plan Association

---

Plan for the New York–New Jersey–Connecticut Metropolitan Region

Robert Yaro

In February, 1996, the Regional Plan Association published its Third Regional Plan for the Tri-state region around New York City, the nation's largest metropolitan area, to the acclaim of the region's media, civic and business leaders, and the area's three governors. The plan sets forth proposals for investments in infrastructure, education, and urban systems required to sustain the region's economic growth in the first decades of the twenty-first century.

More than ever before, metropolitan regions are the competitive unit in national and global markets. Recent research by the National League of Cities and others confirms that regions and their cities and suburbs succeed or fail as a unit. These new realities underscore the importance of a coherent long-range, regionwide plan.

The Third Regional Plan builds on the strong foundation laid by the first metropolitan plan published in 1929 by the Regional Plan Association, a private, nonprofit group established in the 1920s. Many of the region's major systems of highways, bridges, parks, and commuter rail lines were promoted by that first regional plan. The second plan, published in 1968, resulted in creation of the Metropolitan Transportation Authority and the revitalization of the then-failing commuter rail system that links a network of 11 employment centers today involving more than one million jobs.

Developed over a five-year period with foundation and corporate support, the new plan recognized the revolutionary changes taking place in the region's economic, environmental, and social systems. Global competition and industrial restructuring are threatening even the strongest service industries; a generation of immigrants is transforming the region's social structure; and continued suburban sprawl was impacting the region's natural systems. The plan is organized around the three "E's" of economy, environment and (social) equity and their interactions.

(RPA) was founded by business and civic leaders in the 1920s to create a long-term plan for the New York region and promote its implementation across political boundaries. For more than seven decades, the RPA has sponsored highly regarded research studies, formulated three regional plans, and acted as a regional advocate to influence public and private decisions throughout the region. Its 1929 *Regional Plan of New York and Its Environs* provided an authoritative analysis of regional development issues and a breathtaking vision of future growth. The 1968 plan and the newest plan both emphasize needs for maintaining and revitalizing older urban areas and preserving open space.

The plan recommends five "campaigns:"

Mobility Campaign: Proposals to integrate elements of the seven existing rail networks into a regional express (or "Rx Rail") system, to manage highways through incentive tolls, and to improve rail freight movements.

Centers Campaign: Proposals to attract half of future employment growth over the next quarter century to the Manhattan business district and 11 regional downtowns, and to promote "transit-friendly" development in several hundred centers served by the regional rail system.

Greensward Campaign: Proposals to protect 11 "regional reserves," large water-supply areas, estuaries, agricultural districts, and other natural areas that constitute the region's "green infrastructure" and that can serve as a permanent regional growth boundary.

Workforce Campaign: Proposals to provide the region's citizens with skills required by an information- and technology-driven economy by reforming urban education finance, creating a lifelong learning system for adults, and linking urban public schools to private-sector employers.

Governance Campaign: Proposals to restructure regional authorities, coordinate state investments and incentives, improve state growth management systems, and establish a tri-state congressional coalition.

The plan is distinguished from most regional plans by clearly spelling out the costs of needed investments ($75 billion over a 25-year period) and setting forth alternative means to pay for them, including user fees, reduced intraregional tax incentives, reduced costs of sprawl, and other resources. It also estimates the "pay-back" in terms of expanded gross regional product and other substantive and quality-of-life measures that will be produced by adhering to the plan.

The RPA implements these ideas through the hard work of informing, persuading, nudging, and brandishing the banner of regionalism through countless meetings, hearings, discussions, and conversations. Its board and staff put prestige, lengthy experience, and a regional outlook in service for regional development. In a region with few other regional advocates, the RPA provides a constant reminder of the value of thinking regionally.

In addition to business-led organizations, civic federations, coalitions, and alliances promote discussion of regional issues in many areas. Citizens planning and zoning groups, for example, often sponsor regionwide discussions of current development issues. These educational efforts often pay off in an enlarged constituency for regional action.

Lessons for Effective Regional Growth Management

The variety of organizational models and experiences in regional management of growth described earlier provides some general themes for effective regional efforts:

- A broad *constituency of interests* for regional action must be identified and built, admittedly a tough job but one absolutely necessary for overcoming current obstacles to regional cooperation.

- A *clear objective* must be defined for which a persuasive case for regional action can be made; successful regional agencies have been created to preserve highly valued environmental features or solve specific, grave regionwide problems such as water pollution; regional agencies are accepted more readily if they control key components of the development process; multipurpose "regional governments" are beyond the pale and do not exist.[11]

- Effective regional strategic planning and implementation depend on the capability of saying "no" to individual local proposals if necessary; the power to override local governments realistically comes only from *state and/or federal authority* for regional action rather than from voluntary local assent to regional decisions.

- Procedures must be established to make *local governments accountable to regional interests,* such as requiring conformity of local plans to regional objectives; accountability requires *auditing or monitoring* local plans and regulations and providing an *enforcement process.*

- Decision-making responsibilities must be shared in such a way that *local governments retain major responsibilities* for development policies and regulations and day-to-day development decisions; the alternative is the almost certain rejection of regional governance.

State Growth Management

Nine states in the past 20 years have enacted statutes that called for comprehensive statewide planning for growth management. Three states—Oregon, Florida, and Rhode Island—have administered comprehensive, statewide growth management programs for at least two decades. Other states, including Vermont, Maine, New Jersey, Georgia, Washington, and Maryland, have less experience in implementing their more recent laws. Together, however, they illustrate a spectrum of approaches to state leadership and intergovernmental coordination in managing urban development.[12]

State Planning: A Long and Arduous Road

States have been practicing some form of growth management since the early part of the century, when Massachusetts in 1915 prepared a general outline of a state conservation plan. In the 1920s and 1930s, states began establishing state planning offices in response to conservation and economic development concerns. The National Planning Board appointed by President Roosevelt in 1934 urged states to form permanent state planning boards, with the result that, by 1938, 47 boards were in place. With the outbreak of World War II, federal funding and support disappeared and two-thirds of the state planning agencies were dismantled. State planning was revived, however, by the Housing Act of 1954 that gave life to so many regional planning agencies. The act's incentives for state planning, together with needs for channeling funds from federal programs initiated during the 1960s through states to local governments, boosted state planning agencies to 39. However, attempts by state planning agencies to coordinate other agencies' planning efforts were turned away. In the 1970s, federal funds dwindled and the Nixonian emphasis on "New Federalism" instigated widespread reorganization of state governments, during which many state planning offices were absorbed into other agencies or relegated to "back-office" status.[13]

Also in the early 1970s, however, at roughly the same time that Petaluma, Ramapo, and Boulder were pioneering local growth management concepts, several states moved to strengthen public controls over development. Their actions tended to reflect proposals for state planning in the Model Land Development Code then being prepared by the nation's top land use attorneys for the American Law Institute. The code provided for state involvement in planning for areas of critical state concern and for state oversight of local planning. Those concepts and others were highlighted in a highly influential book by Fred Bosselman and David Callies, *The Quiet Revolution in Land Use Control,* which claimed that the time-honored control of land development by local governments was being revolutionized by a variety of new laws with a common theme: "the need to provide some degree of state or regional participation in the major decisions that affect the use of our increasingly limited supply of land."[14]

Vermont's Act 250 was enacted in 1970 in response to rampant resort development and land speculation that sent land prices soaring and threatened the state's bucolic environment. The act required state permits for most sizeable developments and specified criteria for evaluating them. District environmental commissions were established to apply and interpret the criteria for proposed projects.

For over 25 years, the commissions' deliberations have formed a political flash-point for controversial projects. Although typically the commissions granted rather than refused projects, increasingly the approvals come with rigorous conditions attached to mitigate development impacts. During the mid-1990s, the commissions were intensely involved in conflicts over proposals for development of Wal-Mart and similar stores in small Vermont towns, in some cases requiring substantial revisions in site designs and in one or two denying the application altogether due to its probable impact on the town's economy.[15]

Although California had enacted legislation as early as 1955 to require all local governments to plan according to state policies, and subsequent state acts tightened requirements in specific areas such as affordable housing and hazardous waste disposal, state enforcement of these requirements was weak and largely ineffectual. California's big step came when legislation in 1972 established its coastal program that imposed strict restrictions on the use of coastal lands. Regional commissions worked with local governments to conform local plans to state criteria; over many years, this finally transpired. Meanwhile, the commissions took on the job of reviewing major projects, a process that caused extensive controversy among local governments and developers. It was the California Coastal Commission, for example, that issued the requirement for public beachfront access across Patrick Nollan's property, a decision reversed by the U.S. Supreme Court in *Nollan* v. *California Coastal Commission* (cited in the list of growth management cases in Chapter 2).

Also in 1972, Florida initiated a series of land and water management acts that required regional and state approval of "developments of regional impact" and encouraged formulation of plans in areas of critical state concern. Those were followed by the 1975 Comprehensive Planning Act that required all local governments to engage in comprehensive planning.

Later, in 1974, Colorado adopted a limited statewide planning act; it soon met political resistance that led to its demise. North Carolina approved legislation restricting development in 20 coastal-area counties that is still on the books but may be faltering in execution.

Comprehensive State Acts

All these efforts helped set the stage for the initiation of comprehensive state growth management acts, beginning with Oregon's legislation in 1973. Oregon's law established a Land Conservation and Development Commission whose first task was to adopt state goals and guidelines for development to which local governments' plans must conform. Later, the Commission presided over reviews and approvals of those plans, unlike the situation in Florida, where the 1975 requirements for local planning were unenforceable. In 1978 Rhode Island adopted a statewide planning program that consolidated a number of previous actions requiring local planning and adopting a state land use plan.

In the 1980s, a flurry of state enactments occurred as nine states undertook comprehensive planning. Florida led the way in 1985 with legislation to strengthen its local planning requirements and engage in state-level planning. Hard on the heels of that law, in 1986, New Jersey created a state planning commission to formulate a state development and redevelopment plan to which local plans would be made to conform through a "cross-acceptance" negotiation process. The states of Maine, Vermont, and Rhode Island enacted new legislation in 1988 requiring local governments to adopt plans consistent with state planning goals. Maine and Vermont also gave regional councils responsibility for reviewing and commenting on local plans. Georgia adopted a complex law in 1989 calling for multitiered planning.

Washington followed suit in 1990 (expanded in 1991) with a law similar in many respects to previous laws, and Maryland enacted a relatively limited law in 1992. The momentum of new state growth management acts appears to have waned in the wake of the real estate downturn of the late 1980s and early 1990s, but a considerable amount of discussion and legislative activity is taking place in states such as New York, Michigan, and Pennsylvania that may yet lead to additional statutes.

Although the statutes of the nine states vary in detail, they commonly require or encourage local governments, and frequently regional and state agencies as well, to prepare plans that conform to state goals and policies. Most also require consistency between plans and development regulations. In essence, the nine states have fundamentally reconfigured their approaches for dealing with urban development issues to emphasize intergovernmental responsibilities and actions.

State officials and growth management supporters in all nine states understood that they must retain a significant role for local governments in growth management. The legislation reflects that concern: Provisions often express the principle of continuing local control over day-to-day decisions. Maine's law, for example, finds that "the most effective land use planning can only occur at the local level of government, and comprehensive plans and land use ordinances developed and implemented at the local level are the key in planning for Maine's future."[16] But the statutes attempt to weave local decision making into a larger framework of intergovernmental responsibilities for managing growth and development. The state statutes also assert that states have legitimate statewide interests that justify some oversight of local actions.

Why States Should Manage Growth
John DeGrove

An alternative title to this essay might be "Growing Smart Beats Growing Dumb." I assert that collaborative efforts among state, regional, and local governments to manage growth wisely and well is a winner for both the environmental and economic health of states. To achieve that win requires political leadership to bring key public and private stakeholders to the table to reach consensus on structuring a managed growth system that benefits all the players.

Growth management in the 1980s and 1990s has emerged as a powerful concept that can reorder relations among states, regions, localities, and private interests in important ways. State growth management systems such as those long in place in Oregon and Florida and newer systems in Washington and Maryland have introduced important new concepts and given fresh meaning to traditional planning principles such as consistency, concurrency, and compact urban form.

A major benefit of state growth management systems is that they represent the application of common sense to growth challenges. Planning carefully for growth in a way that responsibly balances protection of natural systems with development required to support a growing population is a central theme of all the growth management acts. Properly defined, the state acts are neither pro-growth nor anti-growth. They represent a deep state commitment to securing an equitable and reasonable "fit" between major objectives.

If state growth management systems are so beneficial, why haven't they been adopted by most states? The answer is complex, involving confused notions about private property rights, local home rule, and the difficulty of mobilizing and sustaining broad-based support for adoption and implementation of state acts. Yet new studies are shedding light on the substantial social, environmental, and fiscal costs of sprawling patterns of development, a growth trend that cannot be contained by local governments and regions that insist on planning and regulating in isolation. A compelling advantage of state growth management, reason enough for its adoption in every state, is that managing and limiting sprawl cannot be achieved without it.

The ways in which states have realigned their relationships with local governments in growth management are many and varied, but center on strengthening intergovernmental responsibilities in guiding development and pursuing specific development objectives for the shape and character of urban growth.

The Intergovernmental Imperative for Managing Growth

Broadly phrased, statewide planning for growth management, as defined by the statutes of the nine states, promotes planning at state, regional, and local levels of government and encourages consistency and coordination between resulting plans. Six types of intergovernmental planning responsibilities may be discerned in the statutes: (1) state plans, (2) state agency planning and coordination, (3) requirements for local planning, (4) provisions for regional coordination, (5) processes for achieving consistency between local and agency plans and state goals, and (6) appeals or conflict resolution procedures.

State Plans or Goal Statements. All nine state growth management acts incorporate or provide for preparation of statewide plans to express state interests in growth and development. In every state except New Jersey and Rhode Island, the plans are expressed as statements of goals and policies to guide planning activities throughout the state. Oregon's act in 1973 contained 14 goal statements, later expanded to 19 by the addition of five coastal management goals. Two goals refer to citizen involvement and the planning process to be followed by local governments, regional, state, and federal agencies, and special districts. Six deal with environmental concerns and six with development issues. The goals are spelled out in some detail and include both mandatory and suggested implementation policies—for example, the agricultural lands goal that calls for preserving and maintain agricultural lands cites criteria for determining the appropriateness of converting such lands and guidelines for separating urban from agricultural uses.[17]

These state goal and policy statements define state interests that must be addressed by plans and regulations of local governments, regional agencies, and state agencies.

Although Florida's Comprehensive Planning Act of 1972 required formulation of a state comprehensive plan, it was ineffective; new legislation in 1984 was required to mandate preparation of a draft plan by December 1, 1984.[18] The plan that the legislature rewrote and adopted in 1985 is an extensive statement of goals and policies covering 25 topic areas.[19] Maryland's statute incorporates seven "visions" as the prime policies to be implemented by local plans.

Several states have attempted to go beyond policy statements to geographic determinations of urban growth policies, closer in concept to local comprehensive plans. Hawaii's 1961 plan designated urban, agricultural, and conservation areas—a rural area was later added—that placed the state in the role of directly controlling the location of urban development. Vermont's Act 250 adopted in 1970 required adoption of a state plan in three phases over one year. The first plan contained quite general policies and a map of land capabilities for certain uses such as agriculture. The second depicted land capabilities in more detail; but the third plan, which began in some people's eyes to look like state zoning, was emphatically rejected and the Act 250 provision pertaining to plan preparation was repealed.[20] New York attempted to craft a geographically defined state plan in the mid-1970s but encountered a highly-resistant legislature that killed the plan and dismantled the state planning office.

Of the nine comprehensive acts, those in New Jersey and Rhode Island incorporated maps depicting geographic locations for applications of policies. Rhode Island's Comprehensive Planning and Land Use Regulation Act of 1988 established 11 rather general goals "to provide overall direction and consistency for state and municipal agencies in the comprehensive planning process. . . ." The "Land Use 2010, State Land Use Policies and Plan," published in 1989, however, expands on those goals with explanatory discussions and adds a statement of policies in seven categories (e.g., "Housing"). The plan includes a computer-generated land capability map identifying four categories of land use intensity, from high-intensity development potential to positive conservation potential. The map is to be used by cities and towns in determining allocations of land for development and conservation.[21]

New Jersey's State Development and Redevelopment Plan adopted in 1992 is unique among state growth management programs. The State Planning Act adopted by the legislature in 1985 and signed by the governor in 1986 provided a short list of general goals but also required preparation of a state plan that would "identify areas for growth, agriculture, open space conservation, and other appropriate designations."[22] The plan, adopted after lengthy and controversial negotiations, expands the general goals into dozens of more definitive policies and blends state and local plans into a statewide map depicting growth centers and preservation areas. Applications of policies to geographic areas will be further detailed through continuing discussions and formal delineations of growth centers between local governments and state agencies.[23]

The extent of urbanization and existing planning in New Jersey possibly explains the appropriateness of this approach; whether other states will gradually move toward more definitive locational controls is problematic. Oregon, for example, although it requires local governments to define urban, agricultural, and forest areas around urban centers, has not moved in 20 years of administering the statute to consolidate those mapped areas into anything resembling a statewide plan.

State Agency Planning and Coordination. Many local government officials would like to see state agencies spend more time planning and coordinating their own programs than prodding local governments to plan. State agencies are notoriously independent and reluctant to act cooperatively with each other or with local governments. John DeGrove, the dean of state growth managers, comments: "The notion that state agencies will actually move in the direction of coordinated behavior to further a clear and well-understood set of state goals and policies is no less than revolutionary."[24]

Yet most state growth management statutes promise just that. Vermont's Act 200 is typical: "State agencies that have programs or take actions affecting land use . . . shall engage in a continuing planning process to assure those programs are consistent with [state] goals . . . and compatible with regional and approved municipal plans. . . ."[25] Vermont is one of the few states that has actually responded to this mandate. After two years of discussions, Vermont's agencies pulled together a draft agreement for interagency cooperation and coordination. Now plans have been adopted for 17 agencies and departments.

Oregon's law empowers the Land Conservation and Development Commission to coordinate state agency planning with local plans and state goals. DeGrove reported in 1984 that the Commission was making some progress but observed that it had to move cautiously to avoid the appearance of becoming a super agency.[26] In the mid-1980s, the Commission stepped up efforts to secure interagency coordinating agreements, revising rules to incorporate periodic reviews and conflict resolution procedures. By 1990, according to a recent evaluation, plans of 20 agencies were certified as consistent with local plans and state goals. The report notes, however, "there has not been a concurrent emphasis on coordinating among state agencies or addressing interagency conflicts."[27]

One bright spot in the state agency scene is the evolution in planning approaches of state transportation agencies stimulated by the Intermodal Surface Transportation Act of 1991. The act requires greater consideration of a range of transportation choices, local and regional development issues, and citizen involvement in transportation planning. Secretary David Winstead's description of the Maryland Department of Transportation's response to multi-modal and intergovernmental planning issues demonstrates the route that many state agencies need to follow in building state–local growth management relationships.

In general, state agencies have been slow to respond to directives to prepare functional plans and coordinate them with other agencies and with state goals. Florida has established a process for accomplishing that, but the effort falls well short of being comprehensive. In New Jersey, because the state plan relies on state agencies to implement many of its provisions, the Office of State Planning has worked hard to establish in-

Making Tough Choices: Multimodal Transportation Planning

David Winstead

Transportation infrastructure decisions embody some of the most profound choices governments make. Transportation policy making is inherently political, for it determines who gets what, when, and how—classic definition of politics. Yet transportation decisions affect systems in which arbitrary political boundaries are meaningless, like markets and ecosystems. Transportation infrastructure can determine where economic development occurs, the value of land, where families live, and the condition of the air we breathe. Transportation decisions have a quality of permanence that require a long-range view.

Since the passage of the Intermodal Surface Transportation Efficiency Act (ISTEA), there is a growing awareness that transportation decisions have far-reaching external effects that traditional methods of transportation planning do not take into account. The key features of this evolving planning process are the elimination of barriers between sources of federal funds, making funding more flexible, and the examination of a range of alternative solutions to transportation problems through the Major Investment Study (MIS). ISTEA requires that an MIS be conducted in all metropolitan planning areas for high-cost transportation proposals. The MIS triggers a comprehensive and collaborative planning effort that considers all transportation modes and all levels of government. The process brings together interdisciplinary teams and stakeholders with diverse viewpoints to arrive at solutions. By evaluating many alternatives simultaneously and by eliminating modal bias (e.g., moving cars on highways), the MIS approach promotes a more accurate assessment of fiscal, social, and economic costs and impacts. The result is planning focused on mobility, rather than single modes, and a more rational decision-making process.

Inherently this comprehensive approach also encourages more frequent and earlier consideration of land use impacts, so that decisions can support broader goals such as economic development or historic preservation.

Maryland has engaged in several of these comprehensive studies with much success. Since 1971, the state's unique departmental structure has included all transportation modes within one cabinet-level agency. Inherently this encourages a multimodal perspective, although overcoming modal bias is still a struggle. The Maryland Department of Transportation (MDOT) continues to tackle transportation problems for a multimodal perspective. An ongoing study of the I-270 corridor from suburban Washington, D.C. to the City of Frederick County illustrates MDOT's approach. The corridor, dubbed Maryland's "High-Technology Corridor," is a key component of Maryland's economic-development program. But sprawling development along the corridor is producing congestion and other problems associated with rapid growth that will only get worse over time. Several multimodal alternatives for improving corridor transportation are being evaluated in terms of feasibility, cost, and impacts, including consistency with local land use plans. Public input has been sought through "alternatives workshops" and focus groups. What in past years might have been a simple road-widening project is now subject to much more complex study.

As the twenty-first century approaches, budgetary constraints, environmental degradation, and increased citizen participation require a new method of transportation planning. A multimodal approach will allow us to establish and implement regional visions for an integrated transportation network, one representing the best decisions about the tough choices.

teragency ties, with some initial success. How its program, and those of other states, will fare over future administrative cycles remains to be seen. Generally, then, local governments have yet to notice much benefit from this aspect of state growth management. As the programs mature and the first flurry of securing local compliance with state requirements dies down, more focus on state agency coordination may emerge.

Requirements for Local Planning. The most visible and significant accomplishment of state growth management acts is their prodding of local governments to plan and implement plans in a responsible manner. Moving from simply enabling local governments to plan and regulate future development, the state growth management statutes have mandated or provided incentives for local governments to plan according to defined standards of purpose and content and to implement plans through consistent regulatory programs.

The Oregon model—also employed by Florida, Rhode Island, Maine, Washington, and Maryland—requires local governments to prepare or revise comprehensive plans to conform to state goals and to state requirements for plan elements. (Washington requires counties over a certain population threshold, and cities within them, to plan; others may volunteer to plan.) In Vermont, Georgia, and New Jersey, planning by local governments is voluntary, although in each case the act provides incentives to encourage planning. Vermont's and Georgia's statutes also provide that local governments deciding to plan must meet the act's planning requirements.

Typically, the statutes spell out the required or recommended elements of local comprehensive plans. Rhode Island's statute provides that the local comprehensive plans "shall be a statement (in text, maps, illustrations or other media of communication) that is designed to provide a basis for rational decision making regarding the long-term physical development of the municipality."[28] It should include a statement of goals and policies consistent with the state guide plan and elements for land use, housing, economic development, natural and cultural resources, services and facilities, open space and recreation, and circulation. Rhode Island also mandates preparation of an implementation program, including a capital improvement program and other public actions necessary to carry out the plan.

Securing the cooperation of local governments in meeting these requirements has been difficult and time-consuming. Oregon's program was administered for 12 years before all cities and counties completed state-approved plans. Florida's approval process is still dragging on, some eight years after the statute was enacted. In Maine, enforcement of the requirement is essentially on hold due to lack of state funds to assist in planning. In the meantime, local governments have refused to plan at all, have refused to plan according to state guidelines, have refused to plan according to state officials' interpretation of state goals and objectives, and have gone to court and to the electorate to assert their rights.

The comprehensive plans produced through this process also have come under criticism. Charles Siemon comments that the shortage of funding and the brief time frames allotted to local planning in Florida "led to the use of 'cookbook' approaches and other short cuts that are antithetical to rational, comprehensive planning."[29] He adds that, in the rush to comply with statutory deadlines, many policy decisions were simply postponed to the regulatory phase. Undoubtedly this problem also has appeared in other states.

Have the state requirements resulted in more planning by local governments? Certainly. More public officials have been introduced to planning concepts and more have been pressed to use them in their regulatory programs and other decision making on urban development issues. The state requirements can be and have been used as leverage by citizens and interest groups to curb planning abuses, either through appeals procedures or in the courts. Have the requirements produced better plans? Possibly, although the jury is still out in most states. State requirements clearly have set new standards for planning content and procedures. Whether the requirements stimulated a better quality of development—the bottom line—is discussed in the final section.

The Regional Role in Planning. States also defined a regional role in growth management systems. Regional agencies were required to plan and to coordinate local plans in Florida, Vermont, and Georgia. In those states, also, regional agencies review developments of regional impact, linking them more directly with the development process.[30] In addition, Maine's regional councils are required to comment on plans of local governments within their areas. New Jersey's statute requires counties to coordinate local plans and participate in negotiating compatibility of local with state plans. Although Washington's statute does not specify county coordination of local plans, it does require counties to delineate urban growth areas in consultation with cities, natural resource lands and critical areas, and open space corridors.

Oregon legislation requires regional planning by the Metropolitan Service District in Portland. The Land Conservation and Development Department has worked with the District to establish special standards and procedures for coordinating metropolitan development in accordance with state goals. Nevertheless, a recent evaluation found that "Oregon lacks a framework for systematically introducing the regional perspective in multijurisdictional regions outside of the Portland area." Even in Portland, the report continues, there is no provision for routine regional review of plan amendments.[31]

The effectiveness of regional agencies in reviewing plans is mixed. In

Vermont, at the insistence of local governments, regional councils' authority to review local plans for conformance to state goals was postponed to a future date. According to a recent evaluation of regional councils' activities in Florida, many councils were ineffective and others were too aggressive in pursuing their mandates, resulting in a recommendation that their authority to review developments of regional impact be sharply curtailed. Although legislation to that effect was enacted in 1994, it proved unpopular and will probably be withdrawn in the near future.

The New Jersey growth management program has been given credit for energizing county planning and establishing counties as legitimate players in the growth management process.[32] Georgia's and Washington's experience is too recent to evaluate.

Enforcing Consistency—the Intergovernmental Challenge. One measure of the success of state growth management programs is their effectiveness at achieving consistency of local, regional, and state agency plans with state goals. All nine states have set up some type of review process to encourage consistency between levels of government, compatibility among plans of adjoining jurisdictions, and consistency among plans and implementing programs and regulations within jurisdictions. These procedures provide the ultimate test of intergovernmental relationships in growth management.

State agencies in all states except Vermont review local plans for consistency with state goals. (Vermont reviews only the housing element for consistency with affordable housing policies.) Oregon, Florida, Georgia, Rhode Island, and Maine retain ultimate authority to approve local plans. Washington and Maryland review and comment on plans.[33] New Jersey negotiates agreements with local governments on plan consistency but does not mandate consistency. In Florida and Georgia, regional agencies also review and approve local plans for consistency with regional plans and state goals. In Vermont and Rhode Island, state agency plans must be made compatible with local plans after local plans are approved.

State differences in review approaches led to characterizing some states as "bottom up" and others as "top down." In "bottom up" states (including by most accounts Vermont, Georgia, Rhode Island, Maine, and Washington), state or regional reviewing agencies have relatively little leverage to determine the substance of local plans. In "top down" states, including Florida, New Jersey, and Oregon, state planning agencies exert a considerable amount of leadership in determining the appropriate content of local plans.

Florida's Department of Community Affairs and Oregon's Land Conservation and Development Commission, the administering agencies for the state growth management program, retain ultimate approval authority over local plans. Both agencies were quite aggressive in interpreting applications of state goals to local plans. For example, they turned back plans that permitted densities deemed too low to satisfy the goal of compact development. New Jersey's Office of State Planning, although it negotiated agreements with local governments on compliance with state goals and policies, still retains a considerable amount of influence over the ways future state actions may be used to encourage greater compliance—for example, in future state actions to officially designate growth centers depicted on local plans.

Maryland's status in the review process is ambivalent. The state planning office can only comment on local plan compliance with state goals. But state agencies cannot provide state funding (except under "extraordinary circumstances") for any projects that are not consistent with state goals or local plans. This provides a significant pressure point to ensure that local plans are consistent with state goals.

The sanction written into Maryland's law is echoed in other state statutes, all of which may deny eligibility for various state grants to local governments whose plans are not brought into conformance with state goals. Florida, for example, may suspend recreation and state revenue-sharing grants, as well as federally funded community development grants. Some states allow communities to impose impact fees only if they have achieved compliance. Both Florida and Rhode Island provide for state preparation of comprehensive plans if local governments fail to prepare them. In Maine, recalcitrant municipalities may find their zoning ordinance invalid. Thus far, penalties for failure to comply with state mandates have been used very sparingly. Generally, states have been more interested in negotiating agreements with local governments than issuing politically embarrassing sanctions.

Appeals and Conflict Resolution. State planning review processes frequently have created animosities between state and local officials that can be overcome only through appeals and conflict resolution processes. Most state statutes foresaw this and provided procedures to negotiate agreements or appeal to higher authorities, all of which have proved a boon for the participants as well as attorneys. The earlier acts tended to set up administrative procedures that include litigation; the later statutes emphasize conflict resolution techniques.

The 1973 statute in Oregon provided a Land Use Board of Appeals, with three judges who decide nothing but land use cases. Their decisions may be appealed to state courts. Rhode Island has a similar process. Florida has an elaborate system that allows regional bodies to mediate local conflicts, provides hearing officers at the state agency level, and establishes final authority in the governor and cabinet sitting as an appeals board.

The 1988 act in Georgia, by contrast, emphasizes dispute resolution, directing the state Department of Community Affairs to establish a mediation or other conflict resolution process for resolving state, regional, and local differences over plans. The 1990 Washington statute set up three hearings boards to hear disputes over urban growth boundaries and other matters.

The appeals procedures have been heavily used. Oregon communities were constantly challenging state decisions that rejected local plans for noncompliance with state goals, but the procedures were also used by landowners and developers who felt aggrieved by local decisions; 1000 Friends of Oregon, a watchdog organization that monitored local, state, and private actions, often chose to enter the fray. Florida's appeals process also has heard many objections to state decisions on plan reviews, not least of which are citizen complaints about specific aspects of local plans. The appeals processes are given credit for providing a pressure release valve for complaints, as well as for helping to establish more specific interpretations of state goals.

State Growth Management Policies

All of the state growth management acts are premised on needs to guide development more effectively than local governments can achieve through their individual actions. Legislative findings introducing the statutes refer to needs for greater cooperation and coordination between governments, more efficient land development patterns, less costly infrastructure systems, and more effective protection of natural resources and environmental qualities. Statements of goals commonly include strictures to prevent urban sprawl, protect rural and natural areas from undesirable development, and develop efficient systems of public facilities and services to support anticipated growth and economic development.

In many cases, the statutes promoted these goals by directing local governments and regional agencies to adopt specific growth management mechanisms. The most common are some form of urban/rural demarcation to induce more compact development patterns and protect rural areas, requirements for programming and financing infrastructure to support development, and special provisions for dealing with large-scale development and critical areas.

Urban/Rural Demarcation. Since Oregon in 1973 required all cities to define urban growth boundaries to contain urban development and natural resource areas to promote agriculture and forestry, several other states have required or promoted similar provisions. New Jersey calls for urban development to occur within compact centers designated on local and state plans. Maine requires municipalities to identify and designate growth areas and rural areas. Washington requires counties to designate urban growth areas and counties and cities to designate natural resource lands and critical areas.

Other state statutes include goals that, while less specific, encourage the demarcation of urban from rural lands. Maryland provides that local plans and regulations must implement goals to concentrate development in suitable areas and protect sensitive lands. Florida's state goals contain a number of statements that discourage the proliferation of urban sprawl, on which the Department of Community Affairs has based its policy—enforced through a rule—to insist that local plans promote compact patterns of development. The Department has encouraged local governments to consider adoption of mechanisms such as urban growth boundaries and urban service limits.[34]

Securing local compliance with these requirements is difficult. Market forces and citizen attitudes still favor low-density development: Single-family detached homes and reliance on automobiles remain prime objectives of many Americans. Translated through the political process to local plans and regulations, these attitudes appear rather intractable. Oregon's experience is telling. As described in Chapter 4, although all municipalities adopted urban growth boundaries as required by the state statute, a considerable amount of development still takes place outside them. Widespread development on "exception" lands (deemed unuseful for agriculture or forestry) and waivers by local governments have undermined the state's policy. In addition, in both Oregon and Florida, development within urban growth boundaries has tended toward lower densities than would be appropriate to achieve compact growth. Plans and regulations may permit higher densities but developers often choose to finesse opposition from local residents by proposing lower-density development. Only in Portland, which has adopted special rules to promote higher-density housing, including minimum-density provisions, have densities increased.

The upshot is that state goals and inducements to encourage compact development and preserve rural areas have been only partially successful in the face of countervailing market and political forces.

Infrastructure Planning and Financing. Another purpose of most state growth management acts is to get a grip on infrastructure needs and costs, which in many areas appear to be totally out of control. State statutes refer to the inefficiencies of extending public facilities to serve sprawl development, the advantages of promoting better use of existing facilities, and the need to provide adequate capacities of facilities concomitant with development. The New Jersey state plan expresses the policy in this way:

The essential element of statewide policies for infrastructure investment is to provide infrastructure and related services more efficiently by restoring systems in distressed areas, maintaining existing infrastructure investments, creating more compact settlement patterns . . . , and timing and sequencing the maintenance of capital facilities service levels with development throughout the state.[35]

At least three approaches to achieving these goals have been incorporated in state acts: encouraging more attention to capital facilities programs; requiring "concurrency" of facility capacities with development; and linking infrastructure funding sources to completion of plans that conform to state goals.

Most state statutes have prompted local governments to strengthen the connections between comprehensive plans and implementing regulations and programs, including capital improvement programs. Such provisions not only promote consistency between plans and subsequent actions but also emphasize the necessity of formulating realistic implementation efforts. Rhode Island's statute, for example, incorporates an implementation program in the requirements for local comprehensive plans, including the definition and scheduling of "expansion or replacement of public facilities and the anticipated costs and revenue sources proposed to meet those costs. . . ."[36] Similar requirements are found in all other state acts except Georgia's and Maryland's, although the latter statute requires that funding to achieve state goals must be addressed.

Perhaps the best known state requirement that connects public facilities to development plans is the "concurrency" provision of Florida's statute, later repeated in Washington's act. Although many local governments have enacted provisions requiring that development approvals be contingent on the availability of facilities required by the developments, Florida was the first to raise the requirement to the state level. Florida's act provides that no local government shall issue a development permit unless adequate public facilities are available to serve it. Unfortunately, Florida did so at a time when state highways were demonstrably lacking in capacity and when the state was unprepared to fund improvements to make up deficiencies. The results, as described in Chapter 6, have been a major controversy over the concurrency requirement and highly imaginative calculations of levels of service by local planners to avoid development moratoriums.

Facility funding is another point of leverage by some states to secure compliance with state goals. Maryland's requirement that projects receiving state funds must be consistent with approved plans and state goals has already been referenced. But other states threaten to withhold various types of state funding if local plans remain out of compliance with state goals. New Jersey's plan, for example, suggests that state funding of capital projects will be dependent to some degree on adherence of local governments to state goals.[37] Thus far, however, it does not appear that any states have actually withdrawn funding for this purpose.

On a more positive note, several states permit local governments that secure approval for local plans to levy impact fees. Washington allows local governments to levy an excise tax on real estate transfers to assist in funding capital improvements.

Special Development and Area Concerns. As noted in the earlier section on regional roles in state growth management, several state statutes pay special attention to large-scale developments. Vermont's Act 250 is focused directly on such projects. Florida set up special review procedures for developments of regional impact many years ago. Georgia's statute builds on the Atlanta Regional Commission's past experience with reviewing developments of regional impact by giving all regions that responsibility. Washington's act provides for recognition of large-scale resort developments in delineations of growth areas. These states are concerned with addressing the regional and statewide impacts that major projects may engender.

Similar attention is given to critical natural areas such as wetlands, aquifer recharge areas, wildlife habitats, and flood plains. Washington required an immediate delineation of critical areas to be followed by recognition of such areas within local comprehensive plans. Maryland's act singles out "sensitive" and critical areas for attention in state and local plans.

The Balance Sheet for State Growth Management

Nine states have embarked on programs for managing future development that establish new relationships among state and local governments and, in some cases, regional agencies. Only two states, Oregon and Florida, have gained a substantial amount of experience; others are still working through, or have just completed, initial requirements for achieving consistency between local plans and state goals and policies. They have yet to fully address state agency planning, local regulatory actions, and amendment processes.

The record thus far shows that the tensions and strains that mark most intergovernmental relationships are not allayed by state growth management activities. Indeed, by forcing confrontations between conflicting state and local interests, the state statutes probably have increased at least the perception of divisiveness and disagreement. The state programs also have attracted charges that they engender stultifyingly complex regulations, intractable bureaucracies, and misguided development policies.

To the extent that these program "costs" are real and substantial, they should be matched to the real benefits achieved through the state programs. Whether one agrees that these benefits are without blemish, the programs have accomplished some important objectives.

1. The states succeeded in promoting increased attention to state and regional interests in development issues while retaining significant decision-making roles for local governments in the development process. In all nine states with growth management statutes, local governments still maintain a considerable amount of autonomy in determining the character of future community development.

2. The state programs stimulated a greater understanding of the planning process among local officials, prodding municipalities, regional agencies, and state agencies to define development trends, identify future needs, and plan and program public actions to meet those needs.

3. The state programs structured a framework for coordinating the growth management efforts of all jurisdictions and levels of government and encouraged negotiated agreements among them regarding development issues.

4. State agencies recognize the programs and plans of other agencies and local governments in their own planning for future projects.

5. The private sector gained certainty and predictability from the state requirements that set standards for local governmental planning and implementing programs and regulations, and that provide procedures for ensuring consistency among jurisdictions.

6. The state programs stimulated a growing recognition that plans must be linked to workable implementation programs, and that public guidance of urban development is a long-term process that should be incorporated in every jurisdiction's administrative structure.

7. Experience in Oregon, Vermont, and Florida indicates that state programs take time to mature and require continuous fine-tuning and reevaluation to maintain effective, creative intergovernmental relationships for managing growth and development.

Existing state growth management programs have raised some questions and issues that should be considered in formulating future state programs:

1. In general, state programs have not recognized differences in local governments' planning needs or abilities to respond to state mandates. Although some states such as Washington and Vermont provide for optional participation by local governments, planning requirements in all programs do not distinguish between community size, growth rate, or other characteristics that might affect the nature of planning. This issue was recognized in the recent evaluation of Florida's program, in which

the evaluation committee concluded that Florida should move away from the "one size fits all" type of requirements.

2. State agencies administering growth management statutes have found that statements of state goals and policies require further definition to provide sufficient guidance for determining consistency of state and local plans. The exercise of interpreting broad goals often entails formulation of detailed guidelines and administrative rules to guide preparation of plans and plan reviews. These requirements generally were not foreseen in the original statutes and are just beginning to emerge as significant components of state growth management programs.

3. The long-term nature of state growth management programs demands continuity of administration in a political arena—state government—that traditionally has been highly unsettled. To date, Oregon's and Florida's programs have benefitted from strong constituent support that has maintained staff and budget priorities for growth management programs through several state administrations. Maine's program, severely cut back for budget reasons soon after enactment, illustrates a problem that may be faced by other states in the future.

4. Several states, after issuing mandates for more planning or specific mechanisms for managing growth, failed to provide adequate financial assistance to local governments for meeting requirements. In general, state funding of additional needs for local planning has been unsatisfactory. Florida's example, requiring concurrency but not providing adequate funding to correct state highway deficiencies, remains a sore point in intergovernmental relations.

5. Evaluations of Oregon and Florida programs suggest that their focus on establishing procedures for planning according to state goals has been largely successful but that results "on the ground" have fallen short of desired objectives for urban development and protection of open spaces, natural resources, and environmentally sensitive lands. In the future, state programs may consider the possibility of greater involvement in setting minimum development standards (such as the minimum density provisions adopted in Portland, Oregon) to be incorporated in local plans.

Conclusion

In summary, regional and state growth management is in a revolutionary but also evolutionary stage—revolutionary in establishing new playing fields for managing development; evolutionary in adapting to circumstances and issues that arise during program administration. The programs are suspended not in equilibrium but in a political sea that will push and tug at the forces that both bind and divide public interests in urban development.[38]

9

Balancing the Upsides and Downsides of Growth Management: Conclusions and Guidelines

Public officials manage development to achieve benefits important to their communities. Growth management approaches also may aid the private development process by instilling greater rationality and certainty in public/private decisions on development. Even the best-intentioned regulations, however, generally restrict development choices and increase development costs in some ways. Growth management decisions may limit market choices of locations and types of development, create shortages of developable sites, and lengthen and complicate the development process, all of which may drive up development costs and may act to exclude some types of residents and uses from the community. In the end, however, the effectiveness or success of growth management in specific communities must be measured by the extent to which its benefits outweigh its costs.

Potential Downsides of Growth Management

Since the earliest initiation of growth management programs, critics railed against the effects of these programs on the cost of development and regional patterns of growth. The largest outcry, no doubt due to the number of people potentially affected, is directed at the ways growth management can increase housing costs. Lesser but significant concerns include perceived constraints by growth management techniques on economic growth and choices of living styles, the use of growth manage-

261

ment for exclusionary purposes, increased costs for supporting bureaucracies that administer growth management programs, and, perhaps most serious, the failure of growth management programs to achieve their objectives. Each of these criticisms, taken individually and without consideration of potential benefits, has some basis in fact. Growth management programs do affect the development process in a variety of ways that can raise costs of development and do fall short of perfection in conception and administration.

Effects on the Development Process

Growth management techniques restrict when, where, and how development takes place and expand both public and private costs in some aspects of the development process. They restrict the supply of land available for development, may suppress rates of development, increase infrastructure costs, and raise project approval costs.

Restricting Land Supply. Growth management techniques that restrict the location of development may create artificial shortages of developable land. For example, although growth boundaries are supposed to encompass a 20-year supply of land available for development, politics, policy changes, and bureaucratic inertia may postpone boundary revisions necessary to maintain that supply. Even if enough land in the aggregate is available, suitable sites for specific land uses may be scarce. In Clackamas County, Oregon, for example, developers wanted more sites for campus-style office and industrial parks to promote economic development, while Portland's Metro planners set the boundary to promote more compact development. Developers in Lincoln, Nebraska pressed to extend urban services to make more developable land available in the most desirable sections of the city, while planners tried to steer development to other sections where utilities were available. In other communities, preservation of environmentally sensitive land may prohibit development in key areas. Such shortages of sites in areas deemed desirable by the market tend to inflate land prices.

Suppressing Development. Growth limits and moratoriums that reduce the amount of development below market demands create artificial shortages and quasi-monopoly conditions that can boost development prices. Adequate facility ordinances that impose limits on development can have similar effects. The seven-year sewer moratorium in Montgomery County, Maryland, for example, required developers to install redundant package treatment plants and raised land prices in areas already sewered.

Increasing Infrastructure Costs. The nationwide tendency of local governments to shift responsibilities for funding development-related infrastructure to the private sector, through impact fees and other means, raises direct costs of development while relieving general public costs. In addition, many communities have raised design and construction standards for infrastructure, adding to direct costs of development. Although these costs may be beneficial to both new and existing residents, they add to the cost of development and may price some potential residents and business tenants out of the market.

Raising Approval Costs. By its very nature, growth management tends to enlarge the number of regulatory requirements and approval procedures faced by developers and builders. Frequently, growth management introduces more variety and flexibility into regulations, an advantage for developers and builders who wish to achieve high-quality design. Such techniques, however, usually require more elaborate analyses and detailed documents prepared by professional consultants. They also multiply the number of steps and variety of groups involved in the development process. With more discretion allowed for decisions, opportunities for delays and interventions by new participants increase. The "rule of law" in land use actions is replaced by the "rule of politics."

Consequences of Requirements

The effects of growth management on land supply, production, and costs have important ramifications for community concerns such as housing prices and economic development. During the 1970s and 1980s, housing prices rose rapidly at the same time that growth management programs were expanding in many communities. It appeared to many observers that growth management was a major cause of higher housing prices—and not just of new housing. A market that can pay higher prices for new housing will also pay higher prices for existing housing—the rising tide lifts all boats.

Over several decades, numerous studies have concluded that such growth constraints (1) significantly raise housing costs; or (2) have some effect on housing costs under certain circumstances; or (3) have no long-term effect on housing costs. Seymour Schwartz, David Hansen, and Richard Green, for example, found in a 1984 study that the amount of affordable housing in Petaluma dropped after growth controls were introduced.[1] Lawrence Katz and Kenneth Rosen, in 1987, determined that growth controls significantly raised housing prices in 64 San Francisco area communities.[2] A more recent study by John Landis, however, found that housing price increases varied insignificantly among growth-controlled and noncontrolled communities within regions.[3] Other studies have shown a range of impacts of growth controls on housing prices.[4]

The reason for the variation in study conclusions lies in the economist's favorite dictum: "It all depends." It appears that the imposition of new growth management controls can stimulate increases in housing prices in three types of circumstances: (1) in communities deemed highly desirable in the regional market; (2) when controls are imposed for a brief time during periods of rapid growth, after which the housing market adjusts to the new regulations; and (3) in relatively isolated communities in which homeowners have few options.

The essential factor in understanding effects of regulations on housing prices is that communities usually exist within a multijurisdictional market area offering a variety of market circumstances and a range of regulatory restrictions. Over time, developers and builders can respond to regulatory restrictions in some places by selecting sites in less-regulated communities or by downsizing housing products. The process was demonstrated in Boulder, Colorado after enactment of its growth limits. Studies showed that housing prices briefly rose, then retreated to former levels as builders focused on smaller houses and apartments at prices roughly comparable to former levels of single-family homes. Consequently, Boulder's residents now tend to be small families and individuals. In effect, Boulder's action exported its market for larger houses to surrounding communities with fewer restrictions. A similar trend was found in Petaluma, California, one of the first growth-limiting jurisdictions.

In most communities subject to competition within the region, economists believe that market limits on development cost increases ultimately will drive land prices down. In the short term, however, market inertia, especially in a fast-moving market, will allow developers to pass increases in development costs along to homebuyers. The city manager in Tracy, California, for example, observed that the city's growth limits during the 1980s probably helped drive housing prices to new highs on the outskirts of town; abrupt drops in values caused by the financing debacle of the early 1990s left many homeowners with mortgages higher than their home values, a situation experienced in many western communities.

Thus highly desirable, uniquely situated, or remotely located communities constitute seller's markets in which housing choices are limited and growth management restrictions can raise housing prices. On the plus side, high housing prices may simply reflect homeowners' perceptions of the desirability of the community—its school system, for example, or level of amenities. Fischel points out that growth controls may actually improve residential amenities or prevent impending disamenities, thereby increasing housing values.[5]

Finally, it is important to realize that effects of regulatory pressures on housing prices in specific communities may be relatively insignificant. Some studies demonstrated a regulatory "premium" of 2 to 5 percent; others concluded that regulations caused price increases of as much as 40 percent, taking all factors into account, including sizeable impact fees. However, Deakin concludes that the effects of growth management controls on housing prices "are probably smaller than many have thought and in some circumstances may be negligible or mitigable."[6] Since the late 1980s, housing prices have risen far less rapidly and even dropped from the levels established during the "hot market" days prior to 1990. In addition, a large share of the increased costs found by some studies included higher infrastructure costs and impact fees—costs resulting from policies that shifted basic facility costs once paid by the general public to the specific development benefitting from new facilities.

Growth management constraints also are blamed for inhibiting economic development by limiting site selection or demanding high development standards for new industries and shopping centers. Complaints by developers about the dearth of land available for large-scale industrial and business development in the Portland metropolitan area were noted above. Generally, however, proponents of economic development are unhappy with any regulations that might raise development costs or restrict the locational choices available to new businesses, reasoning that gains in jobs and tax revenues far outweigh any disadvantages that might accrue from new business development. Certainly that is the tack taken by supporters of "big box" retailers, although opponents of such development claim their net benefits are meager, arguable, and undependable in the long term.

Yet it is reasonable to expect that harsh restrictions or substantial add-on costs can make a difference in the competitive position of an area or region. When San Francisco imposed stiff new requirements for contributions to transit, child care, and other public amenities on developers of downtown office buildings, then added an annual limit on the amount of office space constructed, experts forecast a surge in the displacement of low-cost office users to suburban locations. This trend already was evident in many downtowns where rent levels were substantially higher than suburban office rents. Experts have not demonstrated that such restrictions dampen an entire regional market; most simply shift development within a region.

Another perspective on this issue is suggested by an evaluation of growth management techniques that might be used to suppress projected growth in the Portland metropolitan area. The study, commissioned by the Metro regional organization as part of its evaluation of alternative growth strategies, concluded that increasing development costs and restrictions sufficient to slow or stop growth would negatively affect the quality and cost of living for current residents.[7] Another way of interpreting that finding is that the consequences of highly restrictive growth management may be as damaging to current residents and businesses as they would be to new development.

The potential exclusionary effects of growth management programs have received a great amount of attention from both proponents and opponents of growth management. Communities can use growth limits, unreasonably restrictive development standards, and other techniques to screen out unwanted forms of development. The most often cited example is the suburban community that raises minimum lot sizes to levels that assure that new residential development will be affordable only to wealthy families. To achieve the same end, other communities may exclude mobile homes, establish minimum housing space standards, adopt onerous zoning procedures for certain types of development, and take other actions that individually or collectively have exclusionary effects.

In his book *The Environmental Protection Hustle,* Bernard Frieden described numerous circumstances where special interest and community groups successfully opposed projects that promised to provide housing, including affordable housing, to meet growing needs in expanding urban regions. He cited cases in which major projects were whittled down to minor ones, where developers were forced to drop multifamily housing in favor of single-family homes, and where community groups demanded set-asides of huge chunks of land for open space, leaving little room for houses.[8]

As another example, Paul Niebanck documented the exclusionary effects of official actions by the city and county of Santa Cruz that over time substantially raised the price of admission for potential residents. In 1975, the city formulated a housing program that identified areas that could support about 7600 new dwellings. Three years later, a citizen's initiative placed substantial amounts of land in an undevelopable greenbelt and downzoned other areas, effectively cutting in half the capacity for housing and undermining the new housing program. The county, meanwhile, increasingly restricted the pace of housing construction in unincorporated areas, reducing the number of building permits by 10 percent a year since 1978. In addition, the county, according to Niebanck, "actively resisted extending utilities or addressing the capital improvement needs that would facilitate housing expansion." The result, Niebanck concluded, is that homeowners in 1986 paid at least 10 percent more for single-family homes. More important, some 5000 families that might have located in Santa Cruz had to look elsewhere.[9]

The motivations behind these actions of local governments may be difficult to detect, since they are often masked by official statements about "retaining the character of the community" or "preventing incompatible development." The exclusionary results may be evident only over time.

Mismanagement

Growth management programs also fall short of achieving their objectives due to evasions and glitches in program design and administration. In the initial instance, many communities mismanage growth by reacting slowly and inadequately to growth pressures or by refusing to tackle the difficult choices they must make to exercise reasonable control over growth. Then, when decisions to manage growth are finally made, public officials adopt techniques without adequate consideration of administrative requirements, needs for coordination, and potential impacts on the development process.

First, many communities are reluctant to formulate a realistic vision of their future urban status. As rural settlements and small suburbs grow and change, community leaders have difficulty envisioning a future community character unlike their present one. Both new and old residents covet the current qualities of their communities and become committed to the status quo. Often this attitude prompts inadequate attention to evolving conditions. Elected officials neglect to invest in strategic planning and examination of alternative scenarios for growth. In failing to come to terms with their evolution toward future urban centers, such communities miss opportunities to guide and support development in positive ways.

The history of Sarasota County's growth management efforts related in Chapter 3 told how county commissioners delayed responding to urbanization spreading into unincorporated areas, hoping that a lack of infrastructure would turn development away. When that strategy failed to suppress development, the county was forced into intensive administrative and financial reorganization to deal with near crises in infrastructure capacity. A decade or so ago, as another example, city officials in Blacksburg, Virginia refused to pursue annexation of urbanizing areas outside the city. Helter-skelter, poorly designed development beyond the city limits was deemed unsuitable for inclusion in the city. The result was that the city lost an opportunity to control the substantial amount of development occurring in those areas, and perhaps to improve the quality of existing development.

Second, growth management too often means crisis management. In the normal course of events, public officials enact growth management techniques in response to immediate or looming needs. Schools are becoming overcrowded, or a water shortage commences, or a major highway becomes a bottleneck. These kinds of occurrences move community leaders to create and adopt new regulations, ordinances, or programs.

Unfortunately, public officials in many communities remain wedded to the illusory mode of quick-fix, Band-Aid solutions created as problems arise. Instead of structuring a comprehensive growth management program, they seize on one or two techniques, employ them without thought of potential consequences, and fail to relate them to other development policies and regulations. Frequently the solutions exacerbate problems rather than relieve them and introduce needless confusion and complexity into the development process.

The city of Walnut Creek, California, for example, adopted a constructive plan for downtown development, oriented to its access to major highways and its station on the Bay Area Rapid Transit line from San Francisco. The plan was crafted over several years of effort by public and private community leaders. Several years after the plan was adopted in 1975, new buildings began to rise in locations designated by the plan. At the same time, however, traffic on the main highways through town became increasingly congested. The electorate linked one event to the other, although most traffic was passing through the town from other areas, and voted to deny permits to all commercial buildings over 10,000 square feet of floor space until traffic congestion improved.

The action froze further development and scuttled the downtown plan. However, highway congestion continued to increase as growth continued in outlying jurisdictions. With no capacity to welcome growth, Walnut Creek missed opportunities for valuable development in its city center. In 1990, the California Supreme Court struck down the voter initiative on a technicality, but Walnut Creek's quick fix had proved an unworkable solution.[10]

A downzoning enacted by Fairfax County, Virginia offers another example of reactive management. During the 1970s and 1980s, the county's campaign to attract new businesses was remarkably successful, especially in the highway corridor leading to Dulles International Airport. The county's planning and programming of public systems to support development, however, fell well short of rising demands. Resultant traffic congestion, as well as resident concerns over the rapid transformation of the corridor, led to a proposal in 1989 for zoning revisions to significantly reduce development of office space along the corridor.

This action might have been appropriate within the context of a long-range strategy for economic development coupled with a plan for coordinating growth with infrastructure capacity. Among other benefits, such planning might have pointed out the false premise that reducing densities would improve traffic congestion. Lacking long-range strategies, however, the county supervisors quickly moved to lower permitted densities. Most alarming, the downzoning extended to properties for which development agreements had been executed. After a flurry of lawsuits and loud reactions from the state legislature, the country established waivers for many projects.

The excuses given by public officials for such actions really amount to an unadmitted failure to "plan ahead." Local officials have postponed decisions until too late—the Neville Chamberlain approach to growth management.

Third, as practiced in some communities, growth management resembles a grab-bag of assorted programs and regulations rather than a comprehensive, coordinated, and systematic approach to community development. Local governments add new requirements, bit by bit, to basic plans and zoning regulations, without adequate consideration of their consequences or even how they relate to each other. New techniques are hastily concocted and employ simple methodologies to address complex problems. Often they are administered by insufficient staff. No attempts are made to evaluate how the regulations are working.

Revisions to reflect changing needs come slowly or not at all, so that regulations become obsolete and inoperative. Some components work at cross purposes with others. Departments planning for growth management may not communicate well with departments responsible for implementing programs. The management structure simply fails to work properly.

Fourth, growth management programs that expand public control over the development process demand substantial support by elected officials and administrative staff. Elected officials are required to make long-term policy decisions and adhere to them, which cramps the style of many a politician. Almost always, growth management programs require a sizeable and knowledgeable staff for program administration. To do their job well, staff must be educated and experienced in a wide range of development and regulatory methods. Expert staff are not always easy to find and, just as important, easy to fund. Growth management programs require budgetary support that may not always be available or given priority, thus leading to faulty management.

The growth management efforts of the city of San Diego, for example, have suffered over the years from wild swings in the region's economic fortunes. During upward swings of the growth cycle, the planning staff was expanded and ambitious planning programs initiated. The downward part of cycles and their consequences for city revenues generated staff cutbacks and declining attention to managing growth. The lack of continuity and breaks in momentum of the planning program wrought havoc in establishing predictable growth management.

Finally, most local governments manage growth to meet their own objectives, with relatively little consideration of potential impacts of their actions on their neighbors or on regionwide conditions. Growth management in one community may well work to counteract the development intentions of nearby jurisdictions. One fairly common circumstance, for example, is the approval by a community of a revenue-generating shopping center or industry that creates traffic congestion in adjacent communities who receive no revenue gain from the new development.

In addition, regionwide concerns and goals are given short shrift by local governments in all but a few metropolitan areas. Local growth management programs may pay token attention to needs for affordable housing, responsible economic development, fiscal parity among jurisdictions, and efficient delivery of public services. But their actions in approving building, zoning, and subdivision permits usually bespeak other priorities. Commonly, local public officials give the highest priority to acquiring tax ratables and protecting single-family residential neighborhoods despite the needs of other communities and other sectors of the population. In the past decade, as another example, many miles of planned arterial road improvements have been cut from community plans to please neighborhoods that might be affected by the improvements. The ensuing traffic congestion is then cited as a reason to limit growth.

As detailed in Chapter 8, regional and state efforts to promote effective growth management are hampered by inadequate funding and authority. Few regional agencies possess powers to insist on regionally responsible planning and implementation of plans by local governments. Most regional agencies, hobbled by local governmental interests, lack sufficient funding to conduct strategic planning or track local planning. As we have seen in this chapter, state growth management programs are long on instructing local governments about planning and short on coordinating planning among their own agencies. Several state programs also suffer from severe funding and staff shortages that have created hollow shells of major policy structures.

The shortcomings of growth management in practice demonstrate that community programs still suffer from the problems found by a 1974 study of local governments' efforts. Its authors concluded that growth management techniques are seldom conceived as part of an organized, integrated system. To the contrary, growth management practices, they found, usually focused on problem solving with inadequate attention to the side effects that might result.[11] As more and more communities have adopted growth management techniques since 1974, this issue has remained a major concern.

Benefits of Growth Management

Despite the difficulties encountered by communities in formulating and administering growth management techniques, growth management programs can provide important benefits for community residents and workers and all participants in the community development process. Managing growth can improve the overall quality of development and achieve important public objectives such as environmental preservation. Well-managed programs can reduce development risks by increasing the predictability of the approval process. Property owners, developers, and builders also gain value from a well-ordered program of public improvements and from enactment of planning and regulations that ensure a high-quality living environment.

Supporting Community Development

Perhaps the most direct benefit of growth management stems from its positive support of the process of community development. Growth management techniques are intended to anticipate and resolve development issues such as needs for expansion of infrastructure systems and for protection of sensitive environmental qualities. By providing ways and means for communities to accommodate development in a positive manner, growth management programs can reduce conflicts and disruption of the development process and ensure that growth and change are compatible with community standards of development and livability.

The description of the Carlsbad's program in Chapter 4 demonstrates the value of using growth management approaches to deal with development problems. Inundated with complaints about traffic and other effects of recent growth, Carlsbad's public officials slapped stiff controls on development while they formulated a workable process for providing needed public facilities to support growth. With a firm plan in place to fund and deliver infrastructure improvements as development proceeded, city administrators worked with federal and state officials to reach agreement with a developer on a plan to conserve extensive wildlife habitats. The plan permitted a significant amount of development and included an important new arterial street connection. These proactive efforts allowed Carlsbad to continue developing in response to market forces while achieving valued public objectives.

Sarasota County's experience, described in Chapter 3, provides another example. After ignoring growth in unincorporated areas for several years, county officials realized that the future development of the county would be hampered by allowing continued uncoordinated and below-standard development. Although its comprehensive plan spelled out ambitious goals, the county had established little control over the development process. Over several years, the county created and expanded infrastructure systems to support development, including sewer and water facilities, major road improvements, and an admirable park development program. Facility improvements were guided through a detailed capital improvements program undergirded by communitywide funding programs. The county's strenuous efforts made up deficiencies and provided the necessary infrastructure to accommodate continuous growth.

These types of approaches to managing growth prevent problems from occurring or worsening, provide solutions to development issues, and reduce time-consuming and costly conflicts over development issues.

Establishing a Predictable Development Process

By providing public support of development in both policy and practice, growth management programs reduce both public and private risks in the development process. Construction of a recognized public policy framework to guide community development puts everyone on notice about community needs and public objectives to be achieved as growth and change occur. Developers can orient their projects to achieving those objectives, thereby limiting the risks—and costs—that otherwise might attend project approval processes. Definitive public policies also provide measures by which proposed projects can be evaluated by officials and residents. And residents gain the security of knowing what to expect in their neighborhoods.

Growth management programs that spell out expectations for development, in terms of quality, quantity, and location, thus benefit all the stakeholders in communities. Although developers and builders in Oregon initially fought the state growth management program as too restrictive and meddlesome in local affairs, for example, eventually they came to support its continuation. To this day, Oregon's program is widely supported by interest groups on all sides because it is viewed as a predictable policy framework that provides assurances that reasonable development, including higher-density forms often opposed by neighborhood groups, will be publicly supported.

An unusual perspective on the significance of growth management in regulating market forces is provided by a study conducted by Arthur Nelson, a planning professor at Georgia Institute of Technology. Noting that the Congressional Budget Office estimated taxpayer costs at $500 billion for bailout of failed savings-and-loan banks, he allocated those costs among states with functioning state growth management programs and states that have no such laws. The 9 nine states he identified as growth-management states accounted for $1642 in bailout costs per new resident but the other 40 states averaged $5582 per new resident. (The two groups each accounted for just over 11 million new residents.) After analyzing performance in specific states, he concludes that overbuilding in unmanaged states vastly inflated ultimate costs for taxpayer bailout. He gives credit to state growth management acts for moderating the amount of overbuilding in those states.[12]

Protecting Quality of Life

One of the important objectives of most public officials in managing growth is preserving and even enhancing community quality of life. They are keenly interested in maintaining highly valued areas, amenities, and conveniences that make their community a desirable place to live and work. Managing growth and change can protect those qualities against potential impacts of development and ensure that the quality of new development meets community standards. Growth management can protect property owners from losses in value, provide desirable amenities that enhance the character of the community, and widen lifestyle choices for all residents.

The proactive efforts of town officials in Lincoln, Massachusetts to maintain the quality of their community were detailed in several chapters. They constructed a multifaceted program to preserve the town's treasured rural landscapes and diversity of residents, identifying significant open spaces, working with conservation groups and property owners, and using cluster design techniques. In the process, they also negotiated agreements with developers to make housing available to moderate-income homeowners and renters. In the West, the cities of Boulder and Scottsdale both levied taxes to acquire mountains important to residents as natural settings for the communities. Raleigh and Plano enacted design guidelines to improve the appearance of commercial corridors and areas through which many people travel every day. Townships and counties in the Grand Traverse Bay region of Michigan adopted guidelines for site design to retain the visual quality of the area. San Francisco, Seattle, and Bethesda, Maryland provided incentives for contributions of public art, open space, and other amenities in association with downtown development. The small town of Bethel, Maine levied fees and required special project reviews to make certain that major new developments did not harm the livability and fiscal stability of the town.

Improving Social and Economic Opportunities

Local governments and state and regional agencies can manage community growth and change to widen housing and employment opportunities, retain the vitality of older neighborhoods and business districts, and ensure fiscal and social equities among communities. In an ever-changing society, these are important goals. Growth management programs in many communities, for example, include a variety of techniques for ensuring the availability of affordable housing for all residents. Portland's Metro regional housing rule is perhaps the most far-reaching program to establish a measure of housing equity among communities throughout a metropolitan area. But the efforts of Lincoln, Massachusetts described above represent similar initiatives in many communities to improve housing conditions.

Use of growth management techniques also allows communities to leverage housing and job opportunities to improve the daily life of residents. San Jose modified its industrial and residential development policies to reduce commuting distances and improve choices of housing types and industrial sites. The city also promoted development of light-rail transit lines to link residential and employment areas, thus improving travel opportunities within the community. Montgomery County, Maryland has pursued similar policies through its growth management program.

Growth management, then, provides a means of coping with community development to achieve substantial benefits and prevent adverse impacts. Growth management not only can ensure desirable qualities of new development but can retain and enhance the qualities of existing development. For most public officials and residents these benefits far outweigh the costs imposed on development by policies and regulations. Nevertheless a periodic reckoning of the balance of benefits and costs should be built into every growth management program.

Balancing Benefits and Costs

It has been observed throughout this book that effective growth management depends on achieving a reasonable and equitable balance between overlapping and competing interests and objectives. Communities—and hopefully, regions—must somehow reach a reckoning that establishes a clear, balanced strategy for guiding development. Such a process is not easy. Our regulatory systems too often run in parallel with few crossovers that can stimulate reconciliation between conflicting ways and means. Urban development, for example, often requires modification of environmental goals in specific areas to make sense in terms of infrastructure service, economic opportunities, and social cohesion. Environmentalists may need to accept second-best solutions, such as mitigation banks, to allow development of satisfactory patterns of city development. On the other hand, decisions on urban infrastructure extensions may need to recognize broader interpretations of "efficiency" to preserve environmental qualities.[13] Other examples include the current tug-of-war between planners' desires for compact development and Americans' preferences for low-density development, and the car-versus-transit issue.

Yet if growth management is to be successful in guiding community development, it must construct a policy framework in which all the components are mutually supportive and supported by a consensus of the affected constituency.

The ways and means we have invented for reaching consensus on such a framework are well known in most communities. They include extensive technical evaluations of potential development scenarios, community "visioning" exercises, a recent innovation usually termed "benchmarking," and various forms of collaborative planning involving stakeholders. None of these approaches is without problems and none can guarantee perpetual consensus, especially on long-standing and politically charged issues. The alternative, however—nonaction amid continuous conflict—is less attractive by far.

Technical Evaluations of Alternative Scenarios

In planning for future community development, planners and public officials commonly postulate alternative plans for community development to allow evaluation of potential advantages and disadvantages of various courses of action and to test political acceptance of possible policies. For example, in a recent planning effort for the U.S. 301 transportation corridor in five Maryland counties east of Washington, D.C., seven types of transportation options (e.g., highway-oriented, transit-oriented) were tested against three land use scenarios. The purpose of the evaluation was to determine the combination that would produce the most effective travel and land use patterns. The effects of the combinations on travel behavior, transit use, consumption of developable land, impacts on wetlands, and other factors were evaluated during the process.

At a larger, more comprehensive scale, the Region 2040 planning process for the Portland, Oregon metropolitan area evaluated four development scenarios involving various degrees of development density, transit service, and other characteristics. Similar evaluations have been carried out by the Puget Sound Council of Governments, the Metropolitan Washington, D.C. Council of Governments, and many other regional agencies, especially those concerned with regional transportation planning. Analyses of alternatives also play a part in reaching agreement on specific plans for smaller areas and even zoning provisions, all quite common in practice and well documented in the literature.

These kinds of evaluations, which help policy makers determine the best "fit" between infrastructure system development and future land use patterns, have been encouraged by the Intermodal Surface Transportation Efficiency Act of 1991. The act promotes consideration of many factors in determining future transportation plans.

Increasingly, computerized models are being used for such evaluations. Although computer-assisted transportation forecasting models have been used for many years, newer computer capabilities allow urban designers to portray three-dimensional visions of future development. Mapping of tabular data through geographic information systems also aids evaluations of alternative futures. Now a new generation of land use models is promising to provide additional ways of projecting results of alternative land use policies.[14]

In recent years, many evaluations of various development patterns include analyses of fiscal impacts on local governmental revenues and expenditures. Perhaps the most extensive such evaluation was carried out in 1992 by the Rutgers University Center for Urban Policy Research for the proposed State Development and Redevelopment Plan for New Jersey.[15] But similar evaluations on smaller scales are becoming quite common.[16] Paul Tischler's brief essay on fiscal issues in growth management describes a typical approach. (See box on p. 60 in Chapter 3.)

Community Visioning

The necessity of achieving broad consensus on a vision of the future community is an article of faith in the planning community today. Entire books have been written to explain the importance of and techniques for envisioning the desirable characteristics of communities as they grow. "Visioning" is difficult, however. It requires participants to stretch their imaginations beyond simple ratifications of current conditions to embrace needs for accommodating change. Unfortunately, many visioning exercises stop short of defining realistic futures or conclude with statements so broad and inclusive as to be virtually meaningless. Nevertheless, efforts to reach concurrence on the desirable form and character of the future community are immensely significant for establishing objectives that shape day-to-day decision making in managing growth.

Portland's regional planning for 2040, which involved extensive consensus-building among community interests, illustrates one approach to staking out long-term goals for regional development. The new plan for the New York region by the Regional Plan Association represents another attempt to identify major goals for metropolitan development that can influence state and local decision making on major issues. Long Beach's intensive community involvement in defining reachable goals and following through with periodic assessments on achievements exemplifies an effective, practical approach to managing development. Many of the other local growth management programs described throughout the book show how goal-setting combined with well-managed policy implementation produces positive management.

Concurrence on a vision is not a one-time event. For growth management to be successful, community leaders should continue to involve all sectors of the community in constantly reviewing and updating their understanding of future community goals. Communities that commit to goal-tending make extensive use of study and advisory groups, task forces, and outreach forums to refresh attitudes toward growth and change and reconfirm or revise growth strategies.

Consensus-Building and Collaborative Planning

The days of entrusting a selected few civic and political leaders to make decisions without communitywide input are past in most communities. Public officials and planners are accustomed to seeking broad community consensus on vital development issues—a process of participatory democracy. Civic activists are quite skilled in using such processes to promote their own objectives in growth management, as discussed by Ingrid Reed in the accompanying feature box. To reach consensus among all of these stakeholders in the growth management process, a number of consensus-building techniques are employed in many communities.

Consensus-building processes have several aims that translate into phases of effort. First, the issues at stake must be understood and defined well enough to identify the stakeholders who should be consulted. Second, the stakeholder parties themselves must be identified, including those with decision-making power and those who can influence decision makers. Third, relationships among the parties should be explored, and their willingness to participate in consensus-building determined. The process, once launched, can use dispute-resolution techniques where battle lines have been clearly drawn, or more open discussion and negotiation procedures where participants are less wedded to a specific cause.

Techniques for structuring and negotiating dispute-resolution and collaborative planning processes have been described at length in many books. They can become quite convoluted, even to the matter of who designs or convenes the process which, according to one text, "may call into question the motivations of the convenor, threatening the implementation of otherwise fair and wise decisions."[17]

Such consensus-building processes are valuable in reaching decisions on major growth management issues without resorting to harsh political conflicts, litigation, or divisive referendums. As Lindell Marsh points out in the accompanying brief essay on page 280, the processes are also valuable in forming a constituency that has invested time, effort, and ideas to the results and remains interested in supporting subsequent efforts and implementing decisions.

Setting Targets and Objectives: Benchmarking

Visioning statements and strategic policies emanating from planning processes frequently leave room for a great deal of interpretation and po-

Optimizing Citizen Support of Growth Management

Ingrid W. Reed

Throughout the nation, citizen activists have been increasing their efforts to participate in and influence the outcomes of growth management programs at all levels—community, regional, and state. Frustrated and angered by local responses to growth and change, citizen groups tend to focus on opposing specific projects and on pressing for more regulatory restrictions on development. Noisy hearings and messy politics often ensue.

But some activists in a number of places around the country are discovering that they are not getting anywhere by engaging in one fight at a time. Rallying citizens to target a single issue or against a specific project does little to shape policies and programs that can avoid or prevent unwanted consequences of growth, or to steer development to appropriate places. They may be winning battles but not wars.

To truly influence a community's development process demands sustained advocacy and a complex, long-term agenda. Ideally this would be founded on a state policy adopted to provide a framework for local development planning and actions and for guiding state agency decisions. Even in states without those policies, however, it makes sense in the long run for citizens to rally for comprehensive local management of the development process, for a better system of community decision making on development goals and actions, and a coordinated regional approach. To do this, citizens need to develop positions over time and across constituencies.

There is now a record of citizen actions that make a difference in this complex arena where community goals are linked to policies and regulations designed to implement those goals.

Citizen groups that achieve enactment of growth management policies now know that their work really begins when legislation is in place and implementation is initiated. Ironically, experience shows that citizen groups advocating growth management capture attention and attract support for the larger effort when they do what got them started—that is, focus on a specific issue or take legal action on a case that illustrates the broader importance of growth management initiatives.

At the same time, they need to master the behind-the-scenes influencing of state and county officials to keep them true to growth management policies while maintaining their connections to elected leaders whose support is required for success.

It can be done. Groups like 1000 Friends of Oregon, New Jersey Future, and others around the country have a track record of keeping public officials and developers at both the state and local levels aware of basic goals and policies for managing community development and assuring their implementation. These groups have demonstrated that it is possible to win the war as well as the battle.

litical maneuvering. Most planning objectives and policies would benefit from specifying in more certain ways just what was meant and how it should be applied in given circumstances. Perhaps this explains the growing interest in the use of "benchmarks" as methods of establishing measurable targets for guiding the development process. Benchmarks establish broad goals and objectives for community development but also establish specific numerical targets that will allow measurement of progress toward achieving those goals.

One of the best-known examples is the benchmark project created by the Oregon Progress Board, a commission created by the Oregon legislature in 1989 to translate the state's strategic plan for economic development into measurable goals. The Progress Board, after extensive citizen input and review, published *Oregon Benchmarks: Standards for Measuring Statewide Progress and Government Performance* in 1992. When the state legislature adopted the benchmarks later that year it directed the Progress Board to update them every two years. Subsequently, a governor's task force recommended the integration of the benchmarks into state agency goals and budgeting processes, which has been initiated.

Among their uses, the benchmarks provide easily understood indicators for citizens of important goals and movement toward those goals. The benchmarks define measures of current conditions and desired targets at multiyear intervals into the future. Several types of measures are incorporated. Some are indices already available, such as the index of serious crimes. Some, such as traffic congestion or water quality, are based on physical measurements. Other measures are based on sample surveys or various state and federal census surveys.

The state benchmarks are comprehensive in scope, involving social and economic goals as well as physical objectives, but frequently they are germane to growth management. One series of benchmarks, for example, deals with affordable housing; it measures the percentage of Oregon households below median income that spend less than 30 percent of their household income on housing. Percentages of homeowners and renters that achieve that status are given for 1990 (from the U.S. Census), and targets for future years evidence an interest in both categories' achieving a sizeable majority by 2010. Another benchmark measures the percentage of development per year occurring within urban growth boundaries. Endnotes to the tables of measures explain the rationale for each measure and identify data sources for the information.[18]

The benchmark concept also is employed by local governments. Several cities and counties in Oregon are following the state's lead. Communities outside Oregon are also initiating benchmark systems, for example Greenville, South Carolina and Pasadena, California. Jacksonville, Florida has employed "Quality Indicators for Progress" for 10 years.

Noblesville, Indiana provides a small-community example. Public officials and citizens in Noblesville, a suburb of Indianapolis, grew increasingly concerned about updating the 1980 master plan for the community. A facilitated public participation process, beginning in May 1993 and culminating a year later, sought to set measurable goals for the community's future. Now efforts are focused on defining the strategies needed to implement the benchmarks.[19]

Noblesville's benchmarks identify 15 community concerns (e.g., historic preservation, industry) in three general categories (land, people, economy). The "overarching goal" expressed for land is to "retain and enhance our distinctive small-town atmosphere." A subgoal is to protect and improve the environment, for which benchmarks included such

---

Collaborative Planning: A New Paradigm for Reconciling Urban Growth and Conservation
Lindell L. Marsh

Flowing from early colonial policies and concepts of individual rights, decisions about land use in this nation have been fragmented among landowners and local, state, and federal governments. Through World War II, this arrangement worked well to serve the growing nation and promote its economic development. It became apparent in the early 1960s, however, that exuberant economic growth was creating environmental costs, or externalities, that should be controlled to protect the quality of the nation's air, water, and natural resources that form our common heritage. The environmental laws we enacted at the time mirrored our traditional approach to regulation: employing command and control techniques to forbid further impacts on the environment.

While environmental protection has continued to be supported by most people, the command and control approach of the regulatory agencies has proved highly inefficient. In addition, by default, preservation costs were imposed primarily on new development, resulting in reactive efforts to roll back regulations in the early 1990s.

For over a decade, a new and different approach has been emerging to resolve conflicts between environmental and development objectives. Focused on overcoming the inefficiencies and economic disruptions caused by the project-by-project permitting process, the new model respects the underlying goals of environmental protection. It is epitomized by the habitat conservation planning (HCP) process authorized by 1982 amendments to the federal Endangered Species Act and by the critical areas planning process allowed by Section 380 of the Florida Comprehensive Land and Water Management Act. These approaches encourage the constituency of interests—landowners, conservationists, government agencies—to collaboratively design a plan that reconciles their individual concerns, conserving wildlife and wetlands while allowing development to proceed.

measures as the number of septic failures and the *E. coli* levels in the White River. Again, existing conditions and future targets are defined.

The experience to date with benchmarks suggests their adaptability for visioning exercises involving intensive citizen participation, as well as their usefulness in establishing perceptible goals and providing connections to a broad range of existing programs and data sources.

Conclusion: Guidelines for Managing Growth and Change

The description and evaluation of growth management policies and practices in this book demonstrate that many communities have built on fun-

After a slow start, the 1980s and 1990s have seen a blooming of hundreds of conservation planning efforts addressing urban, water, timber, and other development issues in all parts of the nation. Among major initiatives is California's Natural Community Conservation Plan program that is being applied in the ecosystems of virtually all of urbanizing southern California.

The promise of such an approach extends in many directions. It overcomes the nation's historic institutional fragmentation. It is based on the collaboration of interests and shared leadership. Together, stakeholders formulate a plan, a kind of social contract, that reconciles the variety of interests. The process has much in common with ideas such as "partnering," public/private partnerships, "horizontal management," and "management by principle" that now pervade our culture.

The breadth and power of this approach can be expected to extend to broad growth management issues such as central city/suburban conflicts and regional economic development strategies.

For me, the metaphor that best characterizes the evolving notion of collaborative planning is traditional American quiltmaking. Typically a group process, quiltmaking promotes individual creativity in individual sections that are stitched together to reflect broader themes determined through a collective, often facilitated process. De Tocqueville observed these paradoxical qualities in our nation's culture in the eighteenth century: fierce individual independence coupled with a willingness to share ideas and responsibilities when necessary. We are now engaged in evolving the collaborative process—the stitching together—that respects individual creativity while creating a shared vision.

damental planning and regulatory techniques to structure workable policy frameworks and action programs for guiding community development. At the same time, it is evident that growth management, like any political process, is far from perfect. In every community and region, managing growth and change is a difficult, time-consuming, and perplexing chore. Yet communities have found imaginative and reasonable ways to deal with the fact of growth, adapting programs and regulatory techniques to recognize changing conditions and objectives. Their experience tells us that certain understandings and approaches are important to success in managing growth. Three principal considerations may be summarized as (1) comprehensiveness and connectivity, (2) complexity and change, and (3) regional interrelationships.

Aim for Comprehensiveness and Connectivity

This analysis of growth management policies and practices has stressed the importance of viewing growth management both comprehensively and as an interactive system of policies and regulations. The four cornerstones of planning—comprehensive plans, zoning, subdivision regulations, and capital improvement programs—form one level of community policies and regulations. On this broad foundation, other growth management techniques can be added, interlinked to build a strong policy and action framework for guiding community development.

Understanding the linkages and interactions between the components of growth management programs is a key to successful management. This evaluation of experience with growth management techniques demonstrates that growth boundaries, for example, are most effective when accompanied by efforts to promote compact development within boundaries, including revitalization and redevelopment of older areas, minimum density requirements, and other programs. Programs to expand infrastructure systems in efficient ways must take account of needs for protecting environmentally sensitive lands and other forms of open space. One community's growth controls should recognize and mitigate potential effects of those controls on other communities.

The cross-section of community growth management programs described in previous chapters identifies a broad and inventive array of approaches and techniques in use today. The review also reveals the problems that occur when techniques are adopted without fully thinking through their potential consequences. San Diego's and Portland's efforts to curb sprawl by encouraging infill development provoked antagonism from residents unhappy with the quality and incompatibility of new development in their neighborhoods. Those reactions might have been muted by revising obsolete zoning provisions and providing design guidelines. Many communities have adopted requirements for adequate facilities as a condition for development approval without putting programs in place to ensure facility funding and construction consistent with the pace of development.

Public management of community development should recognize the complexity of the development process in enacting policies and regulations to guide that process. Stop-gap measures and borrowed provisions will not suffice. To be effective, growth management programs must establish a comprehensive framework of development policies related to community objectives. Within that framework, public officials must link together individual growth management techniques to recognize interactions and potential secondary effects.

Expect Complexity and Change

"Keep it simple, stupid" may be the watchword of politicians, but growth managers should understand that community development is a complicated enterprise. In practice, growth management programs mirror the ever-changing environment of community attitudes and market forces in which they are formulated. All communities experience shifts in citizen and consumer preferences, real estate booms and busts, changing federal and state policy contexts, and constant turnover among community decision makers.

NB!

Many of the community programs described in this book were afflicted with severe disruptions reflecting these types of problems. Public administrators in Tracy, for example, planned for growth with an unusually proactive program that scheduled and funded public improvements according to a prescribed annexation process. Although the program was quite successful in accommodating substantial development, violent swings in real estate activity, along with administrative complications, caused considerable consternation and reevaluation of the city's program.

This analysis has pointed out that many growth management techniques appear simple in concept but prove difficult and time consuming in execution. Making development contingent on "adequate" facilities, for example, requires technical expertise to establish measures of project impacts, levels of adequacy, and facility capacities over time. Imposition of impact fees necessitates adoption of similar measures and establishment of an accounting system to track payments and benefits. Open space preservation may involve a variety of acquisition techniques, funding sources, and associated organizations. All of these efforts take time and staff resources and can be derailed by technical glitches at any moment.

Even in the best-managed communities mistakes are made, unforeseen consequences occur, needs are shortchanged, and solutions fail to perform satisfactorily. These perplexities must be expected and arrangements made to cope with them, starting with construction of a firm policy base. Communities that have pursued successful programs over many years have learned to institute periodic evaluations of program performance and to adapt policies and regulatory techniques to reflect changing circumstances and objectives.

Recognize Regional Interrelationships

Growth in most communities is occurring in regions unguided by public strategies for accommodating development, although clearly many development issues and their solutions transcend local boundaries. Infrastructure systems, conservation of open space and environmentally sensitive lands, widening choices of living, working, and travel, all can benefit from regionwide strategic planning. As discussed in Chapter 8, regional planning agencies generally possess little authority to influence development decisions of local jurisdictions. Individual local governments tend to go their own way, infrequently cooperating to resolve regional issues. The widening gap between "have" and "have-not" communities described in Chapter 7 further erodes the ability of regions to formulate regionwide development strategies to maintain a desirable quality of life for all residents. That loss leaves regions vulnerable to competition in the global marketplace.

Somehow, *metropolitan* communities should find ways to exert leadership and authority in shaping the course of future regional development. To accomplish that, individual jurisdictions should be held accountable for the effects of their growth management policies on other jurisdictions and regionwide interests.

There is no "one size fits all" solution to this dilemma. Regions must look to leadership from sources that best suit their circumstances. As discussed in Chapter 8, some states have enacted planning and development objectives to which local growth management actions must correspond. In Oregon and Florida, especially, these laws insist on local accountability to regional and state interests and prod local governments to plan and regulate wisely. Cities and towns in some other states, however, might not benefit from state intervention in their affairs.

Some states support establishment of regional planning agencies and urge or require regional coordination of local growth management programs. The limited amount of authority given such agencies could be strengthened by state or local action to allow greater regional leadership in managing growth.

Interlocal agreements or compacts can be useful in promoting coordination and cooperation among jurisdictions. The examples of Raleigh and Fort Collins demonstrate that such agreements can extend growth management outside city boundaries to urbanizing areas. Coupled with favorable annexation laws that support city control over the development process, interlocal agreements can improve the capacity of local governments to manage their future development.

Development in many regions has been guided by business and civic groups that provide discussion forums for regional issues and leadership for achieving targeted solutions. Such groups as the Allegheny Conference in Pittsburgh, the Bay Area Council in San Francisco, and many chambers of commerce in smaller cities encourage regional thinking and action on important development issues.

Finally, regional authorities empowered to manage specific services have proven useful. Ports, airports, transit, and sewerage systems frequently are managed by such authorities. They offer a means of achieving significant efficiencies for a multiplicity of jurisdictions, although they may not prove cooperative in pursuing coordinated growth strategies.

In closing, the evidence is that growth management is here to stay. It is a concept and process that has proven value for communities coping with growth and change. The spirited efforts of many towns, cities, and counties in managing their development demonstrate the potential rewards from anticipating and accommodating development.

Notes

Chapter 1

1. Elizabeth Deakin, "Growth Controls and Growth Management: A Summary and Review of Empirical Research," in David J. Brower, David R. Godschalk, and Douglas R. Porter, eds., *Understanding Growth Management* (Washington, D.C.: Urban Land Institute, 1989), 6.

2. David R. Godschalk et al., *Constitutional Issues of Growth Management* (Chicago: The ASPO Press, 1977), 8.

3. Randall W. Scott, ed., *Management and Control of Growth*, Volume I (Washington, D.C.: Urban Land Institute, 1975), 4.

4. Benjamin Chinitz, "Growth Management: Good for the Town, Bad for the Nation?" in *Journal of the American Planning Association*. Vol. 56, No. 1, Winter 1990, p. 4.

5. Eric Damian Kelly, *Managing Community Growth: Policies, Techniques, and Impacts* (Westport, CT: Praeger, 1993), 1.

Chapter 2

1. James G. Coke, "Antecedents of Local Planning," in *Principles and Practices of Urban Planning*, William I. Goodman and Eric C. Freund, eds. (Washington, D.C.: International City Managers Association, 1968), 13.

2. Randall W. Scott, ed., *Management and Control of Growth*, Volume I (Washington, D.C.: Urban Land Institute, 1975), 6.

3. Rachel Carson, *Silent Spring*, (Boston: Houghton Mifflin, 1962).

4. William K. Reilly, ed., *The Use of Land: A Citizens' Policy Guide to Urban Growth*. A Task Force Report sponsored by the Rockefeller Brothers Fund. (New York: Thomas Y. Crowell Company, 1973), 6.

5. Ibid., 40

Chapter 3

1. Joel Garreau, *Edge City: Life in the Near Frontier* (New York: Doubleday, 1991).

2. Homer Hoyt, *Structure and Growth of Residential Neighborhoods in American Cities* (Washington, D.C.: Federal Housing Administration, 1939).

3. Real Estate Research Corporation, *The Costs of Sprawl: Detailed Cost Analysis* (Washington, D.C.: U.S. Government Printing Office, 1974).

4. James E. Frank, *The Cost of Alternative Development Patterns: A Review of the Literature* (Washington, D.C.: Urban Land Institute, 1989).

5. Robert Burchell, Rutgers University Center for Urban Policy Research, and Paul Tischler, Tischler and Associates, speaking at the American Planning Association annual conference in Orlando, Florida and at a Washington-area workshop, both in April 1996.

6. The literature on sprawl is immense, but one of the most helpful brief discussions of the nature and effects of sprawl is an article based on a report prepared for the Florida Department of Community Affairs by Reid H. Ewing, "Characteristics, Causes, and Effects of Sprawl: A Literature Review" in *Environmental and Urban Issues*. (Published by the FAU/FIU Joint Center for Environmental and Urban Problems in Boca Raton, Florida.) Vol. XXI, No. 2, Winter 1994, 1–15. The article contains an extensive bibliography on sprawl.

7. A detailed explanation of techniques for establishing boundaries is provided by Gail Easely, *Staying Inside the Lines,* in Planning Advisory Service Report Number 440 (Chicago: American Planning Association, 1994).

8. ECO Northwest, *Urban Growth Management Study: Case Studies Report,* prepared for the Oregon Department of Land Conservation and Development, January 1991.

9. Telephone interview with Mitchell Rohse, Oregon Department of Land Conservation and Development, 1994.

10. Randall Arendt and James Constantine, "Urban Growth Boundaries: Do Growth Limits Lead to the Promised Land?" in *Land Development.* (Published by the National Association of Home Builders), Vol. 9, No. 1, Spring/Summer 1996, 9–13.

11. The text of the court's decision can be referenced in Randall W. Scott, ed., *"Robinson v. Boulder*: Utilities and Growth Control Challenges." *Management and Control of Growth* (Washington, D.C.: Urban Land Institute, 1975), vol. 2, pp. 237–50.

12. References for the case study include interviews in 1989 with Garner Stoll, Lincoln Director of Planning; Kent Morgan, Assistant Director of Planning; William Smith, First Tier Bank of Lincoln; Robert Hans, former Chairman, Lincoln/Lancaster County Planning Commission; and Patrick Malloy, Lincoln Chamber of Commerce; in 1993, John Bradley, Assistant Planning Director; and in 1995, Timothy M. Stewart, Planning Director. Documents include the *Lincoln/Lancaster County Comprehensive Plan,* prepared by the Lincoln City/Lancaster County Planning Department, 1985 and 1994.

13. Ibid., 38.

14. See "Growth Management and the Economy" report of the San Diego Economic Development Corporation, September 28, 1987; and ECO Northwest, *Evaluation of Slow-Growth and No-Growth Policies for the Portland Region,* prepared for Metro, 1994. Both studies determined that regional growth could be slowed only by actions that would adversely affect the economy, such as imposing taxes and fees that would increase the price of doing business, or actions that would reduce the quality of living in the area, such as allowing degradation of public services or raising the cost of living. The studies concluded that not only were these actions unlikely to be supported by area residents and businesses but that if adopted were likely to lead to unforeseen consequences—in other words, tampering with regional economic functions was risky.

15. Daniel R. Mandelker, *Land Use Law,* 2d ed. (Charlottesville, Virginia: The Michie Company, 1988), 209 ff.

16. Roger Lewis, "Planning—A More Sensible Choice" in *Urban Land,* September 1989, 37.

17. Eric Damien Kelly, *Managing Community Growth: Policies, Techniques, and Impacts* (Westport, CT: Praeger, 1993), 46.

18. Ibid., 47.

Chapter 4

1. Ian L. McHarg, *Design with Nature*, 2d ed. (New York: John Wiley and Sons, 1992), 56.

2. John W. Rogers and B. Fritts Golden, "Ecosystem Management: The Crucial Role of 'Process'" in *Land Use and Environment Forum*, Vol. 4, No. 1, Winter 1995, 6.

3. Christine Meisner Rosen and Joel A. Tarr, "The Importance of an Urban Perspective in Environmental History," in *Journal of Urban History*, Vol. 20, No. 3, May 1994, 307.

4. Florida Local Government Comprehensive Planning and Land Development Regulation Act, 1985, Section 163.3177(d), Florida Statutes.

5. Maryland Office of Planning, "Achieving Environmentally Sensitive Design." No. 11 of a series on Flexible and Innovative Zoning for Managing Maryland's Growth. (Baltimore: Maryland Office of Planning, 1995), 5.

6. Unfortunately, many people have appropriated the carrying capacity concept as a means of fighting development. Citizens familiar with the traffic capacity concept of "level of service" understand carrying capacity as a means of finitely determining a specific level of development that cannot be exceeded without grave environmental impacts. Their judgments overlook the ways in which carrying capacity—and traffic levels of service, for that matter—can be improved by technical improvements that expand capacity or reduce demands. The widely used standard of prohibiting development on slopes of more than 15 percent, for example, may not make sense for certain types of development such as apartment buildings, which can take advantage of hillside scenic views while employing design and construction techniques to minimize adverse effects on steep slopes. Sitting a 100-unit apartment building on a hillside can be more desirable than allowing 50 single-family houses with associated streets and driveways to sprawl over two or three times as much land.

Carrying capacity, in other words, is a useful initial measure of potential constraints on development but not a precise determination of an absolute limit. An early but still valid analysis of the carrying capacity concept can be found in: Rice Odell, "Carrying Capacity Analysis: Useful but Limited," in Randall W. Scott, ed., *Management and Control of Growth*, Vol. 3, (Washington, D.C.: Urban Land Institute, 1975) 22–28.

7. City of San Diego, *Multi-Species Conservation Plan*, Public Review Draft, 1995. A description of the plan is also published in "Natural Habitats in the San Diego Region: Balancing Development and Habitat Preservation," in *Info* (San Diego: San Diego Association of Governments, January/February 1995).

8. Information about Carlsbad's efforts is taken from Lindell L. Marsh, "Habitat Conservation at Fieldstone/Carlsbad," in *Urban Land*, Vol. 54, No. 6, June 1995, 52–56.

9. For more information on the Chesapeake Bay program, see Erik Meyers, Robert Fischman, and Anne Marsh, "Maryland Chesapeake Bay Critical Areas Program: Wetlands Protection and Future Growth," in Douglas R. Porter and David A. Salvesen, eds., *Collaborative Planning for Wetlands and Wildlife*, (Washington, D.C.: Island Press, 1995), 181–202.

10. Larimer County Planning Department, *A Plan for the Region Between Fort Collins and Loveland*, 1995.

11. Phyllis Myers, "Financing Open Space and Landscape Protection: A Sampler of State and Local Techniques," in Eve Endicott, ed., *Land Conservation through Public/Private Partnerships*, (Washington, D.C.: Island Press and Lincoln Institute of Land Policy, 1993), 223–257.

12. Eve Endicott, "Preserving Natural Areas: The Nature Conservancy and Its Partners," in Eve Endicott, ed., *Land Conservation through Public/Private Partnerships* (Washington, D.C.: Island Press and Lincoln Institute of Land Policy, 1993), 17.

13. Ibid., 21.

14. "New England Conservation Initiatives," in *The Trust for Public Land, New England.* (Published by the Trust for Public Land New England Regional Office.) Summer/Fall 1995, 4.

15. Michael S. Haberkorn, "The Role of Public Conservancies, Joint Powers Authorities, and Nonprofit Land Trusts" in *Land Use and Environment Forum.* Published by the University of California, Berkeley, for the Continuing Education Program of the California Bar. Vol. 4, No. 1, Winter 1995, 21–32.

16. A good roundup of current methods is contained in *Achieving Environmentally Sensitive Design*, No. 11 in the Flexible and Innovative Zoning Series (Baltimore, MD: Office of Planning, 1995).

17. National Association of Home Builders, *Cost-Effective Site Planning: Single-Family Development* (Washington, D.C.: National Association of Home Builders, 1976). For more information on cluster development, also see Ruth Knack, "Selling Cluster," in *Planning*, September 1990, 4–10; and Welford Sanders, *The Cluster Subdivision: A Cost-Effective Approach*, Planning Advisory Service Report No. 356. (Chicago: American Planning Association, 1980).

18. Communication to author from Robert Lemire commenting on the results of the townwide conference on July 19, 1995.

19. The town's experience is further detailed by Robert Lemire, "An Overview of an Innovative Land Protection Technique," in *Exchange* (The Journal of the Land Trust Exchange), Vol. 7, No. 4, Fall 1988, 1, 4–6. The issue also contains descriptions of additional limited-development projects.

20. Much of the Bucks County model ordinance was written by Lane Kendig, then director of community planning for the county. Kendig later expanded the cluster idea in his book, *Performance Zoning* (Published by the American Planning Association), 1981.

21. The Nature Conservancy, *Partners in Protection: Virginia's Eastern Shore Seaside Farms, A Conservation Easement Program* (Richmond, VA: Virginia Council on the Environment Coastal Resources Management Program, 1994).

22. Maryland State Highway Administration, *U.S. 301 Transportation Study, Land Use Technical Supplement.* (Prepared by Douglas R. Porter for the State Highway Administration), 1996.

23. Loudoun County Planning Commission, *Choices and Changes: Loudoun County General Plan, 1990–2010.* Adopted September 17, 1991.

24. For details of Maryland programs, see *TDR Programs in Maryland*, prepared by the Maryland Office of Planning for a workshop convened on April 29, 1994. For a much longer exposition of the concept and its application, see Amanda J. Gottsegen, *Planning for Transfer of Development Rights: A Handbook for New Jersey Municipalities* (Mount Holly, New Jersey: Burlington County Board of Chosen Freeholders, 1992).

25. Robert H. Freilich and Wayne M. Senville, "Takings, TDRs, and Environmental Preservation: 'Fairness' and the Hollywood North Beach Case" in *Land Use Law,* September 1983, 5.

26. For an explanation and critique of mitigation banking, see Lindell L. Marsh, Douglas R. Porter, and David A. Salvesen, eds., *Mitigation Banking: Theory and Practice* (Washington, D.C.: Island Press, 1996).

27. An excellent summary and discussion of conservation implementation techniques can be found in Madelyn Glickfeld, Sonia Jacques, Walter Kieser, and Todd Olson, "Implementation Techniques and Strategies for Conservation Plans," in *Land Use and Environmental Forum.* (Published by the University of California, Berkeley, for the Continuing Education of the Bar, California), Vol. 4, No. 1, Winter 1995, 12–27. The article contains

tables indicating the public acceptability, financial incentives and disincentives, transaction costs, equity and administrative considerations, legal issues, and other factors for 10 implementation techniques such as impact fees and land donations and exchanges. A thoughtful guide to rural conservation planning and implementation is Samuel N. Stokes, *Saving America's Countryside, A Guide to Rural Conservation* (Baltimore: Johns Hopkins University Press, 1989).

28. Aldo Leopold, "Conservation Economics," in Susan L. Flader and J. Baird Callicott, eds., *The River of the Mother of God and Other Essays by Aldo Leopold"* (Madison: University of Wisconsin Press, 1991), 202.

Chapter 5

1. Madelyn Glickfeld and Ned Levine, *Regional Growth—Local Reaction: The Enactment and Effects of Local Growth Control and Management Measures in California* (Cambridge, MA: Lincoln Institute of Land Policy, 1992).

2. William E. Baumgaertner, John W. Guckert, and John J. Andrus, "Leveraging Growth Management with APFs," in Douglas R. Porter, ed., *Performance Standards for Growth Management*, Planning Advisory Service Report No. 461. (Chicago: American Planning Association, 1996), 23–30.

3. Henry Fagin, "Regulating the Timing of Urban Development," in *Law and Contemporary Problems* (Published by the Duke University Law School), Vol. 20, No. 2, 298–304.

4. Chula Vista's program is fully described by its planning director, Robert Leiter, in "The Use of Threshold Standards in Chula Vista's Growth Management Program," in Douglas R. Porter, ed., *Performance Standards in Growth Management*. Planning Advisory Service Report Number 461. (Chicago: American Planning Association, 1995), 13–18.

5. By now, the reader will observe the number of California examples in this chapter. It is no accident that so many California cities have gone to great lengths to manage infrastructure development and funding. State restrictions on levying property taxes, including Proposition 13, have severely hampered California cities' ability to raise revenues for public facility construction. This not only drives those cities to employ impact fees and other user-based funding mechanisms almost exclusively to fund facilities but also to ensure that development occurs only as facilities are made available.

6. Henry Fagin, "Regulating the Timing of Urban Development," 298.

7. For detailed information on methods of calculating and administering impact fees, plus model ordinances, see James C. Nicholas, Arthur C. Nelson, and Julian C. Juergensmeyer, *A Practitioner's Guide to Development Impact Fees* (Chicago: APA Planners Press, 1991).

8. Ibid, 4–8.

9. Detailed discussions of court decisions affecting exactions and fees can be found in the Nicholas, Nelson, and Juergensmeyer book on impact fees and in Nancy E. Stroud and Susan L. Trevarthen, "Defensible Exactions After *Nollan v. California Coastal Commission* and *Dolan v. City of Tigard*," in *Stetson Law Review*, Vol. XXV, No. 3, Spring 1996, 719–822.

10. For more information on trends in special district formation, types of districts, funding approaches, and specific examples, see Douglas R. Porter, Ben C. Lin, Susan Jakubiak, and Richard B. Peiser, *Special Districts: A Useful Technique for Financing Infrastructure* 2d ed. (Washington, D.C.: Urban Land Institute, 1992).

Chapter 6

1. David R. Godschalk et al., *Constitutional Issues of Growth Management* (Chicago: The ASPO Press, 1977), 240–247.

2. Jan Krasnowieki, "The Fallacy of the End-State System of Land Use Control" in *Land Use Law,* April 1986, 1–30, decries the ineffectiveness of zoning to deliver desired qualities of development.

3. The specificity of many development regulations is often based on rather arbitrary measures. Setbacks and side yards for residential lots, for example, establish minimum distances in feet from lot lines to buildings. The distances supposedly are related to health, safety, and welfare—but is a 50-foot setback really more healthy than a 35-foot setback? A 50-foot setback requirement actually reflects official conceptions of desirable neighborhood appearance—spacious lawns, lots of landscaping, mini-estates—all expressive of community perceptions of wealth and stability, rather than health, safety, and welfare. Such requirements also reflect officials concerns about property values that pump revenues into city property tax accounts. "Hard-number" requirements, therefore, often act as surrogates for quality-oriented goals.

4. Publications that offer specific guidance on some of the more common approaches include Eric Damian Kelly and Gary J. Raso, *Sign Regulation for Small and Midsize Communities,* Planning Advisory Service Report No. 419, 1989; Thomas P. Smith, *The Aesthetics of Parking,* Planning Advisory Service Report No. 411, 1989; and Wendelyn A. Martz with Marya Morris, *Preparing a Landscaping Ordinance,* Planning Advisory Service Report No. 431, 1990; all published by the American Planning Association, Chicago. Lane Kendig's *Performance Zoning* (Chicago: American Planning Association, 1980), provides a great deal of information about various types of landscaped buffers.

5. Christopher J. Duerksen and Suzanne Richman, *Tree Conservation Ordinances.* Planning Advisory Service Report No. 446 (Chicago: American Planning Association, 1994). Also see Tovah Redwood, "Tree Time" in *Planning,* September 1994, 13–15.

6. Mark L. Hinshaw, *Design Review.* Planning Advisory Service Report Number 454 (Chicago: American Planning Association, 1995), 4. Hinshaw's monograph provides an excellent overview of design guidelines and design review processes in many types of circumstances.

7. It must be noted that the arguments in these cases usually included basic health, safety, and welfare concerns as well as aesthetic objectives to strengthen the position that the regulations at issue were in accordance with local police powers. The decision on the *Metromedia* case, for example, rested in part on the safety issue that billboards distract drivers. There are signs that the courts are more willing to consider aesthetic arguments on their merits without resort to such excursions in logic.

8. Hinshaw, *Design Review,* 19.

9. Provisions are contained in a number of plans and regulations, including the *General Plan, Scottsdale, Arizona:* "Land Use Element, 1994," "Public Facilities Element, 1992," "Circulation Element, 1991," "Environmental Design Element, 1992;" *Downtown Plan, Land Use,* 1986; *Environmentally Sensitive Lands Ordinance, Citizen's Guide,* undated; *Southeast Downtown Redevelopment Plan,* 1993; and *Waterfront Area Redevelopment Plan,* 1994. All published by the Planning and Economic Development Department, City of Scottsdale.

10. This information was obtained from interviews with Frank Turner, Planning Director, City of Plana, 1989 and 1995, and from *Design Guidelines, Retail Corner and Service Station Development,* City of Plana Planning Department, 1987.

11. A complete discussion of appearance codes, including sample provisions, can be found in Peggy Glassford, *Appearance Codes for Small Communities,* Planning Advisory Report No. 379 (Chicago: American Planning Association, 1983).

12. Grand Traverse Bay Region Guidebook, prepared for the Traverse City Area Chamaber of Commerce by the Planning and Zoning Center, Inc., 1992.

13. Terry J. Lassar, *Carrots and Sticks: New Zoning Downtown* (Washington, D.C.: Urban Land Institute, 1989), 118.

14. See note 9 above.

15. Information obtained from interviews with George Chapman, Planning I 1989 and 1995, and Smedes York, a developer and former mayor, 1989; and from lowing documents: "Resolution to Amend the Comprehensive Plan," CP-11-95, adopted September 19, 1995; *Raleigh Growth and Development,* prepared by the Economic Development Services Office of the Raleigh Planning Department, May 1995; *Housing Element of the Comprehensive Plan,* City of Raleigh, March 1987; "Summary of the Facility Fee Ordinances," effective December 1, 1987; and the case study of Raleigh in Thomas Snyder and Michael Stegman, *Paying for Growth: Using Development Fees to Finance Infrastructure* (Washington, D.C.: Urban Land Institute, 1987).

16. Richard F. Babcock and Wendy U. Larsen, *Special Districts: The Ultimate in Neighborhood Zoning* (Cambridge, MA: The Lincoln Institute of Land Policy, 1990).

17. For a complete discussion of downtown zoning incentives and procedures, see Lassar, *Carrots and Sticks: New Zoning Downtown.*

18. For more information on this process, see Douglas R. Porter, "Washington, D.C. Case Study" in Parsons, Brinckerhoff, Quade, and Douglas, *Transit and Urban Form,* Part IV. TCRP Report 16, prepared for the Transit Cooperative Research Program. (Washington, D.C.: National Academy Press, 1996) 37–70.

19. Terry Jill Lassar, *City Deal Making* (Washington, D.C.: Urban Land Institute, 1990), 2.

20. Lassar, *Carrots and Sticks,* 81. Much of the information in this section is drawn from Lassar's book.

21. Ibid.

22. Bradford J. White and Richard J. Roddewig, *Preparing a Historic Preservation Plan.* Planning Advisory Service Report No. 450 (Chicago: American Planning Association, 1994), 1 and 12. For more information on historic preservation planning, see Marya Morris, *Innovative Tools for Historic Preservation.* Planning Advisory Service Report Number 438. (Chicago: American Planning Association, September 1992).

23. This description is based in part on a detailed case study presented in White and Roddewig, *Preparing a Historic Preservation Plan,* 21–23.

24. Peter Calthorpe, *The Next American Metropolis: Ecology, Community, and the American Dream* (New York: Princeton Architectural Press, 1993), 15.

25. For detailed expositions of these ideas, see Calthorpe, note 24; Suzanne Sutro, *Reinventing the Village: Planning, Zoning, and Design Strategies.* Planning Advisory Service Report No. 430 (Chicago: American Planning Association, 1991); and David Sucher, *How to Build an Urban Village* (Seattle: City Comforts Press). Duany's concepts are well described by Andres Duany and Elizabeth Plater-Zyberk, "The Second Coming of the American Small Town" in *Wilson Quarterly,* Winter 1992, 19–48; and by Ruth Eckdish Knack, "Repent, Ye Sinners, Repent" in *Planning,* Vol. 55, No. 8, August 1989, 4–13.

26. See, for example, *Transit-Oriented Development Design Guidelines,* prepared by Calthorpe Associates for the City of San Diego; Robert Cervero, *Transit-Supportive Development in the United States: Experiences and Prospects,* prepared for the Federal Transit Administration (Berkeley: National Transit Access Center, 1993), 28. Cervero comments that he found 26 publications of design guidelines in a 1993 survey and indications that another 13 were in preparation.

27. Michael Bernick and Robert Cervero, *Transit Villages in the 21st Century* (New York: McGraw-Hill, 1996).

Chapter 7

1. Mary K. Nenno, *Ending the Stalemate: Moving Housing and Urban Development into the Mainstream of America's Future* (Lanham, Maryland: University Press of America, 1995), 67.

2. Evidence for and implications of housing discrimination, as well as other disparity factors, are admirably summarized in Robert W. Burchell and David Listokin, "Influence on United States Housing Policy" in *Housing Policy Debate*. (Published by the Federal National Mortgage Association, 1995), Vol. 6, Issue 3, 559–617.

3. Michael A. Stegman and Margery Austin Turner, "The Future of Urban America in the Global Economy" in *Journal of the American Planning Association*, Vol. 62, No. 2, Spring 1996, 157–164.

4. Calculated from statistics in Mary K. Nenno, note 1, Table 4.3, 89–90.

5. Joint Center for Housing Studies of Harvard University, *The State of the Nation's Housing* (Cambridge, Massachusetts: Joint Center, 1992).

6. Nenno, 41.

7. See note 14 of Chapter 6.

8. S. Mark White, *Affordable Housing: Proactive and Reactive Planning Strategies*. Planning Advisory Service Report Number 441 (Chicago: American Planning Association, 1992), 21.

9. Chapter 13A, "Moderately Priced Housing," Rockville City Code, adopted as Ordinance 29–90 by the Mayor and Council of Rockville, Maryland, September 10, 1990.

10. Sylvia Lewis, "Building Affordable Housing in Unaffordable Places" in *Planning*, December 1991, 24–27.

11. Town of Breckenridge Development Code, Section 21.06, 24.

12. "Boise and Partners Build Affordable Housing" in *Planning*, August 1996, 26–27.

13. Mary Lou Gallagher, "Arlington County's Affordable Housing Protection District" in *Planning*, Vol. 60, No. 4, March 1994, 12–13.

14. For an early description of the various programs and linkage issues, see *Downtown Linkages*, Douglas R. Porter, ed. (Washington, D.C.: Urban Land Institute, 1985). See also Douglas Porter and Terry Lassar, "The Latest on Linkage" in *Urban Land*, December 1988, 24–26; and Lassar, *Carrots and Sticks*.

15. White, *Affordable Housing*, 26–30. White provides a detailed discussion of judicial views on linkage and similar programs.

16. Advisory Commission on Regulatory Barriers to Affordable Housing, *"Not in My Back Yard:" Removing Barriers to Affordable Housing*. Report to President Bush and Secretary Kemp. (Washington, D.C.: U.S. Department of Housing and Urban Development, 1991).

17. See, for example, Welford Sanders and David Mosena, *Changing Development Standards for Affordable Housing*. Planning Advisory Service Report Number 371. (Chicago: American Planning Association, 1982); *Affordable Residential Land Development: A Guide for Local Government and Developers* and *Affordable Residential Construction: A Guide for Home Builders*, volumes 1 and 2, respectively, of *Affordable Housing: Challenge and Response*, prepared by the NAHB National Research Center for the U.S. Department of Housing and Urban Development. (Washington, D.C.: U.S. Department of Housing and Urban Development, 1987).

18. Richard Cowden, "Power to the Zones" *Planning*, February, 1995, 8–10.

19. Allen R. Myerson, "O Governor, Won't You Buy Me a Mercedes Plant?" *The New York Times*, September 1, 1996, Section 3, 1 and 10.

20. Ibid., p.10.

21. Information about Long Beach's experience was supplied by four documents: *Long Beach 2000: The Strategic Plan*, 1986; and *Long Beach 2000: The Strategic Plan, Progress Reports on Implementation*, October 1986 to October 1988, October 1986 to October 1989, and 1986 to 1992. Published in 1989, 1990, and 1993, respectively, all by the City of Long Beach. In addition, James Hankla, City Manager was interviewed in 1990 and Robert Paternoster, Director of the Queensway Bay Project, was interviewed in 1995.

22. Ibid., and an interview with Harry Newman, developer, 1990.

23. For a good description of the program and its accomplishments, see James E. Rosenbaum, "Changing the Geography of Opportunity by Expanding Residential Choice: Lessons from the Gautreaux Program" *Housing Policy Review*. (Published by the Fannie Mae Office of Housing Research, 1995), Vol. 6, Issue 1, 231–269.

24. Michael Porter, "Theory and Practice" *Harvard Magazine*, July/August 1996, 67.

25. John King, "Protecting Industry from Yuppies and Other Invaders" *Planning*, June 1988, 4–8.

26. Elizabeth Collaton and Charles Bartsch, "Industrial Site Reuse and Urban Redevelopment—An Overview" in *Cityscape: A Journal of Policy Development and Research* (Published by the Office of Policy Development and Research, U.S. Department of Housing and Urban Development), Vol. 2, No. 3, September 1996, 18. The article provides an exhaustive overview of the brownfields issue and several examples of cleanup efforts.

27. Deborah Cooney et al., *Revival of Contaminated Industrial Sites: Case Studies* (Washington, D.C.: Northeast-Midwest Institute, 1992), 46–47.

28. Ibid., 15–16.

29. The objectives and additional information are drawn from "Horizon 2000: 1987 Special Review of the General Plan," Executive Summary. Prepared by the San Jose Department of City Planning, October 28, 1987.

30. "San Jose 2020 Focus on the Future: Industrial Land Demand and Land Supply." Prepared by the San Jose Department of City Planning and Building, February 1993.

31. "San Jose 2020 Focus on the Future: Land Use Inventory and Land Use Trends." Prepared by the Department of City Planning and Building, August 1992, 3.

32. B.G. Yovovich, "When the Rubber Doesn't Hit the Road: What Telecommuting Means to U.S. Communities" *Planning*, December 1994, 12–16.

33. Publications that deal with small-town growth management include David J. Brower et al., *Managing Development in Small Towns* (Chicago: Planners Press, 1984); Mark B. Lapping, Thomas L. Daniels, and John W. Keller, *Rural Planning and Development in the United States* (New York: The Guilford Press, 1989); and Judith Getzels and Charles Thurow, eds., *Rural and Small Town Planning*. Prepared for the Old West Regional Commission, Billings, Montana, by the American Planning Association (Chicago: Planners Press, 1979).

34. Rodney C. Lynch, "Bethel, Maine, Tackles Growth Management Planning" *Small Town*, May/June 1990, 19–23.

35. Information about downtown San Diego's plans was drawn in part from Pamela M. Hamilton, "The Metamorphosis of Downtown San Diego" *Urban Land*, April 1994, 32–38.

36. The National Main Street Center provides training, educational materials, and technical advice to small towns interested in improving their downtowns. Write the organization at the National Trust for Historic Preservation, 1785 Massachusetts Avenue, NW, Washington, D.C. 20036.

37. For more guidance on downtown revitalization and descriptions of specific projects, see Susanna McBee et al., *Downtown Development Handbook* (Washington, D.C.: Urban Land Institute, 1992).

38. For more information on the Technology Center, see Douglas R. Porter, "Pittsburgh Technology Center" in *Urban Land*, June 1993, 17–21.

39. Michelle Gregory, "Champaign Neighborhood Wellness Action Plan" in *Planning*, March 1994, 14.

40. For more details on Cleveland's program, see Diane Corcelli and Victor Dubina, "Cleveland's Rejuvenated Neighborhoods" in *Urban Land*, April 1996, 49 ff.

41. Chris Warner, "Attractive Housing for Savannah's Poor" in *Historic Preservation*, May/June 1988, p. 13.

42. "Rehabilitation Award: Commonwealth Development" in *Urban Land*, December 1989, 22.

43. Michele Barrett, "Paul Davidoff Award: City of Anaheim: Avon–Dakota–Eton Neighborhood Association" in *Planning*, March 1994, 16–17.

44. The Fannie Mae Office of Housing Research has been promoting extensive research in the area of housing policy and its relationships to economic and social distress, all reported in the Office's journal, *Housing Policy Debate*. Two articles that shed a considerable amount of light on current conditions in U.S. metropolitan areas are Vincent Lane, "Best Management Practices in U.S. Public Housing" Vol. 6, Issue 4, 1995, 867–904, which describes living, social, and economic conditions of public housing tenants; and Michael H. Schill and Susan M Wachter, "Housing Market Constraints and Spatial Stratification by Income and Race" Vol. 6, Issue 1, 1995, 141–167. Other articles in these issues describe approaches to meeting these challenges.

45. For more information on Orfield's ideas, see Neal R. Pierce, "Mapping a City State's Future" in *National Journal*, October 23, 1993, 2551; and John Kostouros, "Brother, Can You Spare a Dime?" in *Law and Politics*, July 1994, 33.

46. Bob Fitzpatrick, "Tangible Impact of New Jersey's Mount Laurel Doctrine: A Summary of the Matter of Mount Laurel" in *The State Line* (Council of State Community Development Agencies, Washington, D.C.), January/February 1993.

47. For more information on the program, see Edith M. Netter, "From Confrontation to Cooperation: The Massachusetts Approach to Affordable Housing" in *Urban Land*, June 1990, 32–33.

48. Information supplied by Robert Lemire based on the Townwide Conference, July 19, 1995 and excerpts from the *Town of Lincoln Annual Reports* for 1992, 1993, and 1994 pertaining to actions of the Lincoln Board of Selectmen, Lincoln Planning Board, Lincoln Conservation Commission, and the Lincoln Land Conservation Trust.

49. 1000 Friends of Oregon and the Home Builders Association of Metropolitan Portland, *Managing Growth to Promote Affordable Housing: Revisiting Oregon's Goal 10*, Executive Summary (Portland, Oregon: 1000 Friends of Oregon, 1991).

50. Metropolitan Council of the Twin Cities, *Fiscal Disparities Discussion Paper, Staff Report*, 1991.

51. David Rusk, *Baltimore Unbound* (Baltimore: Johns Hopkins University Press, 1995).

Chapter 8

1. This summary is based on a case study by Fernando Aragon, *Why Regional Planning Failed*, Planners' Casebook No. 18 (Chicago: American Institute of Planners, Spring 1996) and a communication to the author by Maria Bello, senior planner for the Countywide Planning Council, April 17, 1992.

2. See Douglas R. Porter, "Tough Choices: Regional Governance in San Francisco" in *Urban Land*, March, 1992, 36–39.

3. Mark Baldassare et al., "Possible Planning Roles for Regional Government: A Survey of City Planning Directors in California" in *Journal of the American Planning Association*, Vol. 62, No. 1. Winter 1996, 26.

4. Lewis Mumford, *The Culture of Cities* (New York: Harcourt, Brace & World, 1938), 47.

5. Historical information in this section is drawn from Carl and Margery Post Abbott, *Historical Development of the Metropolitan Service District*, prepared for the Metro Home Rule Charter Committee, May 1991.

6. The 2040 planning concepts and preferred plan are described in detail in *Concepts for Growth*, Metro Staff Report to the Metro Council, June 1994.

7. The SANDAG concept for regional growth management is described in *Growth Management in the San Diego Region*, Final Report of the Regional Growth and Planning Review Task Force, published by the San Diego County Deparatment of Planning and the San Diego Association of Governments, November 1998; and *Blueprint for the San Diego*

Region, a Progress Report on the Regional Growth Management Strategy, prepared and published by the San Diego Association of Governments, 1993.

8. For an extended discussion of the Council's political and planning evolution, see Steve Keefe, "Twin Cities Federalism: The Politics of Metropolitan Governance" in Douglas R. Porter, ed., *State and Regional Initiatives for Managing Development* (Washington, D.C.: Urban Land Institute, 1992).

9. *Metropolitan Council, Regional Blueprint, Twin Cities Metropolitan Area*. Prepared and published by the Metropolitan Council, September 1994.

10. *Final Recommendations of the U.S. 301 Task Force*. Prepared for the task force by the Maryland State Highway Administration, July 17, 1996.

11. Some will argue that Portland's Metro organization, with an elected regional council, comes close to being a regional government. An analysis of Metro's actual responsibilities, however, demonstrates that it has only a few selected powers to guide development in the Portland region and virtually no general-purpose governmental responsibilities. Moreover, it has attained its present position by carefully building consensus with local governments rather than challenging them on every front.

12. The growth management statutes, by date of enactment, are as follows:

- Oregon: Oregon Land Use Act, Senate Bill 100, 1973. Oregon Revised Statutes 197.005-197.650, 215.055, 215.510, 215.515, 215.535, and 453.345.
- Florida: Omnibus Growth Management Act, 1985, House Bill 287. Laws of Florida Chapter 85-55. State Comprehensive Planning Act, House Bill 1338, 1985. Laws of Florida Chapter 85-57.
- New Jersey: State Planning Act, 1986, Senate No. 1464-L, 1985. New Jersey State Acts 52:18.
- Maine: Comprehensive Planning and Land Use Act, 1988, H.P. 1588 - L.D. 2317. Selc. 4 30 Maine Revised Statutes Annotated 4960-4960-F.
- Rhode Island: Comprehensive Planning and Land Use Regulation Act, 1988. PL 88-601, Chapter 45-22.1, Rhode Island General Laws.
- Vermont: Growth Management Act, 1988, Act 200, General Assembly.
- Georgia: Georgia Planning Act, 1989, House Bill 215. Georgia Laws 1317-1391.
- Washington: Growth Management Act, 1990, House Bill 2929. Chapter 17, 51st Legislature. Growth Management Act Amendments, 1991, House Bill 1025, 52nd Legislature.
- Maryland: Economic Growth, Resource Protection, and Planning Act, 1992, House Bill No. 1195. Article 66B; State Finance and Procurement Article, Sections 5-402, 5-701 through 5-710; and State Government Article Section 8-403(h), Annotated Code of Maryland.

This section was adapted from Douglas R. Porter, "State Growth Management: An Intergovernmental Experiment" in *Pace Law Review*, Vol. 13, No. 2, Fall 1993, 481–503.

13. For a detailed history of state planning, see Robert G. Benko and Irving Hand, "State Planning Today" in Frank So, ed., *State and Regional Planning* (Chicago: American Planning Association, 1986).

14. Fred P. Bosselman and David Callies, *The Quiet Revolution in Land Use Control* (Washington, D.C.: Council on Environmental Quality, 1971), 1.

15. See "Wal-Mart vs. Vermonters" in *The Growth Management Reporter*. Vol. 2, No. 2, 1994, pp. 4,5.

16. Section 4960-A.1.E.

17. Pursuant to Sections 197.225 ff., the Oregon Land Conservation and Development Commission prepared and adopted an administrative rule defining the goals. Published in "Oregon's State Planning Goals" Land Conservation and Development Commission, 1985.

18. Charles L. Siemon, "Growth Management in Florida: An Overview and Brief Critique," in Douglas R. Porter, ed., *State and Regional Initiatives for Managing Development* (Washington, D.C.: Urban Land Institute, 1992), 40.

19. State Comprehensive Plan, Section 2.

20. Jeffrey F. Squires, "Growth Management Redux: Vermont's Act 250 and Act 200" in Douglas R. Porter, ed., *State and Regional Initiatives for Managing Development* (Washington, D.C.: Urban Land Institute, 1992), 14.

21. The original goals are cited in the Comprehensive Planning and Land Use Regulation Act, 45-22.2-3(C). Expanded goals, policies, and the land capability map are included in "Land Use 2010, State Land Use Policies and Plan," Element 121 of the State Guide Plan, published in Report No. 64 by the Division of Planning, Rhode Island Department of Administration, in Providence, 1989. As a note of interest, Rhode Island prepared and adopted a state land use plan, incorporating 12 categories of land uses, in 1975.

22. New Jersey State Planning Act of 1985, N.J.S.A. 52:18A-199.

23. For a detailed discussion of the procedures for delineating growth centers, see "The Centers Designation Process," Document #99 prepared by the New Jersey Office of State Planning, February 1993.

24. John M. DeGrove, *Land, Growth and Politics* (Chicago: Planner's Press, 1984), 288. For an extensive discussion of state agency responses to state growth management requirements, see Douglas R. Porter, "State Agency Coordination in State Growth Management Programs" in *Modernizing State Planning Statutes: The Growing Smart Working Papers.* Vol. 1. Planning Advisory Service Report No. 462/463. (Chicago: American Planning Association, 1996).

25. V.S.A. Chapter 67, Section 4020A.

26. DeGrove, *Land, Growth and Politics,* 284.

27. Deborah A. Howe, "Review of Growth Management Strategies Used in Other States," prepared for the Oregon Department of Land Conservation and Development, 1991.

28. Section 45-22.2-6.

29. Siemon, *State and Regional Initiatives for Managing Development,* 48.

30. Vermont's regional councils were given approval powers over local plans under Act 200 but subsequent legislation postponed these powers to 1996. Vermont's district environmental commissions retain their authority to review and approve large-scale developments.

31. Howe, "Review of Growth Management Strategies," 35.

32. Ibid., 7.

33. Maryland's 1992 law does not expressly call for local governments to submit plans for review and comment by the state agency. Instead, local governments are required to submit a schedule showing when they expect to achieve conformance with state requirements, which include the inclusion of state "vision" goals in local plans. The state agency is required to submit an annual report assessing the progress of state and local governments in achieving the goals and recommending appropriate actions to overcome any problems identified (H.B. 1195, Sec. 5-708). Clearly, in order to prepare the report, it is necessary for the agency to review local plans.

34. The Florida Department of Community Affairs published a "Technical Memo" (Vol. 4, No. 4) in 1989 that cited aspects of the Florida statute that supported compact development, described the legal basis for its position, defined a number of indicators of sprawl found in local plans, and suggested a variety of techniques for avoiding sprawl.

35. *Communities of Place: The New Jersey State Development and Redevelopment Plan,* prepared and published by the New Jersey State Planning Commission, 1992, 35.

36. Section 45-22.2-6(I).

37. See, for example, the introduction to *Communities of Place: The New Jersey State Development and Redevelopment Plan,* published by the State Planning Commission in 1992, which observes that "The State Plan also will be important when the State of New Jersey makes infrastructure investment decisions. The State Plan will serve as a guide to when and where available State funds should be expended to achieve the Goals of the State Planning Act," 6.

38. For an extended critique of existing state programs and proposals for improving state growth management systems, see *Modernizing State Planning Statutes,* Vol. 1 of a research project to improve the statutory basis for American planning. Planning Advisory Service Report No. 462/463. (Chicago: American Planning Association, 1996).

Chapter 9

1. Seymour I. Schwartz, David E. Hansen, and Richard Green. "The Effect of Growth Control on the Production of Moderate Priced Housing" in *Land Economics,* 1984, 110–114.

2. Lawrence Katz and Kenneth Rosen, "The Interjurisdictional Effects of Growth Controls on Housing Prices" in *Journal of Law and Economics,* Vol. 30, 1987, 149–160.

3. John D. Landis, "Do Growth Controls Work?" in *Journal of the American Planning Association,* Vol. 58, No. 4, Autumn, 1992, pp. 489–506.

4. For a roundup of the literature and conclusions on such studies, see Elizabeth Deakin, "Growth Controls and Growth Management: A Summary and Review of Empirical Research;" and William A. Fischel, "What Do Economists Know About Growth Controls? A Research Review," in David J. Brower, David R. Godschalk, and Douglas R. Porter, eds., *Understanding Growth Management: Critical Issues and a Research Agenda* (Washington, D.C.: Urban Land Institute, 1989), 3–21 and 59–86, respectively.

5. See Fischel, p.70.

6. See Deakin, p.18.

7. ECO Northwest, *Evaluation of No-Growth and Slow-Growth Policies for the Portland Region.* Prepared for Metro, February 1994.

8. Bernard J. Frieden, *The Environmental Protection Hustle* (Cambridge, Massachusetts: The Massachusetts Institute of Technology, 1979).

9. Paul L. Niebanck, "Growth Controls and the Production of Inequality" in David J. Brower, David R. Godschalk, and Douglas R. Porter, eds., *Understanding Growth Management: Critical Issues and a Research Agenda* (Washington, D.C.: Urban Land Institute, 1989), 105–122.

10. See Alexander Skaggs, "Walnut Creek Says Nuts to Growth" in *Urban Land,* October 1988.

11. Gleeson et al., 59.

12. Arthur C. Nelson, "Growth Management and the Savings-and-Loan Bailout" in *The Urban Lawyer,* Vol. 27, No.1, Winter 1995, 71–85.

13. Some advocates of sustainable development will decry these statements. They like to believe that urban development and environmental protection can be smoothly meshed without compromise on either side. Although this may be an admirable objective overall, it is unlikely in bounded, higher-density urban areas where something must give. Scott Campbell's recent essay on this dilemma points out that planners "don't have adequate answers" to questions about what needs to be done, what are the consequences of those actions, and what process would arrive at reasonable solutions. He suggests that the current definition of sustainability "romanticizes our sustainable past and is too vaguely holistic." See Scott Campbell, "Green Cities, Growing Cities, Just Cities: Urban Planning and Contradictions of Sustainable Development" in *Journal of the American Institute of Planners,* Vol. 62, No. 3, Summer 1996, 296–312.

14. See, for example, John D. Landis, "Imagining Land Use Futures" in *Journal of the American Planning Association,* Vol. 61, No. 4, Autumn 1995, 438–457, which also lists an extensive bibliography on land use modeling.

15. Rutgers University Center for Urban Policy Research, *Impact Assessment of the New Jersey Interim State Development and Redevelopment Plan.* Prepared for the New Jersey Office of State Planning, Vol. I–III, February 1992.

16. See, for example, the conclusions of a number of fiscal studies demonstrating the comparative fiscal impacts of various types of development with a no-development option, in Frances H. Kennedy and Douglas R. Porter, *Dollars and Sense of Battlefield Preservation: The Economic Benefits of Protecting Civil War Battlefields* (Washington, D.C.: The Preservation Press, 1994).

17. David R. Godschalk et al., *Pulling Together: A Planning and Development Consensus-Building Manual* (Washington, D.C.: Urban Land Institute, 1994) 36. This is an uncommonly clear explanation of the consensus-building processes, with case studies and sample documents.

18. Oregon Progress Board, *Oregon Benchmarks: Standards for Measuring Statewide Progress and Government Performance.* Report to the 1993 Legislature, December 1992.

19. Jamie Palmer, Catherine McCarthy, and Drew Klacik, *Final Benchmarking Report, Noblesville, Indiana.* Prepared by the Center for Urban Policy and the Environment, Indiana University, for the City of Noblesville, September 1994.

Index